# INTEGRATING
# CHINA
## INTO THE
# GLOBAL
# ECONOMY

# INTEGRATING
# CHINA
## INTO THE
# GLOBAL
# ECONOMY

NICHOLAS R. LARDY

BROOKINGS INSTITUTION PRESS
*Washington, D.C.*

*Library of Congress Cataloging-in-Publication data*
Lardy, Nicholas R.
  Integrating China into the global economy / Nicholas R. Lardy.
  p. cm.
Includes bibliographical references and index.
  ISBN 0-8157-5136-2 (cloth : alk. paper) —
  ISBN 0-8157-5135-4 (pbk. : alk. paper)
  1. World Trade Organization—China. 2. China—Foreign economic
relations. 3. China—Commercial policy. 4. China—Foreign economic
relations—United States. 5. United States—Foreign economic
relations—China. I. Title.
  HF1604 L373 2002                                     2001007624
  337.51—dc21                                          CIP


9 8 7 6 5 4 3 2


The paper used in this publication meets minimum requirements of the
American National Standard for Information Sciences—Permanence of Paper
for Printed Library Materials: ANSI Z39.48-1992.


Typeset in Sabon


Composition by Cynthia Stock
Silver Spring, Maryland


Printed by R. R. Donnelley and Sons
Harrisonburg, Virginia

# *Foreword*

CHINA'S ACCESSION TO THE World Trade Organization is a landmark event in China's economic reform and in the evolution of the international trading system. China's leaders expect to leverage the increased foreign competition inherent in its WTO commitments to transform the country's inefficient, money-losing companies and hasten the development of a commercial credit culture in its banking system. Although more competition may eventually help improve productivity, in the short run unemployment will almost certainly increase, potentially contributing to social unrest. Thus the commitment to open its economy further and abide by all WTO rules constitutes a gamble of historic proportions.

Nicholas R. Lardy's book addresses why China's leaders have taken this gamble. He argues that the strong trajectory of reform of the trading system in the run-up to WTO membership has improved the odds for success. By the time China entered the WTO it was already perhaps the most open of all developing countries. Its tariff and nontariff barriers were falling rapidly, and China was leading the world in producing traditional labor-intensive goods such as toys, footwear, and apparel. The nation had also become part of global production networks for computers and other information technology hardware. Indeed by 2000 China had emerged as the world's seventh largest trading country.

Lardy's analysis, however, shows that some parts of the economy remain highly protected and should shrink as China implements its WTO-mandated trade and investment liberalization. This result will be politically feasible only if exports and thus employment expand in certain internationally competitive goods. But as this volume explains, under pressure from industrialized countries, China has granted WTO members unprecedented authority to limit imports of Chinese products. This consent may have led some industries in the United States and elsewhere to expect protection from increased competition from Chinese products, even when they are traded fairly.

Lardy examines the economic effects of China's WTO accession on the world, its Asian neighbors, and the United States. He suggests that even if China meets all of its obligations to provide increased access to its goods and services markets, the politically sensitive U.S. bilateral trade deficit with China is almost certain to increase as China continues to displace other sources of supply of labor-intensive goods.

This book also explores China's likely role in the new round of global trade negotiations initiated at Doha in 2001 and the importance of maintaining open markets in the United States and other economies if China is to be successfully integrated into the global trading system.

The author thanks participants who discussed a draft of the manuscript at meetings convened in Washington and Beijing. Special thanks go to Lu Mai of the State Council's Development Research Center for organizing the meeting in Beijing. Pieter P. Bottelier, Richard B. Cassidy, Adam Cowles, Jeffrey Garten, Jane-yu Ho Li, Will Martin, Richard Seldin, James Steinberg, and an anonymous reviewer read the entire manuscript and offered extremely valuable comments and suggestions.

At Brookings Theresa Walker edited the manuscript, Michael Aller provided research assistance, and Todd DeLelle, Fabian Nierhaus, and Jeffrey Rohaly verified the factual content. Carlotta Ribar proofread the book, and Julia Petrakis prepared the index.

Brookings is grateful to the Carnegie Corporation of New York, the Freeman Foundation, the Henry Luce Foundation, the Loren W. Hershey Family Foundation, PepsiCo, the Smith Richardson Foundation, and the Starr Foundation for support of this project.

The views expressed in this volume are those of the author and should not be ascribed to the organizations whose assistance is acknowledged above or to the trustees, officers, or other staff members of the Brookings Institution.

MICHAEL H. ARMACOST
*President*

*January 2002*
*Washington, D.C.*

# Contents

## Tables

## Figures

## Box

INTEGRATING
CHINA
INTO THE
GLOBAL
ECONOMY

CHAPTER ONE

# China Enters the World Trade Organization

FOR MORE THAN A CENTURY China's promise as a trading and investment partner has lured foreign businesses in search of profit. From the owners of the great English cotton mills of the nineteenth century, who hoped that sales to China could keep their looms operating forever, to the executives of foreign telecommunications companies that sought to break into a potentially lucrative market in the mid-1990s, many foreign business executives have been disappointed. Poor planning by Western firms caused some recent disappointments. The best example may be Occidental Petroleum's joint venture to create China's largest open pit coal mine at Antaibao in the Pingshuo coalfield in Shanxi Province.[1] Oxy's chairman, Armand Hammer, negotiated directly with Deng Xiaoping to establish the venture, overriding his top executives' concerns that some of the parameters in the project's feasibility study were unrealistic.[2] When it was announced in 1983, it was by far the largest foreign joint venture ever established in China. Within a few years it became clear that the assumptions on which the venture was premised were badly flawed. Occidental's losses mounted, and after Hammer's death in 1990 Oxy's new chief executive wrote off the firm's $250 million investment and put its share of the venture on the market.[3]

Chinese bureaucratic restrictions that raised the cost of doing business unnecessarily and limited market opportunities for foreign firms led to other disappointments. Perhaps the best example is the auto industry. In the 1980s and early 1990s Chinese imports of passenger cars rose steadily, and many foreign manufacturers believed that the market for imported cars would explode as China's rapid economic growth began to create a middle class of significant numbers. Then in 1994 the government announced an auto policy to promote the development of the domestic industry at the expense of imports. Almost overnight sales of imported cars,

I

other vehicles, and parts plunged from \$5.5 billion to \$2.7 billion and then sank to a low of \$1.9 billion in 1997.[4]

At the turn of the twenty-first century, however, China's economic promise seemed brighter than ever before. China seemed to have sailed unscathed through the Asian financial crisis of 1997–98. Its trade was expanding at a record-setting pace, and the promise of its market for foreign firms was turning to reality in some sectors. Foreign manufacturers, led by Motorola, Nokia, and Ericsson had captured 95 percent of the market for cellular phones.[5] Coca-Cola was the dominant supplier of carbonated beverages with a market share fifteen times its closest domestic competitor.[6] Its operations in China have been profitable for more than a decade, and Coca-Cola expects China to emerge as its largest Asian market in 2002 or 2003.[7] McDonald's and Kentucky Fried Chicken, with almost 900 outlets between them, dominated China's rapidly growing fast food market.[8] Kodak had captured half the market for film and photographic paper. Volkswagen, through two separate joint ventures, controlled more than half the domestic automobile industry.[9] Carrefour, the French company, had become China's second largest retailer only five years after entering the market.[10] And, as unlikely as it might have once seemed, Proctor and Gamble had more than half of what is undoubtedly the world's biggest shampoo market.[11]

More important than the success of any individual foreign firm, after fourteen years of arduous negotiations, in 2001 China became a member of the World Trade Organization (WTO) under terms that hewed closely to the long-term Western goal of bringing China into the world trading system on "commercially viable terms."[12] China promised not only to reduce significantly tariff and nontariff barriers but also to open up long-closed sectors such as telecommunications, banking, insurance, asset management, and distribution to foreign investment. Equally significant it agreed to abide by all of the WTO rules—from the protection of foreign intellectual property to the elimination of local content requirements that China had imposed on many wholly foreign-owned and joint venture manufacturing companies.[13] In a few important areas China undertook obligations that exceed normal WTO standards. These derogations from WTO rules are sometimes called WTO-plus commitments.

The WTO agreement promised to create tremendous new opportunities for foreign business. For example, China's telecommunications market is exploding. The fixed-line network added 35.6 million subscribers in 2000 alone. Development of mobile telephony is even more rapid, with

42 million new subscribers in the same year, bringing the total to 85 million. In 2000 China surpassed Japan to become the world's second largest mobile phone market, and in July 2001 it surpassed the United States to become the world's largest market.[14] China Mobile, the biggest player in the domestic market, was poised to overtake Vodafone to become the world's largest mobile phone operator in 2002. Its listed arm, China Mobile (Hong Kong), in 2001 was far and away the largest capitalized company in Asia outside Japan.[15] Even before China entered the World Trade Organization Chinese telecommunications companies were buying more mobile telecommunications equipment from multinational suppliers than firms in any other market outside the United States.[16] The WTO agreement, however, holds open the promise that foreign telecommunications companies, for the first time, will be able to enter joint ventures to provide telecommunications services, including Internet, mobile, and fixed-line services.

Foreign financial service providers see a similarly large market. With the world's largest population and the highest savings rate of any major nation, the potential opportunities to provide banking, insurance, securities, and asset management services seem unsurpassed. Even before China's entry into the World Trade Organization, more than 150 foreign branch banks were operating in China, all established with the expectation that eventually a WTO agreement would allow them to offer a full range of banking services. Insurance was seen as an equally lucrative area. European insurance companies were so anxious to expand their toehold in the market that the European Union, in its bilateral negotiations with China on WTO entry, demanded seven new licenses for European firms and stipulated that the Chinese government award the licenses before its WTO entry.[17] Several months later, Switzerland, besides negotiating a big cut in the Chinese tariff on imports of watches, also demanded licenses for Swiss insurance companies as a condition for completing bilateral negotiations with China on WTO entry.[18] Foreign asset management companies also were jockeying for position in advance of China's entry. JP Morgan Fleming Asset Management, Schroders Investment Management, and Invesco were among the early entrants, signing technical cooperation or consulting agreements with Chinese fund management companies in 2000 that the foreign partners hoped would become full-fledged joint ventures in the mutual fund business after China entered the World Trade Organization.[19]

Naturally, its proponents hailed the prospect of bringing China into the World Trade Organization. President Bill Clinton described it as an "opportunity that comes along once in a generation."[20] U.S. Trade Representative

Charlene Barshefsky said the bilateral U.S.-China trade agreement, which was rolled into China's accession package, "will open the world's largest nation to our goods, farm products and services in a way we have not seen in the modern era."[21] U.S. business groups and farm organizations mounted a major lobbying effort to ensure congressional passage of permanent normal trade relations for China, so that when it entered the World Trade Organization the president would have the authority to designate China a normal trading country. Without that designation China would have denied most of the benefits of its market opening to the United States, leaving the field free for competitors from Europe, Japan, and the rest of the world.

Yet critics argue that China remains a state-dominated economy with a mercantilist rather than free-trade orientation and that it will prove incapable of meeting, or does not even intend to meet, its far-reaching WTO obligations.[22] Labor leaders, pointing to the growing U.S. deficit in its trade with China, charge that the agreement will "only lead to further increases in this job destroying trade deficit."[23]

## Shallow Integration and Trade Dualism?

During the 1980s and 1990s China emerged as a major player in the global economy, indeed no other country has ever expanded its role so rapidly. Its foreign trade exploded, from about $20 billion in the late 1970s to $475 billion in 2000.[24] As shown in figure 1-1, after China's inward-looking Cultural Revolution decade (1966–76) drew to a close, China's trade began to grow dramatically faster than world trade. By 2000 its share of total world trade had sextupled compared with its share in 1977, and it was the world's seventh largest trading country.[25]

Simultaneously China attracted record foreign direct investment. For most of the 1990s China was the world's second largest recipient of foreign direct investment, following only the United States.[26] By the end of the 1990s the total stock of foreign direct investment in China accounted for almost a third of the cumulative foreign direct investment in all developing countries. Cumulative foreign investment in China far exceeded the total stock of such investment in countries such as Mexico and Brazil, which opened their doors to foreign direct investment decades before China did.[27]

Less noticed, Chinese firms have become principal investors abroad. As early as the mid-1990s China was the largest outward investor among developing countries and the eighth largest supplier of outward investment among all countries.[28] Finally, China raised significant capital on

Figure 1-1. *The Growth of China Trade vs. World Trade, 1977–2000*

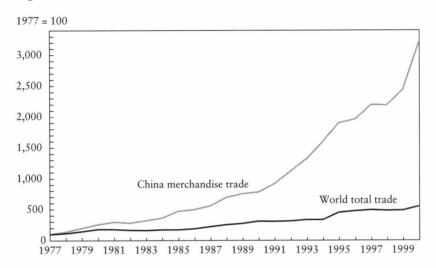

Sources: Nicholas R. Lardy, *China in the World Economy* (Washington: Institute for International Econo-mics, 1994), p. 2; World Trade Organization, *Annual Report 1996: International Trade Statistics* (Geneva, 1996), p. 117, *Annual Report 1997: vol. I,* p. 14, *Annual Report 1998: International Trade Statistics,* p. 18, *Annual Report 1999: International Trade Statistics,* p. 19; National Bureau of Statistics, *China Statistical Yearbook 1999* (Beijing: China Statistics Press, 1999), pp. 578–80; General Agreement on Tariffs and Trade, *International Trade 85-86* (Geneva, 1986), p. 139, *International Trade 90-91,* vol. 2 (Geneva, 1991), p. 77; WTO, *World Merchandise Trade by Region and Selected Economy 1999* (www.wto.org [January 20, 2000]), and *Annual Report 2001* (Geneva, 2001), p. 12.

international bond and equity markets. Initially most of the funds were raised by the sale of sovereign bonds, but by the latter part of the 1990s major state-owned Chinese companies sought listings and raised billions of dollars on overseas equity markets. China Telecom (Hong Kong) led the way with a $4 billion sale of equity in 1997. By 2000 the pace in-creased dramatically as China began to sell off parts of several of its larg-est state-run companies. China Mobile (Hong Kong), PetroChina, Unicom, and Sinopec together raised more than $15 billion through equity sales in New York and Hong Kong in 2000.[29]

Despite this extraordinary performance some have argued that China remained in certain respects only shallowly integrated into the world economy and that its trade regime remains seriously flawed.[30] High tariffs and an array of nontariff barriers mean that some critical sectors of the Chinese economy are relatively insulated from international competition.

More generally, the state attempts to control imports by limiting the type and number of companies authorized to carry out international trade transactions; imposing onerous inspection and safety licensing requirements on imports; developing technical standards designed in part to protect domestic industries; discriminating against foreign goods in government procurement; and imposing high local content requirements on foreign and joint-venture firms producing in China.

The enormous importance of export processing in China's foreign trade also was seen by some as evidence of a dualistic trade regime. China had a liberal set of rules for foreign firms and a few domestic firms engaged in export processing but a relatively closed and illiberal trade regime applying to most domestic companies. Foreign firms began to establish operations in China following the passage of a joint venture law in 1979 and the creation of four special economic zones on the southeast coast in 1980. Naturally, the initial contribution of these firms to China's exports was modest. As shown in table 1-1, not until 1985 did their share of total exports reach 1 percent. But, as foreign investment grew, the share of exports produced by foreign-invested firms expanded, exceeding 10 percent by 1990.[31] By 2000 foreign-invested firms, which accounted for only about one-eighth of all manufacturing output, were responsible for almost one-half of all of China's exports.[32] In addition, some domestic firms produce processed exports, relying on imported raw materials, parts, and components. Since these exports were assembled or processed from duty-free imported parts and components, their rapid growth created only a limited demand for inputs produced by domestic firms. Thus a very large part of the export-producing sector could be seen as an enclave, with limited linkages to the rest of the domestic economy, which remained much more insulated from the international economy.[33]

The share of imports undertaken by foreign-invested firms and domestic firms engaged in processing bears out this perspective. Since foreign firms not only imported large amounts of parts and components but also typically imported the machinery and equipment they needed to equip their factories, these firms were responsible for a third of all imports by 1992 and consistently more than half of all Chinese imports since 1995. Domestic firms engaged in export processing import huge volumes of parts and components as well.

The high share of exports and imports that is accounted for by foreign-invested firms and domestic firms engaged in processing suggests that purely domestic firms were far less involved in international trade than China's

Table 1-1. *Exports and Imports of Foreign-Funded Enterprises,*
*1985–2000*
Billions of U.S. dollars unless noted otherwise

| Year | Total exports | Foreign-funded enterprise exports | Percent | Total imports | Foreign-funded enterprise imports | Percent |
|---|---|---|---|---|---|---|
| 1985 | 27.4 | 0.3 | 1 | 42.3 | 2.1 | 5 |
| 1986 | 30.9 | 0.5 | 2 | 42.9 | 2.6 | 6 |
| 1987 | 39.4 | 1.2 | 3 | 43.2 | 3.0 | 7 |
| 1988 | 47.5 | 2.5 | 5 | 55.3 | 5.5 | 10 |
| 1989 | 52.5 | 4.9 | 9 | 59.1 | 8.9 | 15 |
| 1990 | 62.1 | 7.8 | 13 | 53.4 | 12.3 | 23 |
| 1991 | 71.8 | 12.1 | 17 | 63.8 | 17.2 | 27 |
| 1992 | 84.9 | 17.4 | 20 | 80.6 | 26.4 | 33 |
| 1993 | 91.7 | 25.2 | 28 | 104.0 | 41.8 | 40 |
| 1994 | 121.0 | 34.7 | 29 | 115.6 | 52.9 | 46 |
| 1995 | 148.8 | 46.9 | 32 | 132.1 | 62.9 | 48 |
| 1996 | 151.1 | 61.5 | 41 | 138.8 | 75.6 | 54 |
| 1997 | 182.8 | 74.9 | 41 | 142.4 | 77.7 | 55 |
| 1998 | 183.8 | 81.0 | 44 | 140.2 | 76.7 | 55 |
| 1999 | 194.9 | 88.6 | 45 | 165.7 | 85.9 | 52 |
| 2000 | 249.2 | 119.4 | 48 | 225.1 | 117.3 | 52 |

Sources: Nicholas R. Lardy, "The Role of Foreign Trade and Investment in China's Economic Transformation," *China Quarterly*, no. 144 (December 1995), p. 1,066; Valerie Cerra and Anuradha Dayal-Gulati, "China's Trade Flows: Changing Price Sensitivities and the Reform Process," IMF Working Paper 99-1 (Washington, 1999), p. 25 (www.imf.org [August 23, 2000]); State Statistical Bureau, *China Statistical Yearbook 1995* (Beijing: China Statistical Publishing House, 1995), p. 553; *China Statistical Yearbook 1997*, p. 604; National Bureau of Statistics, *China Statistical Yearbook 2000* (Beijing: China Statistics Press, 2000), pp. 588, 603; "Statistical Communiqué of the People's Republic of China on the 2000 Economic and Social Development (www.stats.gov.cn [March 6, 2001]); and General Administration of Customs of the People's Republic of China, *China's Customs Statistics*, no. 136 (December, 2000), pp. 14–15.

aggregate trade data indicate. For example, in 1999 China was the world's ninth largest exporting country.[34] But if exports of foreign-invested firms are deleted, China's rank falls to fifteenth. China's rank would drop further if processed exports produced by domestic firms were excluded. Foreign firms usually are responsible for product design, the supply of needed parts and components, and the sale of the goods on the world market. In some cases the foreign firm even supplies specialized equipment that is required to assemble the products sold on the world market. In these assembly operations the Chinese firm essentially is a subcontractor. Chinese critics frequently have cited the low ratio of domestic value added in processing activity as evidence of the modest contribution of this activity to economic growth and modernization.

To those who characterize China's trade regime as dualistic, trade liberalization in the second half of the 1990s met with limited success. It was an attempt to move toward a more unified and open set of rules to cover the entire external sector, not just those firms engaged in processing. Consequently limitations on access to the Chinese market are structurally related to the nature of the Chinese trade regime. Domestic firms that are not engaged in export processing are stifled by tariff and nontariff barriers that are still intact, particularly the limited availability of the right to trade. Barry Naughton even argues that the protection provided to the domestic market by the trading system increased somewhat in the second half of the 1990s.[35]

To some the absence of currency convertibility on capital account transactions also highlights the limits on China's integration into the world economy.[36] China notified the International Monetary Fund in late 1996 that it was in full compliance with Article VIII of the Fund's charter, formally confirming the convertibility of the domestic currency in foreign trade and service transactions. That means that Chinese firms have ready access to foreign exchange to pay for imports.[37] And wholly foreign-owned or joint venture firms can convert domestic currency profits into foreign exchange and remit them abroad.[38] But the opportunity for domestic firms and Chinese individuals to legally hold foreign-currency denominated financial assets, such as stocks or bonds, is extremely limited.[39] Similarly, Chinese regulations preclude foreign firms and individuals from purchasing Chinese-currency denominated financial assets, such as government bonds or the stocks referred to as A shares, which are traded on the country's two principal securities markets. Foreign firms and individuals are limited to buying foreign-currency denominated shares of Chinese companies that are known as B shares, sold for U.S. dollars on the Shanghai Stock Exchange and Hong Kong dollars on the Shenzhen market.

Finally China's delayed entry into the World Trade Organization may also indicate the shallowness of China's integration into the world economy. China initiated the process of becoming a member of the General Agreement on Tariffs and Trade, the predecessor to the World Trade Organization, in 1986.[40] But only after a decade and a half of negotiation did China fully embrace the principles of the multilateral trading system, agreeing to terms that brought it into the World Trade Organization.

The central thesis of this book is that China's integration into the global economy increased dramatically after 1978, especially in the decade before its entry into the World Trade Organization. As chapter 2 discusses, in the 1990s the government systematically reduced tariff barriers, giving China the lowest tariff protection of any developing country. Although more difficult to evaluate, it seems that the protective effect of China's nontariff barriers also shrank impressively. By the late 1990s quotas and licensing requirements limited imports for only 4 percent of all tariff lines, and trading rights were widely available for all but a handful of commodities that accounted for only 11 percent of China's total imports. As a result of these and other reforms, between 1995 and 2000 what the Ministry of Foreign Trade classifies as ordinary imports grew much more rapidly than the sum of imports of duty-free parts and components used in processing and the duty-free imports of capital goods of joint venture firms.[41] The rapid growth of ordinary imports undermines the argument of trade dualism. The growing role of foreign-funded enterprises and export processing by domestic firms reflects China's increasing integration into global production networks. The 16 percent share of China's manufacturing output produced by foreign firms is similar to the share in the United States and somewhat greater than that in Germany and Italy.[42] Moreover, by the late 1990s the linkages between foreign and domestic firms engaged in processing, on the one hand, and other domestic firms, on the other, grew significantly. Thus the ratio of value added in export processing almost doubled over the 1990s. That resulted from the displacement of imports by locally produced parts and components and a shift into higher skill levels of processing where wages are higher than in footwear and apparel, the industries that dominated processing in the 1980s and first part of the 1990s.[43] Finally China's lengthy process of accession to the World Trade Organization reflects as much the rising bar imposed by members of the Working Party on China's Accession to the World Trade Organization (hereafter WTO working party) as China's slowness to embrace the principles of the multilateral trading system. Indeed chapter 3 argues that the WTO-plus terms imposed on China, though legally enforceable, are so onerous that they violate fundamental WTO principles. In short China already is more integrated into the world economy than is commonly understood.

## The WTO Decision

Given the rapid growth of the Chinese economy after 1978, the explosive growth of trade, and China's ability to attract record foreign direct investment, it is not immediately obvious why its leadership saw membership in the World Trade Organization as central to the country's economic future. Given the country's apparent success with what some have characterized as shallow integration and a dualistic trading system, why did the leadership agree to go forward on WTO accession when most believed that the result would be heavy costs in the short run, especially to key sectors, and economic growth had already been great without WTO accession? This question is all the more puzzling because the scope and depth of demands placed on entrants into the formal international trading system have increased since the formal conclusion of the Uruguay Round of trade negotiations in 1994. The General Agreement on Tariffs and Trade (GATT), which was established in 1948, reduced barriers to the international flow of commodities by limiting the ability of members to impose tariff and nontariff barriers, primarily on manufactured goods. The focus was primarily on the cross-border flow of goods.

The Uruguay Round of trade negotiations, which led to the formation of the World Trade Organization in 1995, expanded the agenda considerably by covering many services, agriculture, intellectual property, and certain aspects of foreign direct investment, all of which were previously exempt. Since the conclusion of the Uruguay Round the international community has added agreements on information technology, basic telecommunications services, and financial services. Compared with GATT, WTO membership requires liberalization of a much broader range of domestic economic activity, including areas traditionally regarded by most countries as among the most sensitive.

As chapter 3 explains, China's market access and other commitments are not only more far reaching than those that governed the accession of countries only a decade ago, they exceed those made by any member that has joined the World Trade Organization since 1995. The broader and deeper commitments China has made inevitably will entail considerable short-term economic costs. Unemployment will rise in sectors that shrink as they face increased international competition, from imports and from goods and services provided by foreign-invested firms in China. The efficiency gains from restructuring the economy will be significant, but, since they will require the reallocation of labor and capital, are achievable only in the medium and longer term. Political leaders rarely are willing to impose high short-term economic costs in order to reap benefits in the medium and long term. Why does China appear to be an exception?

The answer perhaps can not be fully known to external observers, but several pieces of the answer seem clear. Perhaps the most important background factor is that the regime, during the first two decades of economic reform, increasingly has staked its legitimacy on its ability to deliver sustained improvements in consumption and living standards to the Chinese people. Although China's leaders have hotly debated many of the details of economic reform, the view that economic growth is the sine qua non for retaining political power seems almost unanimous. Appeals to ideology, characteristic of the Maoist era, are long since gone. Appeals to nationalism have increased, but they are distinctly secondary to appeals to economic self-interest. Several factors suggest that the leadership has accepted the stiff demands of the international community in an attempt to continue its ability to deliver rising living standards to the population. What is the evidence that the leadership is concerned about meeting its implicit contract with the Chinese population when its own headline growth numbers have been high for so long?

For one thing China's growth over the past two decades has almost certainly been much slower than reported in official data. The World Bank, the Organization for Economic Cooperation and Development (OECD), and several Chinese research organizations have produced studies attempting to quantify the overstatement. As shown in table 1-2, the World Bank estimates that long-term growth between 1978 and 1995 overstates real growth by 1.2 percentage points per year. Tellingly, the World Bank estimates that overstatement more than tripled between the first subperiod, 1978–86, and the second, 1986–95. Research published by the OECD places the growth rate for 1986–94 even lower, 6.0 percent per year, or 3.8 percentage points below the official data for the same period. China's National Economic Research Center in 2000 released the results of a two-year study estimating a growth rate of 8.4 percent for the years 1978–98, also below the official claim of 9.7 percent for the same period.

Some foreign scholars believe that the degree to which growth is overstated in the official data increased greatly in 1998 and 1999, when China's leadership appears to have taken the decision to meet many of the specific expectations of the international community for China's WTO membership.[44] At that time the overstatement of economic growth was discussed widely in Chinese newspapers and academic journals. In 1998 the authorities identified 8 percent as a mandatory target for the expansion of gross domestic product. Provincial statistical authorities reported growth that averaged well above 8 percent, and the central authorities used an unspecified methodology to adjust these numbers, coming up with national growth of 7.8 percent. Thomas Rawksi has argued that the growth

Table 1-2. *Official and Independent Estimates of China's Growth since 1978*

| Source/period | Official growth rate | Independent estimate of growth rate |
|---|---|---|
| World Bank | | |
| 1978–95 | 9.4 | 8.2 |
| 1978–86 | 9.2 | 8.8 |
| 1986–95 | 9.2 | 7.9 |
| OECD | | |
| 1986–94 | 9.8 | 6.0 |
| China National Economic Research Center | | |
| 1978–98 | 9.7 | 8.4 |

Sources: World Bank, *China 2020: Development Challenges in the New Century* (Washington, 1997), p. 3; Ren Ruoen, *China's Economic Performance in an International Perspective* (Paris: Organization for Economic Cooperation and Development, 1997), p. 108; Tan Hongkai, "Moderate Economic Growth Predicted," *China Daily*, June 12, 2000, p. 4; and National Bureau of Statistics, *China Statistical Yearbook 1999* (Beijing: China Statistics Press, 1999), p. 58.
Note: The data the World Bank give as the official growth rate are about one-half a percentage point below numbers published by Chinese statistical authorities because they were calculated using least squares growth rates. The World Bank data in the original source are presented in per capita terms. The data shown above are the original numbers plus officially reported population growth.

rate in 1998 might have been less than half the official claim, that is, under 4 percent.[45]

Chinese government concern over falsification of economic data reached a new level in the spring of 2000 at a meeting of the Standing Committee of the National People's Congress. Zheng Jianling, who is both the deputy director of the Shanghai Audit Bureau of the National Bureau of Statistics and a deputy of the National People's Congress, proposed that criminal penalties be imposed on officials who falsify statistics.[46] If China's top leadership also believed that official data on economic growth were becoming significantly more upward biased, they may have become more willing to incur the short-term economic and political costs of restructuring associated with increased international competition in order to shore up the medium- and long-term performance of the economy.

Whatever the precise rate of growth of gross domestic product, it greatly overstates the gains in real economic welfare in China during the reform era. The reason is the large buildup of unsold and apparently unsalable goods. In the Western national income accounting system that China has adopted, increases in inventories are counted as part of output and thus contribute to gross domestic product. But unsold inventories, by definition, are not utilized for consumption or for fixed investment, so they do not contribute to improvements in social welfare or to increases in productive capacity of the economy. The real resources that have gone into the production of these goods have been largely wasted. From 1990 through 1999 additions to inventories averaged 5.3 percent of gross domestic product.[47] In the United States the comparable figure was 0.4 percent.[48] Thus, whatever the true rate of economic growth has been, the gains in consumption and productive capacity that China achieved were less notable.

Although some increase in inventories is needed to support higher output over time, the disproportionately large inventory buildup in China reflects continued production of low-quality goods for which there is little or no demand. Chinese society would have been much better off if the goods had never been produced. Although the rate of inventory buildup moderated in 1998 and 1999, it continued to be far higher than would be expected in a market economy. China's premier, Zhu Rongji, in his annual address to the National People's Congress in the spring of 2000, acknowledged that inventory buildup continued to be an ongoing problem and that China must "limit the production of non-marketable products."[49]

China's growth may be explained primarily by extraordinarily high rates of resource mobilization rather than productivity gains associated with more efficiency in the use of scarce resources. Throughout the 1990s investment in China absorbed almost two-fifths of total output, well above the level of from one-fifth to one-quarter that prevailed in other low-income economies.[50] Some studies show that improvements in factor productivity for the economy as a whole that have occurred in the reform era are largely explained by the transfer of labor out of agriculture and improvements in the educational attainment of the work force.[51] The relatively small contribution of productivity gains to economic growth in the nonagricultural sector suggests that significant problems in incentives and other aspects of the institutional structure need to be solved to sustain economic growth over the long run.[52]

The high rate of inventory accumulation and the apparently slow productivity growth in the nonagricultural sector suggest China's economic growth continues to be weighed down by a relatively inefficient state-owned industrial sector. Moreover, despite numerous reform initiatives over two decades, the profits of state-owned manufacturing firms relative to their assets fell through 1998. As shown in figure 1-2, in the early stage of reform, in the late 1970s and early 1980s, the return on assets in manufacturing seemed unusually high, around 25 percent. In fact returns were

Figure 1-2. *Profitability of State-Owned Industry, 1978–99*

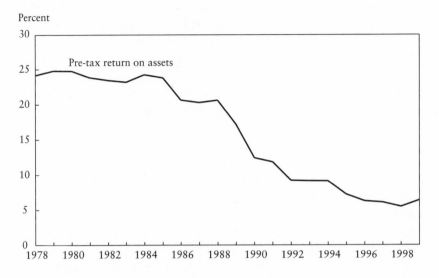

Percent

Sources: State Statistical Bureau, *China Statistical Yearbook 1994*, pp. 392–95; National Bureau of Statistics, *China Statistical Yearbook 1999*, pp. 432–35; and National Bureau of Statistics, *China Statistical Yearbook 2000* (Beijing: China Statistics Press, 1999), pp. 414–17.

Note: Profitability is measured as pre-tax profits divided by the sum of the depreciated value of fixed assets and working capital. Since what the Chinese statistical authorities report as "total profits" is actually profits after payment of sales taxes, sales tax surcharges, and value-added taxes, but before payment of income taxes, pre-tax profits is derived as the sum "total profits" plus sales taxes, sales tax surcharges, and value-added taxes.

exaggerated artificially for two reasons. First, financing for plant and equipment and for a significant share of working capital was provided to state enterprises through the state budget. Firms paid no interest on these funds, reducing their costs of production and thus artificially raising their profitability relative to levels that prevail in market economies. Second, the return on assets in some branches of industry was inflated further as a consequence of the low prices paid by state-owned manufacturing firms for agricultural inputs. The food processing, textile, apparel, and cigarette industries earned extraordinarily high profits, pulling up the rate of return on manufacturing overall to unusually high levels. Ending state budgetary financing of working capital and fixed investment in 1983 and 1985, respectively, and price reforms in the farm sector, which raised the prices of food and fiber crops and tobacco relative to industrial product prices, deflated these supernormal profits.[53] Because of these reforms, by 1990

Chinese data on profitability were much more meaningful, and returns had fallen by half, to a level more characteristic of market economies.

But in the 1990s, after the major adjustment of relative agricultural and industrial product prices had been completed and state budget financing of investment long since phased out, profitability in state-owned manufacturing companies continued to decline. By 1998 pretax profit relative to capital employed was only 5 percent. That is well below rates of return achieved in advanced industrial economies, not to mention emerging markets where such returns are commonly higher. The pretax rate of return on capital in U.S. manufacturing firms in the 1990s, for example, averaged 11 percent.[54]

Some have suggested that because the share of output of state companies has fallen continuously throughout the reform era that their declining efficiency and profitability is of little concern in the long run. According to this reasoning the state-owned sector has become so small that its inefficiency has only modest and thus bearable macroeconomic consequences. It is true that the state has shed its ownership of many small- and medium-sized companies, and the output from firms with other types of ownership has grown more rapidly. Thus the share of manufacturing output produced in state-owned companies fell from about 80 percent at the onset of reform in the late 1970s to only 28 percent in 1998.[55] State-owned industries, however, still controlled more than 70 percent of all of the fixed assets and 80 percent of all working capital used in manufacturing.[56] Given the relatively large claim these firms have on society's resources, if the efficiency in their use of those resources continues to decline, it will become more difficult to maintain robust economic growth. That, in turn, will make it more difficult to sustain employment growth, raising serious political problems for the regime.

China's financial system is not yet prepared to support a market economy. For many years the banks, all of which were state owned, acted as agents of the state, allocating credit according to plan.[57] Although the government since the mid-1990s has adopted policies to encourage the banks to operate on a commercial basis, it still requires them to channel a significant part of their lending in support of state policy objectives. That, combined with the still limited ability of banks to assess credit risk, contributes to the declining financial performance of the banks and the relatively stunted development of the private sector of the economy, which is starved for investment funds. As chapter 3 discusses, China's WTO commitments include a large expansion in the opportunities for foreign financial institutions to operate in China. China's leadership envisages foreign banks and other foreign financial institutions as a source of competition that should improve the ability of domestic institutions to allocate resources to high productivity uses, contributing to greater economic efficiency and thus more sustainable growth. Given the fragility of the banking system, however, judging the pace at which foreign banks and other financial institutions should be allowed to expand is one of the most important decisions that China's leadership faces.

Although it is difficult to judge, perhaps Taiwan was also a factor in the decision of China's leadership to accept the potentially high short-term costs entailed in WTO membership. After Taiwan began to seek membership in the World Trade Organization in 1992, China insisted that Taiwan could not join until China had become a member. Indeed an understanding the GATT Council reached when Taiwan sought membership implicitly supported this position. For a long time the implicit understanding about China's prior membership was not tested since the island resisted some of the economic and trade reforms that the WTO working party on Taiwan's accession was demanding. But by the late 1990s bilateral and multilateral negotiations on Taiwan accession were nearing completion. And U.S. trade negotiators began to reiterate frequently that Taiwan's WTO membership should be considered on its own merits. In short, if Taiwan had completed negotiations, its membership should not be held up by China's delayed entry. Chinese leaders knew they could forestall Taiwan's entry until after their own as long as their own accession negotiations were seen as moving forward. But they may have worried that support for their prior entry would begin to erode if it appeared that little progress was being made.

Finally, it seems that the Asian financial crisis convinced the Chinese leadership of the desirability of accelerating domestic economic reform. The Asian financial crisis, in effect, was a wake-up call. Although some of China's institutional arrangements differed substantially from those in other Asian countries, there were several alarming parallels. China's state-owned companies, like those in Korea and in some countries in Southeast Asia, were too highly leveraged. Its banks had lent excessively to inefficient state-owned companies that in many cases did not earn a high enough return on their investments to be able to service their debt. The resulting buildup of nonperforming loans in state-owned banks and other lending institutions threatened the viability of the entire financial system.[58]

The absence of capital account convertibility, relatively greater reliance on foreign direct investment rather than short-term foreign borrowing and inflows of foreign equity capital, and massive foreign exchange reserves meant that in the short run China was rather insulated from the Asian financial crisis. Unlike the most severely affected countries in the region, China's economic growth remained well into positive territory; the value of its currency was maintained at a fixed rate; and foreign capital inflows in the form of direct investment remained large.

Yet China did not go entirely unscathed by the crisis. The growth of exports, which had tripled between 1990 and 1997, stalled entirely in 1998 as demand for Chinese goods in many of its Asian neighbors collapsed. It was China's worst export performance in more than two decades. Foreign direct investment inflows, which had soared every year earlier in the decade, plateaued in 1998 and then declined in 1999. As a result China's rank as a destination for foreign direct investment on a worldwide basis slipped from number two, a rank it had held for several years, to third in 1998, and then fifth in 1999.[59] Foreign banks reduced their lending to China, first as part of a general retreat from Asia, later in response to the bankruptcy of the Guangdong International Trust and Investment Corporation. GITIC, the investment arm of the Guangdong Provincial government, had borrowed almost U.S.$5 billion (hereafter $ indicates U.S. dollars unless noted otherwise), mostly from international banks. But most of the funds were wasted or lost to corruption, leaving the firm unable to service its debt. From a peak of $90 billion at the end of the third quarter of 1997, foreign bank claims on China declined to $68 billion by the end of 1999.[60] And between September 1998 and December 1999 Hong Kong banks reduced their lending to Chinese-related nonbanks, primarily so-called red chip companies such as CITIC Pacific, by $12 billion.[61] In short, in a period of just over two years Chinese firms and their affiliates in Hong Kong had to repay loans and other external obligations to banks of at least $34 billion. Reduced foreign direct investment and declining foreign bank lending to China contributed to a capital account deficit in 1998, the first such deficit China had recorded since 1992.[62]

China's macroeconomic performance also deteriorated during this period. Economic growth was unsustainably high in the early 1990s, leading to record price inflation. Gross domestic product expanded by a record 14 percent in 1992, setting off an inflationary spiral that peaked in 1994, when consumer prices shot up by about one-fourth. As early as mid-1993

Zhu Rongji, then serving as both vice premier and governor of the central bank, initiated contractionary monetary and fiscal policies that eventually reduced aggregate demand and moderated price inflation. By 1996 growth and inflation were down to a more sustainable single-digit level. But just as a soft landing was in sight, the Asian financial crisis hit. The crisis reduced export growth and put further downward pressure on prices, leading to slower economic growth and deflation.

In response, in August 1998 China shifted from a policy of tightening to one of macroeconomic stimulus, through increased fiscal outlays and expanded lending by state banks.[63] These increased expenditures, which focused largely on public sector infrastructure investment, represented about 2.5 percent of gross domestic product. The World Bank judged that this amount was "sufficiently large to have a major impact on aggregate demand."[64] The fiscal program was supplemented with a relaxation of monetary policy, reflected in multiple cuts in nominal interest rates on loans, and other steps. The government also sought to shore up exports by increasing the share of value-added taxes rebated on goods sold internationally and, for the first time, authorizing private firms to trade directly in the international market rather than working through established state-owned trading companies. In 1999 it also initiated new lending programs by state-owned banks to support export growth.[65]

Besides the fiscal stimulus, monetary loosening, and export promotion measures to prevent a further slowdown in economic growth, China's leaders renewed and in certain respects stepped up their commitment to structural reforms, especially in the financial sector. The government in August 1998 injected 270 billion renminbi (RMB) into the four largest state-owned banks to shore up their sagging capital base; reorganized the branch structure of the central bank along supraprovincial lines in an attempt to insulate banks from political pressure for lending to support local projects; stepped up supervision and regulation of financial institutions, including the closure of a number of insolvent banks and nonbank financial institutions; and brought renewed pressure on state-owned banks to operate on a commercial basis. This was coupled with the creation of four state-owned asset management companies, which by year-end 2000 took about RMB 1.4 trillion in nonperforming loans off the books of the largest state-owned banks in an effort to improve the banks' balance sheets and their profitability. The underlying view, consistent with international experience, was that it is difficult to transform insolvent, unprofitable financial institutions and make them operate on genuinely commercial terms.

Simultaneously, the leadership renewed its commitment to reduce the massive financial losses of state-owned companies. Despite numerous previous reform initiatives, these losses had soared from about RMB 6 billion in 1987 to RMB 83 billion in 1997.[66] The government's initiatives ranged from privatizing smaller state-owned firms to major reductions in employment at core firms that were to remain state owned.

Most interestingly, the party and the government in this period both gradually came to believe that the private sector would have to become a principal new source of output, employment, and export growth. In the early years of reform the party moved cautiously. The concept of private property was still anathema to many of the old guard. Thus at the Sixth Plenum of the Eleventh Central Committee in 1981, the Chinese Communist Party only recognized that the state-managed economy and the collective economy were the two basic forms of economic activity and that a certain scope of economic activity by individual laborers was a necessary supplement of economic activity based on public ownership. This language subsequently was included in article 11 of the 1982 state constitution, passed by the Fifth Session of the Fifth National People's Congress in December 1982. Even this moderate flexibility, which made no mention of private ownership, facilitated the rapid development of firms that were not entirely state owned. Collectively owned firms became an important source of growth and employment in the decade of the 1980s. In 1987 a Chinese Communist Party document, for the first time, included a reference to private enterprises, saying, "For a considerable period of time the existence of the individual economy and a small number of privately-owned enterprises is unavoidable." The following year the 1982 constitution was revised, for the first time supplying the legal basis for private enterprise in China and providing it with a status as a supplement to economic activity based on public ownership. By 1997, at its Fifteenth National Congress, the party went much further, elevating the role of the nonstate sector, defined to include individual and private enterprise, to "an important, integral part of China's socialist market economy." The second session of the Ninth National People's Congress in March 1999 approved the same language in a further amendment to the constitution.[67] By 2000 policy had evolved again, not only acknowledging the contribution that the private sector was making to the economy but also promising that private firms would be put on an equal footing with state-owned firms.[68]

The decision of the Chinese leadership in early 1999 to make the broad commitments to opening of the domestic market that were required to conclude an agreement to join the World Trade Organization was consistent with this evolving attitude toward private economic activity and the earlier decision to accelerate domestic economic reforms.[69] At the time of the summit meeting between President Clinton and President Jiang Zemin in June 1998, China's posture on WTO membership appeared diffident. Premier Zhu Rongji articulated a take-it or leave-it attitude. If the United States would allow China to come in on what were described as reasonable terms, China would join. If the price of entry was too high, China would stay out, perhaps indefinitely. Trade Minister Shi Guangsheng echoed this view as late as December 1998 arguing that "China's market opening can only proceed in a gradual manner and China can not accept excessive or too high demands."[70]

But by early 1999 the view of Premier Zhu and other economic reformers had evolved. They increasingly came to believe that one of the principal benefits of becoming a member of the World Trade Organization was the increased competition it would bring to China's domestic market. More competition was seen as an essential additional source of pressure on state-owned banks and enterprises, forcing them to undertake badly needed structural reforms.[71] In mid-February it was reported that China was preparing to extend "its most credible offer yet for entry into the World Trade Organization."[72] By the time of his trip to the United States in April 1999, Zhu Rongji was openly articulating the view that China's membership in the World Trade Organization could be a lever for promoting domestic economic reform. At his joint press conference with President Clinton in Washington Premier Zhu stated, "The competition arising [from WTO membership] will also promote a more rapid and more healthy development of China's national economy."[73]

More profoundly, it seems that China's top leadership in the wake of the Asian crisis saw that there was no viable alternative to the globalization of production and that, indeed, China through WTO membership would benefit from greater participation in the trend.[74] Long Yongtu, vice minister of foreign trade and China's chief global trade negotiator, has been perhaps the most consistent and articulate spokesman for this point of view.[75] He recognizes that globalization means that production of an increasing array of goods is global rather than national. Although complex products such as automobiles, aircraft, computers, and telecommunications equipment are assembled in only a few locations, their parts and components are made in many locations throughout the world, based on comparative advantage. For computers, for example, some parts and components are relatively labor intensive, while others are more capital intensive. Given declining international transaction costs, it is becoming more and more cost effective to locate different stages of the production process in different countries, depending on the availability of labor and capital. "Thus production chains increasingly cross national borders."[76]

The same phenomenon is occurring in some traditional products. One example is bicycles. Taiwanese manufacturers assemble high-end bikes with aluminum frames produced in China; derailleurs and other accessories made by Japanese manufacturers in Southeast Asia; and a few of the most sophisticated components made in Japan. Countries that wall themselves off with high tariffs and other trade barriers will be excluded from participating in the development of the many industries in which cross-national production chains are critical.

Cross-national production chains have become more important in information technology products. Thus China as part of its WTO commitments has signed the Information Technology Agreement and will reduce tariffs for computers, telecommunications equipment, and integrated circuits to zero by 2005.[77] Quotas on these products were eliminated at the time of China's accession. Alternatively, if China had maintained tariffs and other restrictions that impede the flow of parts and components, that inevitably would have raised their prices, making goods that use those items as inputs in the production process less competitive on world markets. China would be unable to participate fully in the development of the global information industry. Producing many goods entirely within one country also is not viable. Again it raises costs so much that the products would not be competitive internationally. Thus Boeing, the world's premier manufacturer of commercial aircraft, relies on parts and components produced in more than seventy countries, not because they could not be produced in the United States but because they can be acquired externally at a lower cost. Acquisition of parts and components from many countries is occurring for an increasingly broad range of manufactured products.

But in Long Yongtu's view participation in an increasingly globalized economy requires not simply drastically reduced tariffs but also the development of a market economy. In his words, "Countries with planned economies have never been a part of economic globalization. China's economy must become a market economy in order to become part of the global economic system, as well as the economic globalization process."[78]

## Summary of Commitments

China's commitments to further open its economy in order to gain membership in the World Trade Organization are sweeping. They include significant reductions in statutory tariffs that will bring the average level to under 10 percent by 2005;[79] the introduction of a tariff-rate quota system that brings the tariff rate for chief agricultural commodities, such as wheat, almost to zero for a potentially significant volume of imports; the gradual elimination of all quotas and licenses that have restricted the flow of some imports; a large increase in the availability of trading rights, which will reduce the government's ability to use state trading as an instrument to control the volume of imports of agricultural and other key commodities; and the opening of critical service sectors such as telecommunications, distribution, banking, insurance, asset management, and securities to foreign direct investment. China has also agreed to abide by international standards in the protection of intellectual property and to accept the use by its trading partners of several unusual mechanisms that could be used to reduce the flow of Chinese goods into foreign markets.

## Implications

Some studies forecast that China will incur significant restructuring costs in meeting its sweeping WTO commitments. One study, for example, predicts that the opening in agriculture alone will result in the loss of jobs of about 8 million wheat farmers, about 30 percent of the number engaged in wheat production. Substantial reductions in employment and output are also forecast for a number of other products, including rapeseed oil, natural rubber, plastics, and rolled steel.[80]

These projections, however, almost certainly overstate the challenges that China faced when it finally entered the World Trade Organization. The reason is simple. The projections are based on conditions that existed in the mid-1990s and thus do not take into account the huge economic restructuring that occurred in China in the years immediately before its entry into the World Trade Organization.[81] On the external side China began significant tariff reductions in the early 1990s. By the eve of its entry into the World Trade Organization the average statutory import duty rate was only 15 percent, two-thirds less than the peak level of the 1980s. More important, by the second half of the 1990s actual import duties were only a small fraction of the average statutory rate. Similarly, by the eve of China's accession to the World Trade Organization, the state had reduced the number of imports restricted by quotas and licenses by 80 percent compared with the early 1990s. Only 4 percent of all tariff lines remained encumbered by import quotas and licenses.[82]

On the internal side the restructuring of manufacturing companies accelerated after Premier Zhu Rongji's speech to the National People's Congress in the spring of 1998, when he pledged to largely solve the problem of money-losing state-owned companies within three years. More than 36 million state workers, one-third of the total, lost their jobs in the three and a half-year period from1998 through the middle of 2001.[83] Job cuts were focused in sectors that were the biggest money losers for the state.

One example is the spinning and weaving industry, whose origins can be traced to the pre-1949 era, when it was China's largest industry.[84] After 1949 the textile industry continued to be China's largest, employing 7.6 million workers at its peak in 1991.[85] Beginning in the early 1990s the industry went into the red for the first time. In an effort to raise productivity and curtail financial losses, the industry began to shed workers. By 1996 employment in the industry had shrunk to 6.34 million. But the textile industry's losses had grown to RMB 9.6 billion, making it by far the biggest money-losing sector in state-owned manufacturing.[86] The industry, long characterized by outdated equipment and high production costs, initiated a more radical restructuring beginning in 1998 in response to Premier Zhu Rongji's charge to cut losses of state-owned firms. The state closed more than 600 state-owned textile factories (one-fifth of the total), eliminated 9.4 million cotton spindles, and laid off an additional 1.4 million workers by the end of 2000. By 1999 state-owned textile companies recorded a slight profit of RMB 800-900 million, their first in seven years.[87] In 2000 profits surged to RMB 6.7 billion.[88]

The state also aggressively restructured the building materials, nonferrous metals, and railway industries, all of which returned to profitability in 1999.[89] The government closed down money-losing coal mines. Production was cut by several hundred million tons to prevent a further buildup of inventories, but the sector continued in the red. Steel was another big target, but trimming employment and controlling output in that sector proved more difficult.[90]

As a result of this massive restructuring the return on assets in state-owned industrial firms, shown in figure 1-2, turned upward in 1999, ending a twenty-year slide in profitability. Profits turned up even more strongly in 2000.[91]

The gradual convergence of China's domestic prices toward international levels, even in the most sensitive sectors, will also help ease the adjustment process. This reform began in the late 1970s, well before China's entry into the World Trade Organization, when the government reduced disparities between domestic and world prices for key agricultural products by raising the administered prices for products that farmers sold to the state. The government at the same time began to allow parallel free markets, where farmers could sell agricultural products once they had met delivery requirements to the state. The government also liberalized retail prices for a growing range of nonagricultural goods beginning in the early 1980s. The authorities extended price liberalization to producer goods beginning in 1983 by sanctioning the creation of a two-tier market structure in which above-plan output of coal, steel, machinery, and other investment goods could be sold in parallel markets where prices were determined by supply and demand.[92] Over time the share of all types of products sold at market prices rose. Eventually, beginning in the early 1990s, the state raised the fixed prices toward the market level and eliminated fixed prices for most products.

This transformation of the domestic price environment is portrayed in table 1-3, which shows the share of transactions at market, state-guided, and state-fixed prices for various years from the onset of reform in 1978 through 1999.[93] By 1999 market prices prevailed in more than nine-tenths of all retail transactions, more than four-fifths of sales of farm products, and almost nine-tenths of all producer goods sales.

During the same period the government reformed the pricing of imported commodities. In the early years of reform most imports were sold on the domestic market at the same price as comparable domestic goods. But over time the domestic market prices of a growing share of imports were based on international prices.[94] By 1992 the domestic market prices of more than 95 percent of all imported goods were based on international prices.[95] As a consequence of the domestic price liberalization and this change in the domestic pricing of imported commodities, by the mid-1990s the structure of domestic prices of traded goods largely reflected international prices.

For a few important products, however, a significant gap remained between domestic and international prices in the years just before China's accession to the World Trade Organization. One important example was agriculture. In the early years of reform the Chinese government raised domestic grain procurement prices to stimulate grain production and in-

Table 1-3. *Price Reform in China, 1978–99*

| Year | Retail commodities | | | Agricultural commodities | | | Producer goods | | |
|---|---|---|---|---|---|---|---|---|---|
| | Market | State-guided | State-fixed | Market | State-guided | State-fixed | Market | State-guided | State-fixed |
| 1978 | 0 | 3 | 97 | 6 | 2 | 93 | 0 | 0 | 100 |
| 1985 | 34 | 19 | 47 | 40 | 23 | 37 | n.a. | n.a. | n.a. |
| 1987 | 38 | 28 | 34 | 54 | 17 | 29 | n.a. | n.a. | n.a. |
| 1991 | 69 | 10 | 21 | 58 | 20 | 22 | 46 | 18 | 36 |
| 1995 | 89 | 2 | 9 | 79 | 4 | 17 | 78 | 6 | 16 |
| 1999 | 95 | 1 | 4 | 83 | 7 | 9 | 86 | 4 | 10 |

Sources: Ling Bin, "Market Plays Dominant Role," *Beijing Review*, vol. 35 (November 23–29, 1992), pp. 23–25; International Monetary Fund, *People's Republic of China-Recent Economic Developments*, Staff Country Report 97-71 (Washington, September 1997), p. 58; and World Trade Organization, *Draft Report of the Working Party on the Accession of China to the WTO*, rev. 7 (Geneva, July 10, 2001), pp. 15–16 (www.insidetrade.com [July 16, 2001]).

n.a. Not available.

Note: Percentages are calculated according to the value of transactions at different types of prices.

crease farm income. By the mid-1990s market prices for major grains in China were well above those prevailing in the international market.[96] As long as the state controlled imports through its monopoly on international trade in grain, this price disparity could be maintained. Independent importers that could have profited from the spread between domestic and international prices were not allowed to import grain. But under China's WTO commitments world access to China's domestic market will increase significantly. To prepare for this opening the Chinese government took steps to reduce grain prices on the domestic market in 1999. The prices of wheat and corn fell by 20 to 30 percent in 1999 and in both cases converged toward international levels.[97] Since domestic prices of some crops were already converging to international levels before China's entry, there is no reason to anticipate a huge increase in imports of these products in the short run as a result of the agreement. In effect the anticipated substantial adjustment required in China's agricultural sector already was under way more than two years in advance of China's entry into the World Trade Organization. Farmers began moving out of grain and into vegetables, fruit, and other crops that were less land intensive in production than grain.[98]

Another important example of the convergence of domestic and international prices in the period immediately before China's entry into the World Trade Organization was petroleum and refined petroleum products.

In the 1980s the Chinese government maintained rigid and highly distorted prices for crude oil and refined petroleum products. The price of crude oil, for example, was fixed at about one-sixth the international level, depressing the profitability of firms producing crude while providing a financial windfall for Sinochem, the state-owned trading company that had a monopoly on the export of crude. Sinochem captured a significant share of the huge difference between the domestic and international price.[99] Not until the late 1980s did the state begin to ratchet up the domestic price of crude.[100] But it was not until a decade later, in June 1998, that the State Council adopted a policy linking domestic crude oil prices with the international market price. Beginning in July 1998 the government began to adjust the domestic price of crude oil monthly to bring it into line with international prices.[101] Thus when the international price of crude rose sharply in the first half of 1999, the domestic price of crude oil from Daqing, the largest producer rose from RMB 730 per ton in January 1999 to RMB 1,127 per ton in May 1999.[102]

The government, despite its expressed intention to do so, was reluctant to follow a similar policy for refined petroleum products. The state adjusted the prices of refined products only quarterly, and they were not directly linked to international prices. For example, the State Development Planning Commission adjusted prices of gasoline, diesel, and other refined products in November 1999, February 2000, and May 2000. But the upward adjustment of refined product prices was only 30 percent compared with the more than doubling of the price of crude over the same period.[103] This caused a variety of problems. Rapidly rising crude prices combined with less flexible prices for refined products squeezed the profit margins of Chinese refiners, notably Sinopec, China's largest refiner. It also stimulated widespread smuggling of refined products. Finally, in June 2000, the government began pricing refined products in line with international prices, adjusting prices every month.[104]

A similar process of price convergence was well under way for a number of other services and commodities in the run-up to China's entry into the World Trade Organization. Price controls on passenger and cargo water transportation, for example, were dropped on May 1, 2001.[105] The process was formalized in 2001 when the State Development Planning Commission announced the formal termination of price controls for silk, natural rubber, gold jewelry, steaming coal, raw materials used to produce plastic film used in agriculture, and several other commodities.[106] Only thirteen commodities, nine services, and five types of public utilities remain subject to state price control. These include grains, certain chemical fertilizers, important medicines, salt, tobacco, certain transportation charges, some professional service fees, natural gas, water, electricity, and postal and telecommunications services.[107] Even for some commodity categories still subject to state pricing, there has been some liberalization. The state, for example, no longer sets the wholesale price of electricity that is distributed through pooling arrangements.[108] And in 2001 the state announced plans to raise the prices of water and natural gas—perhaps the two most important products for which prices were still well below world levels.[109]

The resulting general convergence of domestic and international prices is crucial to an understanding of the adjustment China faces in meeting its WTO obligations. Much of the process will be stimulated by changes in relative prices in the domestic market as international prices are more fully transmitted to the domestic market as tariffs and other trade barriers are reduced. Because most price distortions gradually were eliminated in the decade before China's entry into the World Trade Organization, much of the necessary industrial and agricultural restructuring already was under way before accession.

The corollary of this analysis is that some predictions of increased Chinese imports following its entry into the World Trade Organization may be overstated. The materials distributed by the Office of the U.S. Trade Representative (hereafter U.S. Trade Representative) in the fall of 1999, for example, stated that as a result of the bilateral U.S.-China agreement, import tariffs on industrial goods in China would fall from 24.6 percent in 1997 to an average of 9.4 percent by 2005.[110] But China already had made a large part of these cuts before the bilateral agreement was reached with the United States in the fall of 1999. An even larger share was made before China's entry into the World Trade Organization. Estimates of additional sales that might be made to China as a result of entry are based on the amount by which domestic prices of the imports are expected to decline as tariff levels are reduced.[111] When these price reductions are calculated based on historic tariff levels, rather than those prevailing immediately before entry, the estimates of the decrease in domestic prices and of the increase in sales of goods into China are biased upward. The same is true for estimates of the macroeconomic implications of China's entry. Since their starting points usually are two or more years before China's entry, other things being equal, they may overestimate the effects on trade and growth that can be expected from the program of liberalization contained in China's WTO commitments.

Although the likely immediate economic gains in the form of increased Chinese imports as a result of reduced tariffs and nontariff barriers may have been somewhat oversold, there is little doubt that China's entry into the World Trade Organization is a landmark event for at least three reasons. First, China's membership commits it to comply with the principles and rules of the international trading system. China was far and away the largest trading country outside the system; its participation is essential for the future effectiveness of the World Trade Organization. Second, China's WTO commitments are a lever that its reform-oriented leadership can use to complete the transition to a more market-oriented economy. The strategy of relying on increased international competition to induce domestic firms to improve their efficiency is not without economic costs and political risks. Even if the strategy is successful, transition costs are inevitable. Increases in unemployment, even if only transitory, could lead to more frequent and more intense demonstrations and urban protest than had already occurred in the 1990s. Third, China's commitment to open markets to increased investment in telecommunications, financial, and distribution services is genuinely revolutionary. This commitment not only offers potential commercial opportunities for foreign firms but also will contribute to the further transformation of the domestic economy.

# CHAPTER TWO

# China's Pre-WTO Trade Reforms

HOW FAR IS CHINA in the transition to a more open economy? If the economy were still fairly closed, one would expect substantial output restructuring and rapidly increasing unemployment as China implemented its WTO commitments. One might anticipate that even with the best of intentions China would fall short of meeting many of its WTO obligations. If market opening is already well advanced, however, one would expect that the required restructuring and increased unemployment would be more modest, and it would be more likely that China would meet its WTO commitments.

Evaluating the openness existing in China as it joins the World Trade Organization is difficult because of the administrative complexity of China's trade regime. Although China is well on the way to becoming a market economy, its institutional structure, including its foreign trade system, still exhibits some continuity with the time when economic planning played a much larger role in resource allocation. In the 1980s and 1990s China, for example, maintained multiple, overlapping forms of nontariff protection—quotas, licensing, limited trading rights, price tendering, and so forth. That gave the appearance of a highly restrictive trade regime. But on closer inspection much of the protection was redundant.[1]

## Foreign Trade Planning before Reform

Before the late 1970s China's commodity trade was determined almost entirely by economic planning. The State Planning Commission's import plan covered more than 90 percent of all imports. The commission designed the import plan to increase the supplies of machinery and equipment, industrial raw materials, and intermediate goods that were in short supply and needed to meet physical production targets for high-priority final goods. The export plan was similarly comprehensive, specifying the physical quantities of more than 3,000 individual commodities. The commission, however, did not regard exports as contributing directly to economic growth but rather simply as a mechanism for financing imports. Typically goods that were expected to be in excess supply were diverted to the export market. If this did not generate sufficient foreign exchange to pay for required imports, planners typically cut back on domestic consumption to free up additional goods for export.

A handful of foreign trade corporations owned and controlled by the Ministry of Foreign Trade was responsible for carrying out the trade plan before 1978.[2] Each of these corporations typically dealt in a narrow range of commodities for which it was the sole authorized trading company. The organization of these trading companies paralleled that of China's industrial production ministries. The China National Textile Import and Export Corporation, for example, handled the import requirements and the export goods of the Ministry of Textile Industry.

Since the planning process was carried out in physical terms, the exchange rate and relative prices were unimportant in determining the magnitude and the commodity composition of China's foreign trade.[3] Export products were sold to foreign trade companies at officially established domestic prices, either ex factory prices for manufactured goods or government procurement prices for agricultural goods. Relative prices in the domestic and international markets thus played little or no role in determining the pattern of exports. Export producers did not share the foreign exchange income from the sale of their products on international markets. Thus they had little incentive to expand production of goods for which there was strong international demand. The exchange rate obviously was irrelevant for most producers of export goods. Devaluation, which normally would increase the profitability of exporting, had no effect on the prices Chinese export producers received. Those prices were fixed in domestic currency.

Pricing of imports was more complex. Most imports were sold on the domestic market at prices similar to those of comparable domestic goods, with adjustments upward or downward allowed to reflect quality differences. This pricing regime protected domestic producers. An inefficient domestic producer, in effect, was protected by what amounted to a variable import tariff that automatically marked up the price of imports to the cost level of the domestic producer. Also, for these goods the exchange rate was irrelevant since changes in the price of foreign exchange had no effect on the domestic currency price of the import. However, for imports for which there was no domestic equivalent, about a fifth of the total, domestic pricing was based on the cost of imports converted to domestic currency at the official exchange rate. Because the government fixed the exchange rate at an overvalued level in the prereform era, these imports were implicitly subsidized. Since most of the imports receiving this implicit subsidy were machinery and equipment for priority state investment projects, the state in effect was using the overvalued exchange rate as a policy instrument to promote rapid industrialization.

The consequences of these peculiar pricing and exchange rate policies were adverse for the efficiency of domestic resource allocation and for economic growth. Exports were not necessarily goods in which China enjoyed a comparative advantage in production. And producers of export goods had no economic incentive to expand their international sales. That in turn impaired China's ability to finance a growing flow of imports that would have embodied technology more advanced than that available domestically, thus contributing to productivity growth and economic expansion.

There were several manifestations of the adverse effects of the prereform trade regime. Most obviously, China's trade grew relatively slowly. China's share of world trade dropped markedly, from 1.5 percent in 1953 to only 0.6 percent in 1977.[4] China simply failed to participate in the rapid growth of world trade after World War II, largely because firms had little or no incentive to produce for the export market. With modest growth of exports, import expansion was fundamentally constrained, particularly in the 1960s and 1970s when China eschewed significant foreign borrowing and remained closed to foreign direct investment. As a result, by the mid-1970s three dozen countries were larger world traders than China.

Not only did this system depress the overall volume of trade, it distorted the commodity composition of foreign trade, especially on the export side. In the late 1970s and first half of the 1980s China's exports did not conform to the country's underlying comparative advantage in labor-intensive products. There was no significant correlation between labor intensity in production, on the one hand, and the growth of exports on the other. Exports of some labor-intensive goods rose sharply; but so did exports of some capital-intensive products. Indeed, the single largest source of increased export earnings in the first half of the 1980s was from the international sale of crude oil and refined petroleum products, among the most capital-intensive goods produced in China. That resulted from a centralized decision taken in the mid-1970s to finance China's turn outward, largely by relying on revenues from oil exports. This policy continued in place, even when domestic oil production grew much less rapidly than originally anticipated. Between 1977 and 1985 the government exported virtually all incremental petroleum production, despite a growing short-age of energy that was crippling the pace of economic growth. In a more market-oriented environment characterized by flexible prices and produc-ers and traders responding to price signals, exporting petroleum would have been far less profitable than it was. One would have expected the growth of exports to be concentrated in products that were relatively la-bor intensive.[5]

## Trade Reform before Accession

The system of physical planning of foreign trade, which was responsible for a relatively irrational pattern of exports, was gradually dismantled in the 1980s. The system was largely transformed by the end of the 1990s. While the government, through its foreign trade companies, maintained direct control of a handful of important commodities, most trade was decentralized and increasingly market determined. This was made pos-sible by a dramatic expansion in trading rights; reforms of pricing of traded goods so that international prices of traded goods were increasingly trans-mitted to the domestic market; and the adoption of exchange rate policies that did not discriminate against exports. As the regime phased out direct quantitative planning of imports and exports, it developed a foreign trade system relying much more on conventional trade policies, such as tariffs and nontariff barriers, to regulate the flow of imports and exports.

### The Import Regime

For much of the reform era China has maintained an extraordinarily complex and highly restrictive system of import controls. Besides the usual policy instruments, such as tariffs, quotas, and licensing requirements, the government has used an array of other tools that are less frequently used by other states. These include restrictions on trading rights by limiting the number of companies authorized to carry out trade transactions and in many cases limiting the range of goods that each of these companies is allowed to trade; import substitution lists; a system of registration for selected imports; and commodity inspection requirements.

The import regime is so complex that it is difficult for outside observ-ers to judge the degree to which the economy was genuinely open to imports and how "openness" was changing over time. The complexity of the controls has been cited as prima facie evidence of a relatively closed trading system.[6] It certainly was a cause of enormous difficulty in negotiating trade liberalization with China. If negotiators eliminated some barriers but ignored others, increased market access would not be achieved. In part in response to these negotiations China reduced tariff and nontariff barriers, and by the late 1990s the protection provided to the vast majority of domestic producers was less extensive than in most developing countries.

TARIFFS. Before the reform era tariffs had little if any effect on the pattern of imports. As already noted, physical quantities of individual imports were determined in the planning process. In any case, as also noted, most imports were sold at the same prices as comparable domestic goods, so for most goods tariff levels had little or no effect on the final price a user paid for an imported good. For many goods imports tariffs simply filled part of the gap between the international and domestic prices. The balance of the gap was profit, which accrued to the foreign trade company handling the good. Tariff revenues in this system were relatively low.[7]

Beginning in the early 1980s, as the state reduced the scope of import planning, it introduced high tariffs for many products and adjusted tariffs upward on others. Import duties on consumer electronics, such as televisions, for example, were raised sharply.[8] As shown in table 2-1, the average statutory tariff stood at the relatively high level of 56 percent in 1982. In 1985 the National People's Congress passed a new customs regulation and overhauled the entire tariff schedule. That reduced the average tariff to 43 percent, a level that was then sustained with only extremely modest adjustments for the next seven years.[9] Beginning in 1992, however, in a series of adjustments outlined in box 2-1, China reduced tariff levels by about two-thirds so that by 2001 the average statutory tariff rate stood at only 15 percent.

As a result of these systematic tariff reductions, China's average statutory import tariff level just before admission to the World Trade Organization was only about one-quarter the level prevailing in the early 1980s and a third the level of the mid-1980s when China first expressed a formal interest in joining the General Agreement on Tariffs and Trade. China's 15 percent average tariff level was about half that prevailing in India and roughly equivalent to that of Brazil and Mexico.

Table 2-1. *Average Statutory Import Tariff Rate, 1982–2001*

| Year | Percent |
|------|---------|
| 1982 | 55.6 |
| 1985 | 43.3 |
| 1988 | 43.7 |
| 1991 | 44.1 |
| 1992 | 43.2 |
| 1993 | 39.9 |
| 1994 | 35.9 |
| 1996 | 23.0 |
| 1997 | 17.0 |
| 2000 | 16.4 |
| 2001 | 15.3 |

Sources: Yin Xiangshuo, *Progress and Results of China's Foreign Trade Reform* (Shanxi: Shanxi Economic Publishing House, 1998), pp. 94–95; Long Yongtu, "Entering into the World Trade Organization; Integration into the International Social Mainstream," *Guoji maoyi wenti* (Journal of International Trade), no. 9 (1999), p. 3; "WTO Membership Promotes China's Reform of Tax System," *China Economic News*, vol. 21 (October 30, 2000), p. 1; and  Xiao Xu, "Nation Fulfills Commitment to Cut Tariffs," *China Daily*, December 30, 2000, p. 1.

Note: Average tariff rates shown are calculated on an unweighted basis.

As the average statutory tariff rate fell, the dispersion in the rates on individual tariff lines also declined significantly.[10] This is important because for a given average tariff rate, greater dispersion in the individual rates generally increases the protection provided to domestic producers.

China's system of exempting goods from import tariffs is a third element that must be considered in assessing the degree to which domestic producers are protected by import duties.[11] Two major categories of goods have been eligible for tariff exemption for much of the reform era—raw materials and intermediate goods used to produce or assemble goods that are then exported and capital goods used in joint venture and wholly foreign-owned factories. The legal framework for export processing activities in China was established in 1979. It provided various incentives for the processing of raw materials for export and the assembly of imported parts and components to produce finished goods for export.[12] Beginning in 1987 these incentives were expanded to provide for the duty-free import of all raw materials, parts, and components used in the production of goods for export. This gave an enormous boost to processed exports utilizing imported components, since it meant that producers of these goods in China operated at international prices and were freed from the distortions of the exchange rate as well.[13]

## Box 2-1. *History of Tariff Cuts*

**Jan. 1, 1992:** Sizable reductions on 225 tariff lines, 4.4 percent of the total.

**April 1, 1992:** Import regulatory tax on 18 product groups eliminated. For 16 of these groups, covering 168 tariff lines, overall import duties fell by amounts ranging from 28.6 percent to 61.5 percent. For two product groups, sedans and video cameras, the basic tariffs were raised when the regulatory tax was eliminated, but overall tariff rates for these two product groups still were reduced somewhat.

**Jan. 1, 1993:** Tariffs reduced on 3,371 tariff lines, 53.6 percent of the total, bringing the average tariff down by 7.3 percent.

**Jan. 1, 1994:** Tariffs reduced on 2,898 tariff lines.

**March 1, 1995:** Tariffs reduced on 19 tariff lines covering wine, liquor, and tobacco. Initial rates ranging from 120 to 150 percent were cut to a uniform rate of 80 percent.

**April 1, 1996:** Tariffs reduced on 4,971 tariff lines; average tariff rate of 35.9 percent fell to 23 percent.

**Oct. 1, 1997:** Tariffs reduced on 4,874 tariff lines, 73.5 percent of the total; average tariff rate of 23.2 percent fell to 17 percent.

**Jan. 1, 1999:** Tariffs reduced on 1,014 tariff lines in the textiles, toy, and forestry sectors; reductions ranged between 0.2 and 11 percentage points.

**Jan. 1, 2000:** Tariffs on 819 tariff lines covering textile products were reduced by amounts ranging from 0.6 to 2 percentage points. Reduced tariffs on 202 tariff lines covering chemicals, machinery, and other goods. For example, the 15 percent tariff on digital processing units for personal computers was cut to 6 percent; the 18 percent tariff on flight data recorders cut to 1 percent.

**Jan. 1, 2001:** Tariffs cut on 3,462 tariff lines, 49 percent of the total.

Sources: Editorial Board of the Almanac of China's Economic Relations and Trade, *Almanac of China's Foreign Economic Relations and Trade 1992/93* (Hong Kong: China Resources Advertising Co., Ltd., 1993), pp. 178–87; *Almanac of China's Foreign Economic Relations and Trade 1993/94* (Hong Kong: China Resources Advertising Co., Ltd., 1993), p. 74; *Almanac of China's Foreign Economic Relations and Trade 1994/95* (Hong Kong: China Resources Advertising Co., Ltd., 1994), p. 40; *Almanac of China's Foreign Economic Relations and Trade 1997/98* (Beijing: China National Economy Publishing House, 1997), p. 51; *Almanac of China's Foreign Economic Relations and Trade 1998/99* (Beijing: China Economics Publishing House, 1998), p. 48; Liu Xiangdong, ed., *Zhongguo duiwai jingji maoyi zhengce shouce (1994–1995)* (A Handbook of China's Foreign Economic and Trade Policies [1994–1995]) (Beijing: Economic Management Press, 1994), pp. 408–96; "China Readjusts Import Tariff Rates of Tobacco and Wines," *China Economic News*, vol. 17 (March 20, 1995), pp. 3–4; Zhang Yan, "Import Tariff Schedule Adjusted," *China Daily*, January 4, 2000, p. 5; Chen Chen, "China's Open Market Again Reduces Tariff Rates," *Guoji shangbao* (International Business Daily), January 7, 1999, p. 1; "Notice of the General Administration of Customs of the People's Republic of China," January 1999, in Editorial Board of the Almanac of China's Foreign Economic Relations and Trade, *Almanac of China's Foreign Economic Relations and Trade 2000* (Beijing: China Foreign Economic Relations and Trade Publishing House, 2000), pp. 217–54; The General Administration of Customs of the People's Republic of China, "Interim Tariff Level of Part of the Raw Materials and Spare Parts in 2000," *China Economic News*, vol. 21, supplement 1 (March 20, 2000); and Xiao Xu, "Nation Fulfills Commitment to Cut Tariffs," *China Daily*, December 30, 2000, p. 1.

Besides exempting parts and components used in export processing, capital goods brought into China by joint venture and wholly foreign-owned companies usually have been exempt from import duties.[14] The value of this machinery and equipment rose in parallel with the dramatic increases in foreign direct investment in the 1990s.

Finally, beginning in 1997 a number of special government initiatives exempted domestic institutions and firms from paying import tariffs on a broader range of imported goods. For example, beginning in 1997 scientific research and teaching institutions were allowed to import scientific equipment and other items used in research free of duty, when these items were not available in China. Similarly in the same year the import of special equipment used by the disabled was exempt from import duties.[15] Beginning in July 2000 Chinese software companies were exempted from paying duties on all imported equipment, technology, accessories, and spare parts.[16]

As a result of these exemptions the share of imports subject to any import duty has become surprisingly small. In the first half of 2000, for example, less than 40 percent of imports were subject to any tariff.[17] Thus actual tariff collections as a percentage of total import value have been much lower than the average statutory tariff levels shown in table 2-1 would suggest. As shown in figure 2-1, even at its peak in the mid-1980s, tariff revenue was only about 16 percent of the value of imports. This percentage subsequently fell steadily for four reasons. First, the share of duty-free imports rose as foreign direct investment expanded and export processing became more important and as the privilege of duty-free imports was extended to a broader range of domestic industries, such as software (table 2-2).

Second, fraudulent use of import duty exemption programs expanded over time. The most common forms of fraud were the sale on the domestic market of goods embodying duty-free imports and the illegal resale of parts and components imported on a duty-free basis. By 2000 fraud had become so pervasive that the government proposed that only export processing firms located in bonded zones would be eligible for duty-free import of parts and components. The use of bonded zones would reduce the task of ensuring that parts and components brought in duty free under processing contracts were all embodied in goods that were re-exported rather than leaking into the domestic economy.[18] But given the large number and geographic dispersion of firms utilizing the import exemption programs, it is not clear that this proposal is practical.

Figure 2-1. *Tariff Revenue as a Percentage of the Value of Imports,*
*1978–2000*

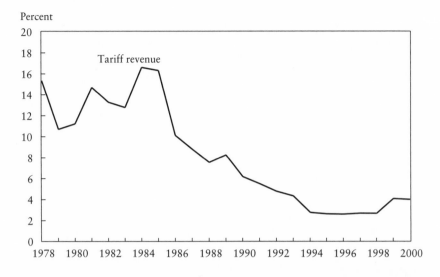

Percent

Sources: State Statistical Bureau, *China Statistical Yearbook 1993* (Beijing: China Statistical Publishing House, 1993), p. 633; *China Statistical Yearbook 1998*, pp. 274, 620; National Bureau of Statistics, *China Statistical Yearbook 2000* (Beijing: China Statistics Press, 2000), pp. 258, 588; Xinhua, "Tax Commissioner Announces 'Unprecedented' Increase in Tax Revenue," January 4, 2001, in Foreign Broadcast Information Service, *Daily Report: China,* 010104 (http://wnc.fedworld.gov); Li Honghai, "Constructing a Modern Customs Administration" (speech by Wu Yi to National Conference of Customs Directors), *Guoji shangbao* (International Business Daily), January 15, 2001, p. 1.

The third reason import duties fell relative to the value of imports was that statutory import tariff rates fell dramatically after 1992 (table 2-1). That reduced the import tariff revenue collected on those goods on which import duties were collected. Finally, it appears that imports subject to high duties or other stringent import restrictions, such as quotas, increasingly entered China illegally, entirely escaping import duties. Thus the mix of legally imported goods shifted toward commodities on which the average statutory tariff was lower.

As a result of these four factors, by 1994 the tariff collection rate had fallen to 3 percent of the value of imports, almost certainly the lowest rate of tariff collection of any developing economy. The ratio remained at that very low level for several years until China's custom service launched a crackdown on smuggling beginning in the later part of 1998, leading to a

Table 2-2. *China's Processing Trade, 1987–2000*
Billion of U.S. dollars unless noted otherwise

| Year | Total export | Processed exports | Percent | Total import | Processed imports | Percent |
|------|------|------|------|------|------|------|
| 1987 | 39.4 |      |    | 43.2  | 10.2 | 24 |
| 1988 | 47.5 | 12.9 | 27 | 55.3  | 13.7 | 25 |
| 1989 | 52.5 |      |    | 59.1  | 16.4 | 28 |
| 1990 | 62.1 |      |    | 53.4  | 18.7 | 35 |
| 1991 | 71.8 | 32.4 | 45 | 63.8  | 25.0 | 39 |
| 1992 | 84.9 |      |    | 80.6  | 31.5 | 39 |
| 1993 | 91.7 | 44.2 | 48 | 104.0 | 36.4 | 35 |
| 1994 | 121.0 | 57.0 | 47 | 115.6 | 47.6 | 41 |
| 1995 | 148.8 | 73.7 | 50 | 132.1 | 58.4 | 44 |
| 1996 | 151.1 | 84.3 | 56 | 138.8 | 62.3 | 45 |
| 1997 | 182.8 | 99.7 | 55 | 142.4 | 70.1 | 49 |
| 1998 | 183.8 | 104.5 | 57 | 140.2 | 68.6 | 49 |
| 1999 | 194.9 | 110.9 | 57 | 165.7 | 73.6 | 44 |
| 2000 | 249.2 | 137.7 | 55 | 225.1 | 92.6 | 41 |

Sources: Barry Naughton, "China's Emergence and Prospects as a Trading Nation," *Brookings Papers on Economic Activity*, 1996, no. 2, p. 300; Nicholas R. Lardy, *China in the World Economy* (Washington: Institute for International Economics, 1994), p. 113; Customs General Administration, *China Monthly Customs Statistics*, December, 1993, p. 11, and December, 1994, p. 13; *China Customs Statistics Yearbook 1994* (Hong Kong: Economic Information and Agency, 1995), p. 12; *China Customs Statistics Yearbook 1997* (Hong Kong: Goodwill Information Ltd., 1998), p. 64; Editorial Board of the Almanac of China's Foreign Economic Relations and Trade, *Almanac of China's Foreign Economic Relations and Trade 1996/97* (Beijing: China Economics Publishing House, 1996), pp. 524–25; *Almanac of China's Foreign Economic Relations and Trade 1997/98* (Beijing: China National Economy Publishing House, 1997), p. 43; *Almanac of China's Foreign Economic Relations and Trade 1998/99* (Beijing: China Economics Publishing House, 1998), pp. 442, 444; Ministry of Foreign Trade and Economic Cooperation, *Zhongguo duiwai jingji maoyi baipishu 1999* (China's White Paper on Foreign Trade and Economic Cooperation 1999) (Beijing: Economic Science Publishing House, 1999), pp. 75–76; "Composition of China's Foreign Trade in 1999 (I)," in Editorial Board of the Almanac of China's Foreign Economic Relations and Trade, *Almanac of China's Foreign Economic Relations and Trade 2000*, pp. 524, 534; General Customs Administration, *China Customs Statistics Yearbook 1999*, p. 68; and *China's Customs Statistics (monthly edition)*, December 2000, p.13.
Note: The data for processing imports exclude the value of equipment provided by foreign firms to Chinese firms engaged in processing contracts. These amounts in the latter half of the 1990s were usually between $1 billion and $1.5 billion annually.

large increase in recorded imports of high-tariff items. When the antismuggling campaign was in full swing in 1999, there was an 80 percent increase in the absolute value of tariff revenues collected. But these revenues were equal to only 4.2 percent of the value of imports, still an extraordinarily low rate. In 2000 the value of tariff revenues collected jumped an additional 30 percent, but the tariff revenue dropped to 4 percent of the value of imports—despite great gains, growth in tariff collection did not keep pace with the 36 percent growth in China's imports in 2000.

NONTARIFF BARRIERS. The Chinese government has used a broad array of nontariff measures to control and regulate imports. Both U.S. trade negotiators and many U.S. exporters have long regarded China's nontariff barriers as more significant in restricting the inflow of foreign goods than tariffs. The most important are import licenses and quotas and limits on trading rights. The use of import substitution lists, registration and tendering requirements for selected imports, and quality and safety standards have also been important nontariff barriers.

The system of import licensing and quotas was introduced in the early 1980s. Although licenses and quotas are normally thought of as a departure from free trade, in the Chinese context their introduction reflected liberalization of foreign trade. They were less restrictive than the system of direct planning of all trade, which quotas and licensing increasingly replaced in the first decade of reform. By the late 1980s the number of commodity categories subject to licensing expanded to fifty-three, and the share of all imports subject to licensing requirements hit a peak of 46 percent.[19]

Even at their peak, however, quotas and licenses on imports in China were much less pervasive than in India. In 1990–91 more than 90 percent of all imports in India were subject to quantitative restrictions. In effect import licenses were granted only for goods for which there was no domestic source of supply.[20] Moreover, in the 1990s liberalization of quantitative restrictions in China proceeded much more rapidly than in India. Partly in response to external pressure, the Chinese Ministry of Foreign Trade in a few years drastically cut the scope of licensing and quotas. The share of imports subject to licensing fell to about 18 percent by 1992.[21] As part of the market access agreement concluded with the United States in October 1992, the Chinese government committed to a further reduction in the scope of import licensing over a period of several years.[22] By mid-1997 only thirty-five commodity categories, defined in 374 separate tariff lines or about 5 percent of the total, required import licenses.[23] The number fell further, so that by the end of the decade fewer than 4 percent of all tariff lines were subject to import licensing restrictions.[24] These products accounted for only 8.45 percent of all imports.[25]

Although the number of tariff lines subject to quotas and licenses on the eve of China's WTO accession was small, their restrictive effect on the few commodities they cover was frequently extreme. Cigarettes are a good example, especially since China has 310 million smokers, about one-quarter of the world's total. The annual quota on cigarette imports prevailing just before China's entry into the World Trade Organization was only 50,000 cases, the equivalent of one-tenth of 1 percent of domestic cigarette consumption.[26] The quota on auto and other vehicle imports was similarly restrictive. In 1999 the imports of cars, trucks, buses, and other vehicles were only 35,000, less than 2 percent of domestic vehicle production.[27] Because of rampant smuggling of these and other products subject to tight quotas, however, the foreign market share was much higher than these numbers suggest.[28]

Limitations on the right to trade traditionally have been one of the most important nontariff barriers maintained by the Chinese government. Trading rights, frequently also discussed under the rubric of state trading, refer simply to the availability of the right to import and export goods.

When reform began in 1978, trading rights were extremely limited— twelve foreign trade corporations that were effectively subsidiaries of the Ministry of Foreign Trade conducted all foreign trade. Each corporation had a monopoly in the import and export of a well-defined range of commodities. During the 1980s and 1990s this system was partially transformed by increasing the number of companies authorized to trade and, more important, by reducing the number of commodities for which trading rights were limited to one or a tiny number of state trading companies.

From the outset of reform, all foreign-invested companies, including joint ventures and wholly foreign-owned firms, automatically had the right to trade directly without using the services of a state trading company. These foreign-funded firms, however, were only allowed to import inputs needed for their own production and could only export their own goods. Thus the progress in granting trading rights to domestic companies, which almost always were authorized to import and export a relatively broad range of goods, is probably a better indicator of the availability of the right to trade.

As early as 1985 the ministry had approved the creation of more than 800 separate corporations authorized to engage in foreign trade (table 2-3). These included new trade corporations set up by national-level ministries. For example, the Ministry of Metallurgical Industry established the China National Metallurgical Import and Export Corporation, enabling it to bypass the China National Metals and Minerals Import and Export Corporation, an old-line central trading company dating from the 1950s.[29] The ministry authorized provincial governments to establish foreign trade corporations to handle trade in a broad range of commodities in their regions. Beginning in the 1980s the ministry allowed some large individual

Table 2-3. *Chinese Domestic Companies Authorized to Conduct Foreign Trade, 1978–2001*

| Year | Number of companies |
|------|---------------------|
| 1978 | 12 |
| 1985 | 800 |
| 1986 | > 1,200 |
| 1988 | > 5,000 |
| 1996 | 12,000 |
| 1997 | 15,000 |
| 1998 | 23,000 |
| 1999 | 29,258 |
| 2000 | 31,000 |
| 2001 | 35,000 |

Sources: Nicholas R. Lardy, *Foreign Trade and Economic Reform in China, 1978-1990* (Cambridge University Press, p. 39); Zhang Yan, "Access to Trade Rights Expands," *China Daily*, February 23, 2000, p. 5; Editorial Board of the Almanac of China's Foreign Relations and Trade, *Almanac of China's Foreign Economic Relations and Trade 1987* (Hong Kong: China Resources Advertising Co., Ltd., 1987), p. 48; *Almanac of China's Foreign Economic Relations and Trade 1990* (Beijing: Finance and Economic Publishing House, 1990), p. 38; *Almanac of China's Foreign Economic Relations and Trade 1997/98* (Beijing: China Economics Publishing House, 1997), p. 50; *Almanac of China's Foreign Economic Relations and Trade 1998/99* (Beijing: China Economics Publishing House, 1998), p. 48; Ministry of Foreign Trade and Economic Cooperation, *Zhongguo duiwai jingji maoyi baipishu 1999* (China's White Paper on Foreign Trade and Economic Cooperation 1999), p. 192; Chen Yao, "Trade with Northeast Asia Countries Bounces Back," *China Daily*, June 8, 2001, p. 4; and World Trade Organization, *Draft Report of the Working Party on the Accession of China to the WTO*, rev. 7 (Geneva, July 10, 2001), p. 21 (www.insidetrade.com [July 16, 2001]).

state-owned manufacturing enterprises to trade directly, letting them bypass state foreign trade corporations.

Further liberalization occurred in the 1990s. In 1997 China allowed the first Sino-foreign joint venture trading companies to be formed. In October 1998 the State Council authorized the creation of the first private trading companies, and the first private companies were licensed by the end of the year.[30] The state authorized selected scientific research institutes to trade beginning in 1999. The same year the state also introduced a system that allowed large industrial enterprises to register to receive trading rights on a streamlined basis. As long as the firms met the announced criteria, they received the right to trade within fifteen days of the time they applied.[31] In 1999 the state also announced it would lower the size threshold for private firms to be eligible to apply for trading rights.[32] The goal is to use the same eligibility standards for state and private firms, in effect creating a level playing field.[33]

Over time these reforms led to a dramatic increase in the number of trading companies. By 1998 more than 23,000 domestic companies of various types were authorized to engage in foreign trade. These included 8,425 foreign trade companies at various administrative levels, 10,215 manufacturing firms, 493 scientific research institutes, 61 private trading companies, and 2,998 companies authorized to engage in border trade. There were also more than 150,000 foreign-invested enterprises that had the right to engage in foreign trade.[34] At year-end 1999 an additional 6,294 domestic companies were authorized to engage in foreign trade, bringing the total to 29,258.[35] By 2000 the state had granted the right to import and export to more than 1,000 private enterprises.[36] In 2001 there were 35,000 domestic firms of all types that had the legal right to trade.

Although the right to trade has increased compared with the prereform period, the share of companies with trading rights remains tiny.[37] However, firms without trading rights are not restricted from importing or exporting because they can contract with a company with such rights to conduct their import or export transactions. Because the number of firms competing to offer such services is large, the market appears to be competitive, and transaction costs are probably low. Indeed, for many firms with limited international trade experience and market knowledge, contracting out their international transactions to specialized trading companies may be more efficient.

Once there is a competitive market in international trading services, a better measure of the availability of trading rights is the number of commodities for which the right to trade is extremely limited. As already noted, at the outset of reform the right to trade every commodity was monopolized by a single state trading company. In 2001 only for grain, vegetable oil, sugar, tobacco, crude oil and refined petroleum products, chemical fertilizer, and cotton are trading rights restricted to a single state trading company or, as in the case of petroleum, a few state companies.[38] Moreover, for these commodities the annual quantity of imports is subject to approval by the State Council.

Trading rights for six other products—natural rubber, timber, plywood, wool, acrylics, steel and steel products—are limited by a system the Chinese refer to as "designated trading."[39] Although the state does not plan the quantity of imports of these goods, the right to import them is limited to trading companies designated by the central government. For example, in 2000 there were 159 companies authorized to import steel and steel products.[40]

By the measure of the share of imports for which trading rights are tightly controlled by the central government, China's trade system was transformed during the 1980s and 1990s. The share of import goods for which trading rights were either monopolized or limited through the system of designated trading fell from 90 percent in 1980 to 40 percent in 1988, and then 11 percent in 1998.[41]

China in 1987 introduced an import substitution list covering 170 products for which the authorities had determined there were acceptable domestic substitutes.[42] According to the U.S. Trade Representative, Chinese firms frequently found it difficult and often impossible to receive government authorization to import these items. Because of the lack of transparency in the operation of this system, however, there are no systematic studies of how significant an import barrier the list was.[43] In early 1992 Tong Zhiguang, vice minister of foreign trade, announced at a meeting of the GATT working party on China's accession in Geneva that the Chinese government had decided to abolish the import substitution list, which by then had expanded to cover 1,751 commodities. Instead, he explained, China would rely primarily on tariffs or, if administrative measures were still required, they would be transparent and predictable.[44]

Only two years later, in April 1994 the State Planning Commission and several other government agencies introduced a system requiring the registration of certain imports.[45] Initially the requirement applied to only nine commodities, including rolled steel, steel billet, scrap steel, copper and aluminum, out-of-service ships, certain plastic materials, paper, fruit, and cosmetics. The 1994 regulation establishing this system was titled "Provisional Procedures for the Administration of Automatic Registration for the Import of Special Commodities." The word automatic in the title of the regulation seemed to imply that registration could not constitute a nontariff barrier. In fact, the detailed provisions of these regulations make clear that the registration system was not simply a special mechanism for measuring the volume of these imports as they passed through the customs system. Rather, would-be importers of these goods had to apply in advance to designated state entities approved by the State Planning Commission, before signing an import contract directly with a foreign supplier or with an authorized Chinese trading company. Importers had to present certificates verifying approval of their application before the customs cleared their goods. This system was still in use in the late 1990s.[46]

Some have argued that the timing of the introduction of automatic registration provides circumstantial evidence, beyond the provisions of the regulations just summarized, that the system constituted a potential barrier to imports, particularly for steel. Under the bilateral market access agreement signed with the United States in 1992, China had to eliminate the system of licenses and quotas on imports of steel and steel products at the end of 1993.[47] Automatic registration, introduced early the following year, seems to have filled the gap left by the removal of licensing.[48]

A closer examination of the pattern of steel imports, however, suggests that neither the licensing system nor the system of automatic registration provided a system of binding quantitative constraints on imports of steel and iron products.[49] Imports of steel products, for example, almost doubled in 1992 and then quadrupled in 1993 to reach 30 million metric tons, making China far and away the largest importer of steel in the world. The huge increases and high level of imports suggest that the system of quotas and licensing, which was in effect throughout 1992 and 1993, was not much of a constraint on steel purchases by Chinese firms from the international market. After the automatic registration system was introduced, steel imports fell. But in 1994 and 1995 steel product imports still averaged more than 18 million metric tons, several times the average level of imports immediately before 1993.[50]

In retrospect the magnitude of China's steel imports seems more closely tied to changes in domestic investment activity than changes in the system of nontariff barriers. Fixed investment jumped by three-fifths in 1993, the single largest annual increase since economic reform began in the late 1970s. Investment as a percentage of output soared to 43 percent, the highest rate since the Great Leap Forward in the late 1950s.[51] The dramatically higher investment activity created a major increase in demand for steel and other producer goods, satisfied in large part by increased imports. As the government introduced restrictive monetary and fiscal policies to reduce economic overheating, which had led to an almost unprecedented surge in prices, investment fell and steel imports moderated.[52]

China is also believed to use tendering as another mechanism to control imports. The Ministry of Foreign Trade maintains a list of products that, while not subject to import licensing or quotas, cannot be purchased abroad except through a process in which bids are sought from international suppliers. The scope of tendering is limited to a few specialized products rather than broad product categories.[53] For example, in 1998 the Ministry of Foreign Trade expanded this list to include eight additional items, such as asphalt and concrete spreading machines and escalators.[54] Once the tendering process is completed, the importer has to submit details of the transaction to the State Machinery and Electrical Products Import and Export Office.[55] That office must approve the transaction before the goods can be imported. The U.S. Trade Representative believes that the Chinese government frequently refuses to approve such proposals, forcing would-be importers to purchase inferior domestic substitutes.[56]

Quality and safety standards acted as a nontariff barrier to foreign goods. On the eve of China's accession to the World Trade Organization, China imposed statutory inspection requirements on 144 different import products, covering about 10 percent of all import tariff lines. Many of these products were subject to separate safety standards. There were 21 products not subject to statutory inspection that were subject to safety standards.[57] These quality and safety standards range from the specifications for cold-rolled steel plate to various safety standards on imported vehicles.

Critics charge that the lack of transparency, difficulty in determining the appropriate standard for a particular imported good, the use of standards for imports that differ from those imposed on domestic goods, and the adoption of unique standards that differ from international standards for no identifiable reason mean that China's system of standards constitutes a significant nontariff barrier to imports.[58] The standards preclude imports or raise their price because of the time and expense involved in obtaining quality licenses and meeting safety standards.

SUMMARY. During the two decades leading up to China's entry into the World Trade Organization China's import regime was impressively transformed. Statutory tariff rates, which through the 1980s were among the highest of all developing countries, fell to relatively low levels, and collection rates by the mid-1990s were almost certainly the lowest of any developing country. The scope of quotas and licensing also shrank dramatically, restricting imports of less than 5 percent of all tariff lines by the end of the 1990s. The restrictive effect of China's other very important nontariff barrier, limited trading rights, also diminished substantially. By 1998 products for which trading rights were limited accounted for only 11 percent of all imports. In 1999 only 1.4 percent of all tariff lines were restricted by a tendering requirement. The restrictive effect of the remaining barriers—import registration and quality and safety standards—is difficult to judge but appears to be little different from similar programs used by many trading countries. Certainly the U.S. Trade Representative has never presented any evidence supporting its frequently asserted claim that these constituted major trade barriers. The case of steel suggests that underlying macroeconomic conditions in China were at least as important as its system of licenses, quotas, and automatic registration in determining the level of steel imports.

### The Export Regime

In the two decades before China joined the World Trade Organization the transformation of its export regime was as profound as the reform of the system governing imports. The direct physical planning of exports gradually was replaced by decentralized, market-oriented transactions. The bias against exports that characterized the prereform system gradually ended as the government decentralized foreign trade and introduced exchange rate policies that no longer discriminated against exports.

The most dramatic change was the expansion of trading rights for exporting. As already noted, shortly before reform, planning was pervasive—physical quantities of more than 3,000 commodities were specified in the annual export plan, and the right to export just about all of these commodities was tightly controlled. By 1998 the Chinese continued to plan export sales and limit export rights to only a single state foreign trade company for only thirteen commodities—tea, maize, soybeans, tungsten, coal, crude and refined oil, silk and unbleached silk, cotton, cotton yarn, cotton cloth, and antimony. Designated trading, in which trading rights were limited to authorized foreign trade companies but for which the state did not fix export quantities, applied to exports of the same list of commodities as on the import side. In 1998 the share of export goods for which trading rights were monopolized or limited through the system of designated trading was less than 4 percent of all exports.[59]

EXPORT LICENSING AND QUOTAS. The Chinese government reintroduced export licensing, which had been abolished in the early 1950s when the state established direct control over trade through foreign trade corporations, as trade was liberalized beginning in the early 1980s. As was true of import licenses, the introduction of export licenses and quotas was an important policy instrument in the movement away from physical planning of trade. As the scope of export planning shrank, the number of exports requiring licenses or subject to quotas initially grew, reaching a peak in 1991. But, as market-determined prices came to dominate all types of commodity transactions in the 1990s, the state dismantled the system of export licensing and quotas (table 1-3).

Export quotas and licensing served three functions. First, especially in the early years of reform, when price reform was just getting under way, quantitative controls were used as a mechanism to control the outflow of products that were still underpriced on the domestic market. In the absence of such controls profit-maximizing traders would have exported large quantities, leading to shortages on the domestic market.

Second, China restricted exports of several commodities in which it had or believed it had market power, globally or in nearby markets. Without such controls excess exports would have depressed world market prices for minerals such as tungsten, antimony, and tin and certain rare earths for which China was a major or even the major source of world supply. The absence of export restrictions would have reduced China's earnings from the sale of these products. And since China was the chief source of supply of foodstuffs for Hong Kong and Macau, the state controlled the flow of products such as live cattle, hogs, and poultry and their frozen meats to those markets through quotas.

Third, as China reentered the world market in the 1970s it was forced to negotiate with developed market economies to limit exports of textiles and garments. China, for example, signed its first bilateral textile agreement with the United States in September 1980, the same year it first gained most favored nation trade status in the U.S. market. The agreement restricted China's exports to the United States of six types of textile and apparel products. The Chinese enforced this agreement domestically by requiring that firms apply for licenses to export the restricted products. When the bilateral textile agreement was renewed in August 1983, it was substantially expanded. The 1986 agreement continued this trend, expanding the restrictions to cover more than 90 percent of all categories of textile and apparel exports. China faced similar restrictions on its textile and apparel exports to the European Union and a few other countries.

As a result of these factors, apart from textiles and apparel, the number of commodities subject to export licensing and quotas rose from 24 in 1981 to a peak in 1991 when these restrictions included 235 product categories, covering two-thirds of all exports.[60] Including the quotas China imposed as a result of agreements reached with other governments brought the total to about 258 product categories, accounting for a huge share of total exports.[61]

But the Ministry of Foreign Trade subsequently drastically cut the scope of export controls. By 1993, apart from textiles and apparel, only 114 products accounting for 30.5 percent of exports were subject to export quotas and licenses.[62] By 1999 the number had shrunk to 59 products, accounting for only 8 percent of all exports.[63] In 2000 the number was cut to 50 products.[64] The reduction in export restrictions after 1991 was made possible by the rapid liberalization of domestic prices, almost eliminating the large differentials between domestic and world prices.

FOREIGN EXCHANGE REFORM. Reform of the pricing and allocation of foreign exchange was another important element undergirding the growth of exports in the years before China's accession to the World Trade Organization. In the prereform era the state had fixed the exchange rate at an overvalued level to implicitly subsidize the import of high-priority capital goods that could not be produced domestically. The losers, of course, were producers of export goods that were forced to sell their output to the state at low domestic prices. Overvaluation of the domestic currency, naturally, led to excess demand for foreign exchange relative to supply, necessitating a rigid system of exchange control. The key elements of this control system were the requirement that exporters surrender 100 percent of their foreign exchange earnings to the government, tight limitations on the rights of individuals to hold foreign currency, and strict controls on the outflow of capital.

Beginning in the early 1980s the state gradually modified these features of the foreign exchange system. Exporters were allowed to retain a share of their foreign exchange earnings. That gave them the ability to finance imports without the need to seek permission to purchase foreign exchange, which was a very attractive incentive to sell to the international market. Individuals, starting in the mid-1980s, were allowed to open foreign currency accounts at the Bank of China and other banks authorized to deal in foreign currency. And it became more possible for domestic firms to invest abroad in light of a modest relaxation on capital outflows.

And, perhaps most important, over time the government substantially devalued the domestic currency. Historically the currency had been overvalued, meaning that for most products exporting was a money-losing proposition. However, the overvaluation of the domestic currency meant that for many products imports were highly profitable. When trade was entirely controlled by a handful of foreign trade corporations, these corporations could use their profits on imports to subsidize their losses on exports. Since all of these foreign trade corporations were subordinate to the Ministry of Foreign Trade, when necessary the ministry could redirect earnings from its most profitable corporations to those with net losses.

These intracorporation cross-subsidies of individual products and the intercorporation financial transfers helped the foreign trade companies to meet their import and export plans. But this system of cross-subsidies was entirely unsuited to the more decentralized trading system that was being introduced.[65] Thus the government had to address currency overvaluation more directly.

The government sought to remedy the problem in January 1981 by introducing an internal settlement rate of RMB 2.8 to the dollar. Since the official exchange rate at the time was RMB 1.5, that effectively cut the value of the domestic currency almost in half in trade transactions.[66] The authorities at the same time gradually began to devalue the official exchange rate and at the end of 1984, when the official rate reached RMB 2.8, the internal settlement rate was abolished. The authorities continued a steady and gradual devaluation of the official exchange rate to RMB 3.2 by mid-1986 and then devalued the currency by 15 percent on July 5, taking the rate to RMB 3.7.[67]

Although the official exchange rate remained fixed for the next three and a half years, the state took two steps that from the point of view of exporters effectively devalued the currency further. The state allowed exporters to retain a much larger share of their foreign exchange earnings and, beginning in late 1986, they introduced a formal secondary market for foreign exchange, frequently referred to as the swap market. Since the price of foreign exchange in the swap market was much higher than the official exchange rate, export earnings measured in domestic currency for each U.S. dollar of sales abroad rose even though the official exchange rate was unchanged. In December 1989 the official exchange rate was devalued by 21.2 percent. There were also more minor adjustments, and then in January 1994 the government unified the two rates at the secondary market exchange rate of RMB 8.7.[68] Following a modest appreciation, since mid-1995 the nominal exchange rate has fluctuated within a narrow range around RMB 8.3.

The cumulative loss of more than 80 percent in the nominal value of the RMB between 1978 and 1995 represented a large depreciation of the RMB in real terms. Adjusting for relative price trends in China and in the world the International Monetary Fund estimates that in real terms China's currency lost just over 70 percent of its value between 1980 and 1995.[69] The official rate was fixed in 1994 at the market-clearing rate, however, suggesting that the cumulative change in the official exchange rate up to that time was necessary to eliminate the historic overvaluation of the currency.[70]

REBATE OF VALUE-ADDED TAXES ON EXPORTS. Another important policy step to reduce the bias against exporting was the decision of the State Council in 1984 to rebate the indirect taxes that reduced the profitability of exporting.[71] The World Trade Organization allows the rebate of indirect taxes, such as value-added taxes. That allows firms in countries such as China, which rely heavily on indirect taxes, to compete fairly with firms in countries such as the United States, which generate fiscal revenue primarily by direct taxes, such as the corporate and personal income tax. Because of the many indirect taxes in use in China, calculating the rebate firms should receive on export products was complex, but by the end of the 1980s the annual rebate of indirect taxes exceeded RMB 10 billion. Because indirect taxes fell unevenly on different products, rebates allowed expanded production of some products whose international comparative advantage had been obscured by the effect of cumulative layers of indirect taxes on the final price.[72]

As the value-added tax, which had only two basic rates, became more important as a revenue source in the 1990s, the rebate program became easier to administer. In 1994 the State Council ruled that export products were entirely exempt from value-added taxes, and rebates grew sharply in value terms.[73] The expanded rebate program, however, quickly ran into difficulties. It was subject to abuse as firms claimed rebates on goods that were never exported, and the central government lacked sufficient funds to rebate the full amount of value-added taxes on exported goods, leading to a large accumulation of arrears. The central government clamped down on corruption and cut rebate rates on the value-added tax in 1995 and again in 1996. But in the wake of the Asian financial crisis, as export growth slumped, the government raised the portion of the value-added tax that was rebated. Rebate rates were raised in several steps starting in January 1998. By 1999, for example, the 17 percent value-added tax on electronic and light machinery products was fully refundable. In the first nine months of 2000 rebated value-added taxes reached a total of RMB 71 billion, almost double the amount rebated in the same period of 1999.[74] The higher rebate rates presumably contributed to the all-time record high growth of exports that year, dramatically reversing the export slowdown that had occurred since the Asian financial crisis of 1997.

DUTY DRAWBACK SYSTEM. Another policy that helps to explain the rapid expansion of China's exports during the past two decades is the duty drawback system that supports China's export processing program. The legal framework for the production of exports by assembling imported parts and components was introduced at the outset of reform in the late 1970s. There are two variants of export processing. In the first the inputs and components are supplied by a foreign firm to a Chinese company that undertakes the assembly or processing and is paid a processing fee. In the second type the inputs and components are purchased from abroad and assembled for export. The first type of processing is undertaken primarily by indigenous firms; the second primarily by foreign-invested firms.[75]

The Chinese government initially supported the second type of processed exports by providing foreign exchange on favorable terms and preferred access to domestic raw materials, fuel, and electricity, which then were in short supply.[76] It was not until 1987 and 1988 that the State Council initiated programs to rebate import duties on raw materials, parts and components, and so forth used for export processing by foreign-funded and domestic enterprises, respectively.[77] This was a critical development because it allowed export processing to take place at world prices, free from tariff or domestic pricing distortions.

The effect of these incentives on the pattern of trade, both exports and imports, was remarkable. As shown in table 2-2, when duty-free import of inputs was formalized in 1987–88, export processing already accounted for about one-quarter of both exports and imports. Export processing grew rapidly in the 1990s, accounting for half of exports by 1995 and almost three-fifths by the end of the decade. The share of imports used in processing activity grew to one half in 1997 and 1998 before declining to two-fifths in 2000. The development of export processing reflects China's increasing participation in the global production networks of transnational corporations, sometimes referred to as production sharing. In the 1990s production sharing expanded at a much faster pace in Asia than in North America or Europe. One measure of this growth is the rapidly expanding trade in components, which account for one-fifth of exports of manufactures in East Asia. Most trade in components in East Asia is concentrated in telecommunications, office machines (including computers), electronics, and motor vehicles.[78] China, because of its low wages compared with Japan, Singapore, and Taiwan, has become deeply involved in this process, initially primarily as a major assembly site.

The computer industry provides a good example. China by the mid-1990s emerged as a major production base for Taiwanese companies, producing computer keyboards, PC mice, switch power supply units, motherboards, and monitors. The world market share of Taiwan firms for these items was impressive, ranging from one-third for switch power supply units to two-thirds for motherboards and keyboards, and almost three-quarters for PC mice. For many of these computer hardware items the dominant world market position of Taiwanese firms was based on off-shore production. In 1995 offshore production roughly was equal to on-shore production of monitors; for keyboards offshore production was six times onshore output. The major offshore production locations for Taiwanese PC hardware firms were Malaysia, Thailand, and, after 1990, increasingly China. As early as 1993 China was the source of production of one-third of offshore production of PC hardware by Taiwanese firms. For example, joint venture or wholly Taiwanese-owned companies produced more than 2 million monitors in China that year, more than half their total offshore production.[79]

In the second half of the 1990s Taiwanese firms such as Acer Computer, Mitac, and First International Computer (FIC) began to shift the production of desktop personal computers to the mainland. By the first half of 1999, 28 percent of all Taiwanese PCs were made in China; a year later the share rose to 42 percent.[80] Some information technology firms entirely discontinued production in Taiwan. For example, King Computer, a major manufacturer of monitors, announced in the summer of 2000 that it was closing its computer monitor plant in north Taiwan and moving all of its production lines to Shunde in Guangdong Province.[81]

Largely as a result of the relocation of Taiwanese firms to the mainland, China's production of information technology hardware soared in the second half of the 1990s. By 2000 China displaced Taiwan to become the world's third largest producer of information technology hardware, after the United States and Japan. Taiwanese firms accounted for 72 percent of $25.5 billion in computers and related equipment produced that year.[82]

China's share of world production of information technology hardware is likely to rise. In 2000 Taiwanese computer firms, anticipating a loosening of government restrictions on investments in the mainland following the entry of China and Taiwan into the World Trade Organization, began to plan to shift their notebook PC production to China. This was a significant development since by 2000 Taiwan had emerged as the world's foremost producer of notebook PCs. It was expected to supply 15 million units, about 60 percent of world production. In most cases Taiwanese firms were original equipment manufacturers, producing notebook PCs marketed by Sony, Fujitsu, Toshiba, NEC, and Sharp as well as U.S. labels.[83]

Compaq, for example, estimated that it would purchase $9.5 billion in computers and related equipment from Taiwanese companies in 2000 and planned to purchase $10 billion in 2001.[84] Even Legend, China's largest computer manufacturer, outsources all of its notebook computers to Taiwanese companies.[85]

By 2000 four of the five most important Taiwanese notebook PC makers, Inventec, Acer, Compal Electronics, and Arima Computer, had plants producing computer components in China. The fifth, Quanta Computers, in 2000 announced plans to open a motherboard production line in China.[86] Quanta in April 2001 became the first Taiwan computer company to begin notebook computer production in a new facility in Shanghai. The firm expected to make 1 million notebook computers in the first year of operations in Shanghai.[87] Quanta's move is important since it is Taiwan's largest notebook computer maker, and its competitors—Inventec, Compal, and Arima—will almost certainly follow its move to the mainland. One other top five producer, Acer, as well as FIC and Mitac, is well positioned to begin notebook production in China. These firms' largest overseas production bases are there.[88]

Taiwanese semiconductor manufacturers are starting to invest in China. Taiwanese chip design and chip packaging companies already have established a presence in China. Firms such as VIA Technologies, Taiwan's largest integrated circuit design company, have set up testing and support facilities to service the Chinese computer manufacturer Legend, as well as Chinese companies producing motherboards and other computer components. Four or five Taiwanese chip design firms had chip design teams in place in China by year-end 2000.[89] Chip packaging firms, for example Kingmax Technology, will be the next to invest in China.[90] Chip design and chip packaging are much less capital intensive than semiconductor manufacturing, but there is little doubt that Taiwanese semiconductor companies believe that investments in China are critical to the successful development of the industry. Grace THW has already broken ground on a $1.6 billion fabrication plant for made-to-order computer chips. It is China's first computer chip foundry.[91] Although the company's chairman has argued that his firm can undertake the investment without violating existing government regulations restricting investments in China, other leaders in the industry, notably the chairman of Taiwan Semiconductor Manufacturing Corporation, are pressing the Taiwanese government for regulatory changes.[92] Taiwan Semiconductor Manufacturing Corporation is the world's largest producer of made-to-order computer chips.

Figure 2-2. *Chinese Information Technology Trade: Computers and Computer Components, 1995–2000*

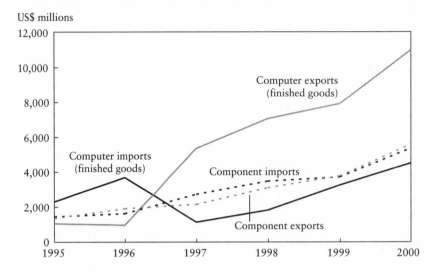

Sources: General Administration of Customs of the People's Republic of China, *China Customs Statistics Yearbook 1995* (Hong Kong, 1996), pp. 484–86, 863–65; *China Customs Statistics Yearbook 1996*, pp. 530–33, 941–44; *China Customs Statistics Yearbook 1997*, pp. 618–21, 1,063–64; *China Customs Statistics Yearbook 1998*, pp. 746–50, 1,217–20; *China Customs Statistics Yearbook 1999*, pp. 869–75, 1,409–13; and *China Customs Statistics Yearbook 2000*.

China's increasing integration into the global production network for computers and computer components is shown in figure 2-2. Chinese exports of computer components, most of which were produced by the Taiwanese companies just discussed, quadrupled between 1995 and 2000, when they stood at $5.6 billion. But at the same time, China was an equally large importer of computer components. These items included components used to produce the motherboards, monitors, and other component exports, and components going directly into finished computers produced by domestic manufacturers and foreign firms, notably those from Taiwan. Exports of finished computers took off after 1996, when they were valued at only $1 billion, to reach $11 billion in 2000. This rapid expansion of trade in computer components and the export of finished computers would have been impossible without the duty drawback system prevailing for processing. If imported components were subject to tariffs, then Taiwanese companies would have found China a less attractive location for producing PC hardware. And the finished computers of Taiwanese and Chinese companies, both of which use imported components, would have been much less competitive on world markets.

## Pattern of Trade

The reforms summarized above led to great changes in the behavior of Chinese companies. Through the mid-1980s the volume of exports and the volume of imports generally were not responsive to changes in the real exchange rate. Because the government specified quantitative targets for most imports and exports, changes in relative domestic and international prices had no discernible effect on the volume of exports or imports. Once foreign exchange retention ratios were raised, the secondary market for foreign exchange was well established, and tariff and nontariff barriers eroded significantly, the relative price elasticities for imports and exports became significant. That is, exports rose and imports fell in response to a devaluation of the real exchange rate. In short, trade liberalization, combined with serious reforms of the system of foreign exchange, "appears to have made export and import behavior more responsive to market signals."[93]

Economic incentives to export such as a more realistic exchange rate, the rebate of indirect taxes on processed exports, the duty drawback on inputs used in processed exports, the reduction of barriers to export, and the growing role of foreign-funded firms as exporters fueled an explosion of Chinese exports. That in turn provided the foreign exchange to finance a dramatically higher volume of imports. Trade turnover soared from less than $15 billion in 1977 to $475 billion in 2000. China's share of world trade grew more rapidly than that of any other country in the world, rising from 0.6 percent in 1977 to 3.85 percent in 2000.[94] Between 1992 and 1999 China's share of the world export market expanded by about 10 percent per year. Japan, in contrast, was the biggest loser of world market share, with a decline of 4.6 percent per year.[95]

Less obvious than the growth of export volume, but equally important, as the reforms took hold export growth became more concentrated in labor-intensive products in which China has a relatively strong comparative advantage.[96] In the early years of reform, China exported primarily agricultural products, petroleum, and petroleum products. Later China shifted into manufactured goods, particularly light manufactures. Thus the share of primary product exports fell by almost four-fifths, from an average of 45 percent of total exports in the first half of the 1980s to only 10 percent by 1999.[97]

China's fastest growing exports have been labor-intensive manufactured goods—textiles, apparel, footwear, and toys. Despite the import restrictions imposed in many important foreign markets, the largest absolute gains have been in apparel and textiles. Textile exports rose from $2.54 billion in 1980 to $12.81 billion in 1998. China's apparel exports soared from $1.48 billion in 1980 to $27.1 billion in 1998. The apparel share of China's total exports more than doubled to reach 15 percent in 1998.[98]

Footwear exports, which were restricted by only a few importing countries, grew even more rapidly.[99] From $173 million in 1980 footwear exports grew almost fiftyfold to $8.4 billion in 1998. The share of footwear in China's total exports expanded from under 1 percent to almost 5 percent.[100] The expansion of exports of toys, for which there were no restrictions in foreign markets, was most rapid of all, growing from $71 million in 1980 to $5.1 billion in 1998. The share of toys in total exports rose from under 0.4 percent of China's total exports in 1980 to 2.8 percent in 1998.[101]

For each of these products China captured a rapidly rising share of total world exports. In textiles China's share almost doubled, from 4.5 percent in 1980 to 8.5 percent in 1998. The increase was even faster for apparel. China's share more than quadrupled, from 4.0 percent to 16.7 percent during the same period.[102] Faster yet was the expansion in the world market share for toys—from 2.3 percent in 1980 to 17.9 percent in 1998.[103] China's share of the world market for footwear rose the fastest of all, soaring from 1.9 percent in 1980 to 20.7 percent in 1998.[104]

These trends obviously are related closely to China's opening to foreign investment and the migration of a great deal of labor-intensive production, mostly from elsewhere in Asia, to China. The best example is probably Hong Kong. As China's opening got under way Hong Kong still had a significant manufacturing sector. In 1981 manufacturing employment hit a historic high of more than 900,000 workers, accounting for almost two-fifths of all jobs.[105]

Slowly at first, but then more rapidly, much of Hong Kong's most labor-intensive manufacturing shifted across the border into China. The migration of jobs in toy manufacturing was rapid. Employment fell from 56,400 in 1981 to only 2,000 in 1999.[106] Employment in textiles and apparel shrank more slowly, since their migration was constrained by the quotas imposed first under the Multifiber Arrangement and later under the Agreement on Textiles and Clothing. Hong Kong's textile and apparel industry developed rapidly in the postwar era. As restrictive arrangements on trade and textiles were put in place in the 1950s, Hong Kong firms were required to observe quotas, imposed by the United States and other industrial countries, on their exports. Although these firms could have easily moved most or even all of their production capacity to China, their Hong Kong export quotas were not transferable, so the shift of the industry to lower-wage China was slower than that for toys. Nonetheless employment in textile and apparel production fell from 382,000 in 1981 to only 75,000 in 1999.[107]

By the end of the 1990s manufacturing employment in Hong Kong had dwindled to under a quarter of a million, only 7.5 percent of the labor force.[108] Few countries have experienced such a rapid reduction in the importance of employment in manufacturing in such a short time. But the reduction in manufacturing employment did not reflect the bankruptcy or shrinkage of Hong Kong manufacturers. These firms maintained their global competitive positions by moving production over the border into China, where labor costs were lower. By 2000 Hong Kong-invested companies in China employed 5 million workers, several times more than they had employed in Hong Kong.[109] A similar, if proportionately somewhat smaller, transformation occurred in Taiwan's labor force as firms moved labor-intensive manufacturing operations to China. By 2000 Taiwanese firms employed an estimated 3 million workers on the mainland.[110]

## Institutional Reforms

China steadily reduced tariff and nontariff barriers during the two decades leading up to its accession to membership in the World Trade Organization. Furthermore, China adopted several important laws and regulations reflecting its transition from a planned economy to a more market-oriented system with a trade regime broadly consistent with international trading practices.

### Antidumping

China promulgated its Antidumping Regulations in the spring of 1997, well in advance of entry into the World Trade Organization.[111] It provided

China, for the first time in the reform era, with a mechanism to deal with the inflow of products being sold in China for less than their normal value. The first case was initiated in late 1997. Interestingly, in this respect China was far ahead of the transition economies of central and eastern Europe, which, with the exception of Poland, still lacked any market-oriented trade remedies such as antidumping.[112]

Although they are far less detailed, the provisions of China's Antidumping Regulations are broadly consistent with the WTO principles.[113] Its definition of "normal value" as the price of the good when it is sold in the exporting country, is identical with the WTO definition. Similarly the injury standard that must be met before antidumping duties can be applied is the cause or threat of material injury to the domestic industry, consistent with the WTO standard. The procedural rules for investigations and collection of evidence are also consistent with WTO practices. Notably, if the authorities determine, in response to a written application from domestic firms, that there is cause for a formal investigation, known foreign exporters or domestic importers of the commodity in question must be notified and subsequently given an opportunity to present relevant information in the case. If an investigation establishes that a good is being dumped, the antidumping duty that is applied cannot exceed the dumping margin found in the investigation. This feature of the Chinese regulation also conforms with WTO practice.

The first important antidumping case was newsprint imports from several firms in the United States, Canada, and Korea. The case seems to have been conducted in conformity with the provisions of the new antidumping law. In November 1997 nine Chinese domestic newsprint producers applied to the Ministry of Foreign Trade for an antidumping investigation. The ministry, after examining the application, publicly announced a formal investigation on December 10. The evidence seems to have warranted a formal investigation. A huge surge in newsprint imports had taken place, starting in 1996. Imports rose from 47,000 metric tons to 356,000 metric tons, an increase of 660 percent in a single year. Imports of newsprint from the United States, Canada, and Korea in 1996 increased 1,335 percent, 743 percent, and 15,660 percent, respectively, over 1995 levels. Imports continued to rise, although only at double-digit rates in 1997.[114] The Chinese firms that filed the case reported substantial reduction in output, a considerable buildup of inventories, reduced capacity utilization, and a sharp drop in profits.[115]

Ministry officials met with officials from the United States, Canadian, and Korean embassies the day after the formal investigation was announced. The companies involved were notified. The ministry issued formal interrogatories to all interested parties a month later, in January 1998. After reviewing the evidence presented by domestic and foreign firms, in July 1998 the ministry announced antidumping margins and imposed temporary antidumping duties.[116] The antidumping margins were confirmed in a final ruling in June 1999.[117]

PUBLIC BIDDING AND GOVERNMENT PROCUREMENT. China began competitive bidding for projects financed by the World Bank in the 1980s. The practice then spread to major domestically funded infrastructure projects.[118] By the mid-1990s government administrative units in some regions began, on a trial basis, to use open, transparent bidding procedures for purchases.[119] Government administrative units spend about RMB 700 billion annually on procurement of goods and services. The government hopes to save up to 10 percent of this amount by uniform application of bidding and tendering procedures.

Important steps in this direction were taken in 1999. In April the State Council promulgated provisional regulations on government procurement, and in August the Standing Committee of the National People's Congress adopted a formal Competitive Bidding Law.[120] The procurement regulations cover government purchases of goods, engineering, and other services, whether by bidding, competitive negotiation, or purchase from a sole supplier, while the Bidding Law applies specifically to engineering projects, including survey, design, construction, and procurement of major equipment and materials for construction. Implementing regulations, which took effect as of May 1, 2000, clarify that the scope of the Bidding Law is unusually broad.[121]

There is little doubt that these regulations and laws are a serious effort to improve efficiency in the expenditure of public funds. Both require considerable transparency in government bidding and purchase. They compel substantial publication of information related to most government procurement in order to attract a large number of bidders. Announcements of projects open for bidding must be published in designated media outlets such as *China Daily*, *China Construction News*, or a newly established website www.chinabidding.com.cn.[122] Moreover, there are certain standards on the use of sealed bids and public opening of bids, and professional

standards must be met to be eligible to serve on bid evaluation committees. The law and regulations forbid linkages between government entities
purchasing goods and services and potential suppliers, as well as kick-
backs and other corrupt practices. There are provisions for huge fines and
criminal penalties and automatic disqualification or suspension from future government bidding and contracting for bidders and suppliers who
violate these provisions. If fully implemented, these procedures would go
a long way to eliminate the corruption that has become endemic in government purchases, especially in large-scale engineering projects.

The structure and many of the provisions of the regulations on procurement and the Bidding Law are consistent with the WTO Agreement
on Government Procurement. For example, the regulations on government procurement follow the lead of the WTO agreement and define the
scope of procurement to include not only outright purchase but also leasing, rental, and hire purchase. Similarly, like the WTO agreement, it covers the procurement of engineering and other services, as well as of goods.

Chinese regulations, however, diverge from the WTO Agreement on
Government Procurement on some points. For example, the Chinese regulations state that government procurement organizations may not purchase foreign goods or engineering and other services without advance
permission. Foreign goods are defined to include not only all imports but
also goods produced in China from imported parts or components in which
the domestic value added is less than half of the total value of the good.[123]
The regulations do not specify which government office is authorized to
give permission for the purchase of foreign goods and services, but it appears that it is the Ministry of Finance, which has the general responsibility for the administration and supervision of government procurement.
More important, the regulations are silent on the criteria the ministry must
use in reaching its decision. Since the procurement regulation requires
approval for purchases of foreign goods but imposes no similar requirement for domestic goods, it clearly fails to provide for national treatment
and most favored nation treatment, the most important tenets of the
WTO code.

Since each signatory to the WTO Agreement on Government Procurement negotiates liberalization of its government procurement market with
other signatories on a reciprocal, bilateral basis, the existence of some
features of the 1999 government procurement regulations that are inconsistent with the WTO Agreement on Government Procurement means little.
China's vice minister of finance, Lou Jiwei, stated in 2000 that the Chinese

government purchase market would be opened up step by step on a reciprocal basis once China entered the World Trade Organization.[124] The vice
minister's comment suggests that China now will be willing to negotiate
bilaterally with the small number of WTO members that are signatories
to the Agreement on Government Procurement. The timing and extent of
liberalization of Chinese government procurement will depend on the details of these bilateral agreements. Since liberalization is negotiated bilaterally, one should not expect China to promulgate regulations that would
give firms from other countries unimpeded access to China's market before the Chinese government has negotiated to secure access to foreign
markets by Chinese firms.

## Summary

China's trade reforms before its entry into the World Trade Organization
were far reaching but incomplete. The rapid decline in tariff revenues relative to the value of imports and the reduced scope of quotas and licenses
were perhaps the most obvious changes. But the increased availability of
trading rights, as reflected in the increase in companies authorized to trade
and the sharp drop in the number of commodities for which trading rights
were limited to one or only a few state trading companies, also was very
important. Eliminating the overvaluation of the domestic currency and
achieving current account convertibility in 1996 were key parts of trade
liberalization. Exporters were no longer penalized, and the availability of
foreign exchange was no longer a factor inhibiting imports. Chinese firms
responded to these reforms in ways consistent with a market-oriented
economy. Exports of labor-intensive manufactures, particularly apparel,
footwear, and toys, soared. China was increasingly drawn into global production networks as foreign firms took advantage of the combination of
low labor costs and a liberal foreign investment environment. Indeed, because it depends on a liberal foreign investment regime, the large role of
transnational companies in generating exports reflects China's deep rather
than shallow integration into the world economy.

However, substantial elements of protection remain. Average tariff rates
are low, but they remain quite high on some important individual items.
Import quotas and license requirements cover only 4 percent of all tariff
lines, but they severely limit the market for a few principal commodities,
for example, automobiles, other vehicles, and parts. Automatic registration, tendering, quality and safety standards, and other nontariff measures

at a minimum have the potential to be used to protect domestic industries. More important, while China had reduced its protection of the domestic goods market through the reforms just discussed, it lagged in providing foreign firms access to its services market. It also imposes many requirements on foreign firms that were inconsistent with WTO standards on intellectual property and other principles that are covered by the terms under which China became a member of the World Trade Organization.

# CHAPTER THREE

# China's Accession to the World Trade Organization

CHINA BECAME A MEMBER of the World Trade Organization more than fifteen years after it first formally requested membership in the predecessor organization, the General Agreement on Tariffs and Trade, in July 1986. Initially the process of accession seemed to be working smoothly. China submitted a memorandum describing its trade regime, the first step in the process, and the GATT Council voted to establish a working party of member countries to conduct the negotiations. Beginning in February 1988 the working party began to meet frequently. At the seventh meeting in April 1989 talks on the protocol of accession began, and many expected that at the eighth meeting of the working party, which was scheduled for mid-July 1989, China would agree to terms that would lead to its membership.

But a confluence of events delayed China's membership. First and most obvious, in the wake of the mass killings in Tiananmen Square in early June of 1989, most Western governments imposed economic sanctions on China.[1] Export credit and economic assistance programs, for example, were suspended. No Western government was willing to send representatives to meet Chinese trade negotiators in Geneva, so the scheduled July 1989 meeting of the working party was canceled. A pro forma meeting was finally held in December that year, but little was accomplished.

Then in 1991 the breakup of the Soviet Union and the collapse of the Council for Mutual Economic Assistance, the economic and trading system that had tied the countries of eastern Europe closely to the Soviet Union, raised the prospect that a large number of additional transition economies would seek to become GATT members.[2] Since the terms of China's membership increasingly were seen as a template that would apply to other transition economies, Western governments implicitly adopted the strategy of bringing China in on relatively rigorous terms.

By the early 1990s China was seen as so successful in expanding its trade and in attracting foreign investment that many members of the working party came to believe that China was not entitled to membership as a developing country. That status automatically would have allowed it to enter on less demanding terms. China's low per capita income clearly qualified it as a developing country. But China's rapid export growth in the early 1990s was taken as evidence that it already was internationally competitive in many products, and thus it did not require the so-called special and differential treatment accorded to developing countries. Not just industrialized countries but also many developing countries that now regarded China as a serious new competitor held this view.

The Uruguay Round trade negotiation, completed in 1994, greatly expanded the scope of the multilateral trading system. As a result the international community increased the demands placed on China to include services, agriculture, protection of intellectual property, and certain aspects of foreign direct investment.

Finally, particularly after the United States released the details of the April 1999 bilateral agreement that President Bill Clinton rejected at the last minute, domestic interest groups in China mobilized against China's WTO membership.[3] Once the agreement was posted on the website of the U.S. Trade Representative, apparently without the prior agreement of the Chinese government, the details of its commitments became widely known in China for the first time. At least temporarily this was not only a setback for the government but for Premier Zhu Rongji personally. In response the government launched a massive educational campaign setting forth the benefits of WTO membership. The accidental U.S. bombing of China's embassy in Belgrade a few months later only compounded the problem of the Chinese government in generating support for the agreement, the terms of which were seen domestically as driven largely by U.S. demands.

The first and last of these five factors simply delayed the negotiation process. But the other three led the members of the working party to place far greater demands on China. The United States took the lead in toughening the conditions under which it would vote support for China's membership. In 1990 U.S. negotiators informed the Chinese government that a final agreement would have to include several items not previously discussed by the working party, including a special safeguard that could be invoked against China in the event of a surge of imports from that country. U.S. negotiators also put forth the view that China should be subject to special periodic reviews of its compliance with its trade commitments.[4]

These items and many others remained under negotiation for more than a decade. Chinese negotiators, perhaps for domestic political reasons, were especially reluctant to forgo developing country status on almost every substantive issue. But in the end the Chinese had little choice but to accept most of the demands of the United States and other members of the working party.

The protocol of accession and the report of the working party governing China's accession to the World Trade Organization provide for additional liberalization of China's trade regime and further opening up of opportunities for foreign direct investment. These provisions, broadly speaking, fall into two categories. The first provides for greater access to China's market through reductions of tariff and nontariff barriers as well as commitments to open foreign investment in the service sector. The second category specifies the terms under which China will interact with the international economy. The second category frequently is referred to as rules-based issues.

## Market Access

China's market access commitments cover goods and services.

### Goods

China agreed to cut average tariff levels for agricultural products to 15 percent and for industrial products to 8.9 percent.[5] For most products new lower tariff levels will take effect by 2004. For some important products tariffs will be eliminated. For example, as noted in chapter 1, China has agreed to participate in the WTO Information Technology Agreement, which requires eliminating all tariffs on semiconductors, telecommunications equipment, computers and computer equipment, and other information technology products. For many of these products tariffs will reach zero by 2003; for the balance in 2004 or 2005. Moreover, China has agreed to bind all of its tariffs. That means it has accepted a legal commitment not to raise tariffs in the future above the agreed-on low rates that will be progressively phased in through 2005 or, for a very few items, such as autos, through July 2006.

China has agreed to eliminate all quotas, licenses, tendering requirements, and other nontariff barriers to imports no later than 2005. In some cases, for example, aircraft, medical equipment, distilled spirits and beer, certain types of fertilizers, and other goods of importance to U.S. firms, import quotas were eliminated on accession. For others a phaseout of import quotas began on accession, when China agreed to large increases in the quotas restricting the import of motor vehicles, various types of synthetic fibers, and other products with significant potential for increased exports by U.S. companies. For some of these products, for example, polyester fiber, China will eliminate quotas one year after accession. The government will raise quotas for all other goods by 15 percent each year and then eliminate them in 2004 or, for motor vehicles only, in 2005.

China has agreed to modify its import registration system to make it consistent with the WTO Agreement on Import Licensing. Among other adjustments Chinese firms will no longer have to demonstrate a need for a specific imported product, a standard that the U.S. Trade Representative believes was used to arbitrarily block the import of products subject to registration.

### Services

Cuts in tariffs and the elimination of nontariff barriers on imports are only the beginning of China's WTO commitments. China has agreed to open important service markets, including telecommunications, banking, insurance, securities, audiovisual, and many professional services.[6] Most important China agreed to grant trading rights and distribution rights to foreign firms, meaning they can import and export as well as engage in wholesale and retail trade, after-sale service, repair, maintenance, and transportation.

TELECOMMUNICATIONS. The opening in telecommunications services is potentially one of the most far reaching. For the first time China will allow direct foreign investment in firms providing telecommunications services, including Internet content and Internet service providers.[7] Before China joined the World Trade Organization, foreign firms were important suppliers of telecommunications equipment, but they were frozen out of the business of providing telecommunications services. Given the sensitivity of the sector, however, the right of foreign firms to invest directly in the provision of various telecommunications services is phased in over time, and majority foreign ownership is precluded in all types of telecommunications services. Upon accession China allowed 30 percent foreign ownership in firms providing paging and value-added services.[8] The permitted foreign share will rise to 49 and 50 percent in the first and second year after accession, respectively. Investment in mobile services also was allowed upon accession, but the foreign share initially is limited to 25 percent. It will rise to 35 percent and then 49 percent one and three years after accession, respectively.[9] For domestic and international wired service foreign investment will not be allowed until the third year after accession and initially will be limited to 25 percent. This share will not rise to 49 percent until six years after accession. Initially foreign-invested firms can offer telecommunications services in the Beijing, Shanghai, Guangzhou service corridor, which accounts for about three-quarters of all domestic telecommunications traffic. The rest of the country will open up over time: two years after accession for paging and value-added services; three years for mobile and data services; and six years for domestic and international wired services. These provisions are summarized in table 3-1.

China's acceptance of the principles of the 1997 WTO Agreement on Basic Telecommunications is at least as important as its easing of foreign investment restrictions. Consistent with this commitment China is transforming its regulatory regime to embrace procompetitive principles. Formally China already has separated the regulatory and operating functions of the Ministry of Information Industry.[10] Historically the Ministry of Post and Telecommunication, one of the predecessors of the Ministry of Information Industry, served as the regulator of the telecommunications industry and the operator of the long-time monopoly service provider, China Telecom.[11] China has adopted the principles of cost-based pricing and rights of interconnection. The effective implementation of these principles is essential if foreign-invested firms are to have a real opportunity to compete with China Telecom. Through most of the 1990s China Telecom refused to provide interconnections to its system, thwarting even potential domestic competitors, such as Unicom, from obtaining a significant market share of the wireless market.[12] Finally China has committed to allow the provision of any basic telecommunications service, including local, long distance, and international service by any means of technology, that is, cable, wireless, or satellite. This technology-neutral commitment underscores its commitment to procompetitive principles.

FINANCIAL SERVICES. The second critical service sector opened through the negotiations leading to China's accession to the World Trade Organization is financial services. China has committed to substantially open its market in banking, insurance, securities, fund management, and other financial services. Historically China precluded or narrowly restricted the ability of foreign firms to compete with domestic firms in these areas. In

Table 3-1. *China's Commitment in Telecommunications Services*
Maximum allowed foreign ownership, percent

| Type of service | Year of accession | +1 year | +2 years | +3 years | +5 years | +6 years |
|---|---|---|---|---|---|---|
| Value added and paging | 30[a] | 49[b] | 50[c] | | | |
| Mobile and data services | 25[a] | 35[b] | | 49[c] | | |
| Domestic and international | | | | 25[a] | 35[b] | 49[c] |

Source: "Agreement on Market Access between the People's Republic of China and the United States of America," November 15, 1999; and "The Sino-EU Agreement on China's Accession to the WTO: Results of the Bilateral Negotiations," p. 3 (www.europe.eu.int/comm/trade/bilateral [June 13, 2000]).

a. Beijing, Shanghai, and Guangzhou only.

b. Beijing, Shanghai, Guangzhou, Chengdu, Chongqing, Dalian, Fuzhou, Hangzhou, Nanjing, Ningbo, Qingdao, Shenyang, Shenzhen, Xiamen, Xian, Taiyuan, and Wuhan only.

c. All geographic restrictions phased out.

banking, for example, the People's Bank of China, the country's central bank, limited the number of cities in which foreign banks could operate and severely restricted the ability of foreign banks to provide local currency services.[13] Thus for many years the primary activity of foreign banks in China was to provide foreign currency banking services, mostly to foreign-invested companies, foreign embassies, and individual foreign citizens. Beginning in early 1997 the central bank licensed eight foreign banks to conduct renminbi business in the Pudong district of Shanghai. The number expanded to nineteen by mid-1999 and to twenty-four in March 2000.[14] In August 1998 the People's Bank of China extended the right to conduct domestic currency business to a few foreign banks in Shenzhen, the special economic zone adjacent to Hong Kong.

But four important additional restrictions severely limited the ability of foreign banks in Pudong and Shenzhen to expand their domestic currency business. First, the business scope of foreign banks in Pudong and Shenzhen was extremely limited. Initially the regulator licensed them to provide domestic currency services only to wholly foreign-owned and joint-venture firms, not to Chinese companies or to Chinese households. The sole exception was that beginning in 1998 the People's Bank allowed foreign banks to participate with domestic banks in extending syndicated loans to Chinese firms.[15]

Second, foreign banks licensed to do domestic currency business in Pudong and Shenzhen were authorized to conduct these transactions only with businesses located within those two small geographic regions. Not until the late summer of 1999 was this narrow franchise slightly expanded.

Foreign banks based in Pudong authorized to conduct domestic currency business were allowed to deal with firms based in the adjoining provinces of Jiangsu and Zhejiang, while those based in Shenzhen were authorized to deal with firms located in Guangdong and Hunan provinces as well as the Guangxizhuang Autonomous Region.

Third, since foreign banks licensed to do domestic currency business had little access to domestic funds, it was difficult for foreign banks to develop domestic currency lending to foreign-owned and joint venture firms. The regulator allowed each foreign bank that it licensed to enter the domestic currency business to increase its capital by at most an amount equivalent to RMB 30 million.[16] These funds, described as operating capital, as well as domestic currency deposits taken from foreign-invested companies, became the sources of domestic currency for foreign bank lending denominated in renminbi. In May 1998 the People's Bank of China took a modest step to ease this constraint by authorizing nine foreign banks, all based in Pudong, to borrow renminbi funds in the domestic interbank market. An additional twelve banks received the same authority early in 2000.[17] This permission gave the banks an alternative to deposits as a source of funds for lending.[18] A second modest step occurred in August 1998 when the central bank raised the ceiling on the banks' RMB operating funds from RMB 30 million to RMB 100 million.[19]

The fourth restriction on the development of the domestic currency business of foreign banks is that the regulator limits the ratio of domestic to foreign currency liabilities of foreign banks. The People's Bank initially set this proportion at 35 percent but raised it to 50 percent in 1999.[20] This limits the domestic currency deposits that foreign banks can accept to an amount equal to half their foreign currency deposits. As long as this regulation remains in effect, once the 50 percent ratio is reached, the rate of growth of domestic currency deposits of foreign banks will be limited to the rate of expansion of their foreign currency deposits. Since banks generally rely primarily on deposits to fund their lending, this means that over the long run the rate of growth of foreign banks' domestic currency lending will be limited to the rate of expansion of their foreign currency lending.[21] Effectively, foreign banks will not be able to shift predominantly into domestic currency lending until this regulation is modified or lifted.

The result of these regulations and restrictions is that while there were large numbers of foreign banks operating in China in the 1990s, their ability to expand their domestic currency business was extremely limited. At the end of March 1998, about one year after foreign banks first were

licensed to conduct domestic currency business in Pudong, the total domestic currency lending of the nine foreign banks licensed to conduct domestic currency business was only RMB 591 million. That was only 0.01
percent of total domestic credit outstanding from all financial institutions.[22]
By the end of 1999, the first full year in which they had the right to borrow domestic funds in the interbank market, the nineteen foreign banks
authorized to extend domestic currency loans in Pudong had an outstanding loan balance of RMB 6.701 billion. Although this was a more than
tenfold increase in a little under two years, it represented only 0.07 percent of credit outstanding from domestic Chinese financial institutions.[23]
Foreign banks have remained marginal players in renminbi lending in a
huge domestic market.

Under the terms of its commitments in services, China is required to
gradually ease all of these restrictions on foreign banks. The number of
cities where foreign banks can offer domestic currency services will systematically increase, and in January 2005 all geographic restrictions on
where foreign banks can offer domestic currency services will be lifted.[24]
As of January 2005, there are to be no numerical limits on the number of
foreign banks that will be licensed.[25] China's central bank must license all
applicants that meet its prudential criteria. The scope of business that can
be offered by foreign banks also will be widened gradually. Two years
after entry foreign banks will be able to conduct local currency business
with Chinese firms. Three years later they will be able to take deposits,
make loans, and offer other local currency services to Chinese individuals.
Five years after accession foreign banks will also enjoy full national treatment. At that point the central bank will no longer be able to restrict the
growth of the domestic currency business of foreign banks by limiting
their ratio of domestic to foreign currency liabilities or use any other
nonprudential ratios to restrict ownership or operation of foreign banks.

The market opening in insurance is similarly broad. Before China's accession to the World Trade Organization, access of foreign insurance companies to the Chinese market was extremely limited. Beginning in the early
1980s the government allowed foreign insurance firms to establish representative offices but, like representative offices of banks, they were not
allowed to conduct any business. The government in 1992 issued the first
license to a foreign firm to American International Assurance Co., Ltd., a
unit of American International Group (AIG). It was licensed to sell a single
line of insurance—life insurance—only in a single city—Shanghai. By the
end of the decade China still had licensed only a handful of foreign insur-

ance companies to sell a limited range of insurance products in only three cities: Shanghai, Guangzhou, and Shenzhen.[26] Firms licensed to sell life insurance were allowed to sell policies to individuals only; group sales were banned. Property and casualty insurers could sell policies to foreign, but not domestic, firms.

As a result of these restrictions, foreign firms have a very limited role in the national insurance market. In 1999 the assets of foreign insurance companies accounted for less than 2 percent of all insurance company assets, and their premium income was only 1.3 percent of total insurance premium income.[27] The dominant firm in the market remains the People's Insurance Company of China (PICC) and, after late 1998, the four specialized companies spun off from PICC.[28]

Under the terms of its accession, China will gradually phase out most of the existing restrictions on foreign insurance companies. Since accession the China Insurance Regulatory Commission is required to consider only prudential criteria when licensing insurance companies, meaning the numerical limitations that have long prevailed are being swept away.[29] Geographic restrictions also are being phased out. Two years after accession twelve additional cities will be opened—Beijing, Chengdu, Dalian, Chongqing, Shenzhen, Fuzhou, Suzhou, Xiamen, Ningbo, Shenyang, Wuhan, and Tianjin. A year later all geographic restrictions will be lifted.

China is gradually phasing out limitations on the scope of business of foreign insurance companies. Since accession foreign insurance companies can offer property and casualty insurance on a nationwide basis and offer certain services on a cross-border basis, that is, from offices outside of China.[30] These services include reinsurance and international marine, aviation, and transport insurance. Foreign insurance companies will be able to offer health insurance three years after accession and group policies, pensions, and annuities two years later.

Unlike in banking, however, the government will not fully lift ownership restrictions in the insurance industry. A foreign firm may have a 51 percent equity share of a nonlife insurance business. Wholly foreign-owned subsidiaries offering nonlife insurance may be established starting two years from the date of China's accession. In life insurance a 50 percent foreign ownership ceiling now applies, but there is no provision for any increase. American International Group, which has operated a wholly foreign-owned insurance company in Shanghai since 1992 and in Guangzhou since 1995, is an exception. It will be allowed to continue to operate under the grandfathering provision for trade in services that was negotiated in the 1999 U.S.-China bilateral agreement and built into China's accession package. This clause provides that the conditions of ownership, operation, and scope of activities of foreign service providers operating in China before its entry into the World Trade Organization will not be made more restrictive.[31]

China's commitment in securities and fund management is less far reaching than in banking or insurance. Foreign ownership restrictions, for example, are more severe. Foreign companies can initially own up to one-third of an asset management company, but this share rises to only 49 percent three years after accession. In securities operations foreign ownership is limited to one-third, with no provision for any increase over time. There are also limits on the scope of business. For example, since accession foreign-invested securities firms can deal directly in B shares, and within three years of accession they will be able to underwrite B shares, underwrite and trade government and corporate debt, and underwrite A shares. But they will not be allowed to participate in the business of trading A shares, which historically has been the source of the largest share of the income in the Chinese securities industry. There are, however, no geographic restrictions on securities. Since accession, foreign-invested securities and asset management firms have been allowed to establish businesses in any location in China.

DISTRIBUTION. Although the State Council promulgated provisional regulations allowing foreign retailers to enter the Chinese market in 1992, the legal right of foreign firms to distribute goods in China remained extremely limited. Restrictions covered wholesaling and retailing, as well as franchising, commission agents, and repair and maintenance services. Foreign retailers were limited to minority-owned joint ventures, able to operate in only six cities and five special economic zones, and faced a host of other restrictions.[32] By 1998 Beijing had approved fewer than twenty Sino-foreign retail joint ventures.[33] Before accession firms that produced goods in China, in wholly foreign-owned factories or in joint venture arrangements, could negotiate to establish networks to distribute their products. But they were not allowed to bring into these distribution networks goods produced outside of China. Thus Shanghai Volkswagen could establish a dealer network to sell and provide repair and maintenance services for Santana automobiles produced in Shanghai, but the same network could not be used to distribute any Volkswagen vehicles imported from Germany or other countries. The same constraint applied to the distribution network established by Shanghai Buick under the terms of its 1996 joint venture with Shanghai Automotive Industrial Corporation.

Under the terms of China's accession to the World Trade Organization most of these geographic, ownership, and other restrictions on all types of distribution services are being phased out over a three-year period.[34] Zhengzhou and Wuhan, two major urban centers in Henan and Hubei provinces, respectively, were opened on accession to joint venture retailing. Two years after entry all provincial capitals, as well as Chongqing, a huge municipality in southwest China that now has provincial-level administrative status, and Ningbo city on the coast south of Shanghai, will be opened to foreign retailers. Moreover, foreign majority equity ownership will be allowed in all cities that have been opened to foreign retailers by that time.[35] All geographic restrictions on retailing will be lifted three years after entry. Joint ventures to provide wholesale services have been permitted since accession; foreign majority equity shares in these ventures will be allowed two years from accession; and three years after accession wholly foreign-owned wholesale companies will be allowed. Most product restrictions in China's distribution commitments will be phased out. The wholesale distribution of books, magazines, newspapers, pharmaceutical products, pesticides, and plastic film used in agriculture is not granted until three years after accession; chemical fertilizers, crude oil, and refined petroleum products not until five years after accession. China has denied in perpetuity the right of foreign firms to wholesale salt and tobacco. Foreign firms will never be allowed to sell tobacco products at the retail level.

The government will liberalize services related to distribution, such as maintenance and repair, rental and leasing, advertising, technical testing and analysis, freight inspection, packaging, courier, storage and warehousing, transport, and freight forwarding. In most cases joint ventures to provide such services have been allowed since accession and restrictions, such as those on the foreign equity share, will be eliminated in periods varying from three to six years after accession. Repair and other distribution services affiliated with a manufacturing establishment in China have been allowed since accession. Thus Shanghai Buick can use its dealer network to sell and service not only the vehicles produced in its factory in Shanghai but also other General Motors models produced outside of China.

PROFESSIONAL SERVICES. Before accession to the World Trade Organization China strictly limited the ability of foreign firms to provide legal, accounting, management consultancy, architectural, engineering, urban planning, medical, computer, and other professional services in China. Its accession terms lift most of these restrictions. Majority foreign ownership of joint ventures offering professional services was allowed on accession, and in some fields wholly owned subsidiaries may be established five years after accession. Geographic restrictions that have limited foreign law firms to nineteen cities and have precluded them from operating simultaneously in more than one of these cities, will be eliminated one year after accession. More important, in its negotiations with the European Union (EU), China eased its long-standing prohibition on foreign lawyers practicing Chinese law and the terms under which they can hire Chinese nationals as lawyers to represent clients in Chinese courts. Foreign lawyers will be able to advise clients on Chinese legal matters, a significant easing of the long-standing, if not usually enforced, restriction that foreign lawyers in China could only provide advice on their home countries' legal matters.

Foreign lawyers continue to be proscribed from representing clients in Chinese courts. However, some improvement has occurred in the terms under which they can enter into long-term relations with the Chinese law firms that provide these services to the client of the foreign firm. Foreign lawyers may now instruct individual Chinese lawyers on how to represent the client of the foreign lawyer. At least in principle this is an improvement over the former system in which the foreign law firm could only maintain "entrustment relations" with Chinese law firms. Whether it will "in practice be equivalent to full employment" of Chinese lawyers by foreign lawyers remains to be seen.[36]

AUDIOVISUAL SERVICES. China historically has restricted the number of foreign films for theatrical release and precluded foreign firms from distributing video and sound recordings or constructing and operating cinemas. These restrictions are now eased. China has allowed up to twenty foreign motion pictures annually for theatrical release on a revenue-sharing basis since accession.[37] China will allow joint ventures with up to 49 percent foreign ownership to enter the film distribution business and to construct and operate movie theaters.

CONSTRUCTION SERVICES. In the bilateral agreement with the United States, China simply confirmed the right of foreign investment in joint venture construction companies. The EU, in its bilateral negotiations with China, improved on this commitment, getting agreement that on accession joint ventures in the construction industry could be majority foreign owned, and that three years after that China would allow the operation of wholly foreign-owned construction companies.[38]

### Agriculture

China's commitments in agriculture are perhaps more far reaching than those on manufactured goods. They encompass provisions on market access, which include tariff reductions and minimum access opportunities under a tariff-rate quota system, limits on domestic support for agricultural producers, and limits on export subsidies for agricultural products. Furthermore, China eliminated long-standing technical barriers to the import of several important agricultural products.

China agreed to reduce the average statutory tariff rate for agricultural products from 22 percent to 15 percent by January 2004.[39] These tariff reductions probably are more significant than those for manufactured goods because before China's WTO accession import tariff exemptions were common for manufactured goods but far less frequent for agricultural products, primarily because most processed exports are manufactures that do not utilize imported agricultural inputs directly.[40]

China's tariff-rate quota system commitment for key products such as wheat, corn, rice, soybean oil, cotton, and a few others is probably more important than the reduction in the average statutory tariff on agricultural imports.[41] The Agreement on Agriculture in the Uruguay Round required all members of the World Trade Organization to eliminate all nontariff barriers to the import of agricultural products and replace them with tariffs that provide equivalent protection, a process referred to as tariffication. In most cases the replacement of quotas and other nontariff barriers with equivalent tariffs led to a rather substantial increase in tariff levels on agricultural products. The objective was to use a tariff-only regime to make the protection provided to agriculture more transparent and to provide a common basis among countries for negotiating future tariff reductions.

To offset the trade-reducing effect of these higher tariffs, the agreement also requires countries to offer minimum access opportunities for agricultural products subject to tariffication. Countries must apply much lower tariffs to the minimum access opportunities. For products for which imports were less than 5 percent of domestic consumption in the base period, the minimum access opportunity began at 3 percent of base period consumption and rose to 5 percent of base period consumption at the end of the implementation period. For commodities for which imports were more than 5 percent of domestic consumption in the base period, WTO members were required to set minimum access opportunities that maintain access equivalent to average imports in the 1986–88 base period.[42]

China's tariff-rate quota system commitments reflect these general principles. For several important agricultural imports China agreed to establish extraordinarily low tariffs, 1 percent for wheat, corn, rice, and cotton, for a fixed initial quantity of imports, referred to as the minimum access opportunity or quota amount.[43] These quotas, which are shown in table 3-2, then rise at preagreed rates through the year 2004 or, for soybean oil, 2006. The quotas are much higher than the level of Chinese imports of these products in 1998, the year before the bilateral agreement with the United States was reached on China's accession. That means that if the demand for imports rises, significant additional amounts of these commodities could enter China at extraordinarily low tariff rates.

China's quota for wheat rises from 6.1 percent of base period consumption in the first year to 7.8 percent in the final year. For rice the initial quota of 2.66 million metric tons is the equivalent of 1.4 percent of consumption in the base period, and the ultimate quota is 2.7 percent. For corn the figures are 4.7 percent and 6.4 percent, respectively.[44] The commitments for wheat and corn are higher than the minimum access standards specified in the Agreement on Agriculture. Corn imports in the base period, for example, composed only 0.6 percent of the base period of consumption, so China's required initial minimum access opportunity should have been only 3 percent, far below the 4.7 percent agreed to in the protocol. Moreover the quota in the final year is 6.4 percent, far more than the required 5 percent. China's minimum access opportunity for rice, however, falls far short of the levels specified in the WTO Agricultural Agreement. Rice imports in the base period averaged only 2.1 million metric tons. That was only 1.1 percent of consumption, meaning that the initial minimum access opportunity should have equaled 3 percent of domestic consumption or 5.9 million metric tons, more than twice China's actual minimum access opportunity. For the final year the opportunity should have been 5 percent of consumption in the base period, also almost twice the actual commitment.

Although some of the minimum access opportunities fall short of the standard set in the Agriculture Agreement, the increase in China's quotas over the period of implementation looms relatively large in world market terms. As a result of the Uruguay Round negotiations, global increases in market access under minimum access opportunity commitments for wheat

Table 3-2. *Tariff-Rate Quotas for Bulk Agricultural Commodities*
Millions of metric tons unless noted otherwise

| Commodity | 1998 imports | Quota tariff (%) | Initial quota | Ultimate quota |
|---|---|---|---|---|
| Wheat | 1.55 | 1 | 7.30 | 9.30 |
| Corn | .25 | 1 | 4.50 | 7.20 |
| Rice | .26 | 1 | 2.66 | 5.32 |
| Soybean oil | .83 | 9 | 2.50 | 3.60 |
| Cotton | .21 | 1 | .743 | .894 |

Source: "Agreement on Market Access between the People's Republic of China and the United States of America"; and "China Promises Agricultural TRQ Regulations upon WTO Accession," September 28, 2001 (www.insidetrade.com [September 28, 2001]).

(0.807 million tons), coarse grains, principally corn (1.757 million tons), and rice (1.076 million tons) summed to 3.64 million metric tons.[45] The increases in China's minimum access opportunity commitments for the same three important crops, which can be calculated from data in table 3-2, sum to 7.4 million metric tons, fully twice those of the rest of the world combined.

No WTO member is required to import its minimum access opportunities. To increase the probability that China will import the quota amounts, U.S. negotiators demanded, and the Chinese government agreed, to modify significantly the long-standing state monopoly on trade in important grains, such as wheat and rice. China agreed to allocate part of the import quota for each commodity to private traders. The initial private share varies, from as low as 10 percent for wheat to as much as 67 percent for cotton. For corn and soybean oil the shares allocated to private traders will rise over time by an agreed schedule. Because wheat is the most sensitive of these commodities, the share of the quota allocated to private traders is relatively low and does not rise over time. But the Chinese government agreed to an additional special provision under which any portion of the minimum access wheat opportunity that is not used by the state trading company responsible for wheat imports will be reallocated later in each year to private grain traders. Thus private traders could handle more than 10 percent of within-quota imports of wheat.

The underlying intent of the U.S. negotiators in these seemingly complex provisions for trade in these important agricultural commodities was to limit the ability of the Chinese government to maintain domestic agricultural prices significantly above world levels. In the absence of significant minimum access opportunities and a specific provision for private trade, over time the government could severely limit imports simply by instructing the responsible state trading company to import only specified small volumes or even forgo imports of any of these commodities. Instead of importing significant amounts from world markets, the government could seek to meet the rising demand for these commodities by raising the domestic price sufficiently to induce local producers to increase production. This in effect has been the strategy pursued by the Japanese government to maintain basic self-sufficiency in rice. By the time the Uruguay Round negotiations were completed in 1994 the Japanese government had raised the price of rice paid to farmers to several times the world level. Japanese trade restrictions precluded would-be importers from taking advantage of this huge disparity in prices between the world and domestic markets.

Requiring the Chinese government to authorize private, profit-oriented trade in these commodities limits this policy option. Whenever domestic prices rise significantly above the world level, it will be profitable for private traders to meet rising domestic demand through imports. At least for some period of time that will constrain the ability of the government to raise domestic prices significantly above the world level.[46]

Only when the quota is exhausted will a higher tariff become relevant for greater imports. For wheat, corn, and rice the out-of-quota tariff is initially 80 percent but falls to 65 percent, 51 percent, and 43 percent, respectively, in 2004.[47] For cotton the level is initially 76 percent, falling to 40 percent by 2004. For soybean oil the level is 85 percent, falling to 9 percent in 2006 when tariff-rate quotas on soybean oil will be removed.[48]

The tariffs China has agreed to for the agricultural commodities subject to tariff-rate quotas are far below the levels many countries committed to in the Uruguay Round negotiations and the commitments made by countries that have become WTO members since then. Latvia, for example, when it entered the World Trade Organization in 1999 set its in-quota tariff rates on wheat, barley, and oats at 25 percent, twenty-five times the level agreed to by China.[49] Even China's above-quota tariff rates, which are much higher than the base rates, are low by international standards. The EU, for example, imposes an above-quota tariff of 150 percent on wheat, well over twice China's rate. The above-quota tariff rate on sugar in the United States is 200 percent, and on dairy products the rate is 250 percent in the United States and Canada and nearly 500 percent in the EU.[50]

Although comparisons are difficult, it seems that China's market access commitments for agricultural products are more far reaching than those of Japan. Historically the Japanese government protected the market for rice, Japan's most sensitive agricultural import. Because other WTO members had little confidence that a minimum access opportunity would lead to any sales of rice, Japan in the Uruguay Round agreed to import a minimum amount. For 1995–96 for the minimum access commitment was set at 379,000 tons, 4 percent of total consumption. That was far less than China's 6.1 percent commitment on wheat, its most sensitive agricultural import. Moreover Japan was exempted from converting its protection of the domestic rice market to a tariff. Instead Japan was allowed to impose an import mark up of 292 yen per kilogram of within-quota rice.[51] Since the average price of rice entering world markets at the time was $346 per metric ton, 292 yen per kilogram was the equivalent of an ad valorem tariff rate of 900 percent, compared with the 1 percent that applies for China's minimum access commitment for wheat.[52] When the Japanese government finally converted specific duties to tariff rates in December 1999, the government set the tariff rate on both out-of-quota rice and wheat at more than 350 percent, many times the out-of-quota tariff rate on Chinese grain imports.[53]

### China's Market Access in Comparative Perspective

The scope and depth of China's market access commitments compare favorably with those of other WTO members. For example, China has committed to reduce its average statutory tariff on industrial products to 8.9 percent by 2005; for Argentina, Brazil, India, and Indonesia, four other large countries, the comparable figures are 30.9, 27.0, 32.4, and 36.9 percent, respectively.[54] As already noted China agreed to much lower tariff levels on its most sensitive agricultural products than has Japan. And China agreed to bind all tariffs at the new low statutory rates as they are phased in. As the U.S. Trade Representative pointed out, "Very few countries have done this."[55] India, for example, has bound only about two-thirds of its tariffs.[56] And some industrialized economies that have agreed to binding have set the bound levels well above their statutory or applied rates. Either approach, failing to bind or binding above the statutory rate, provides the opportunity to legally raise tariff rates.

Similarly China's market access commitments on services also compare favorably with most WTO members. China has made commitments in all of the services covered by the WTO General Agreement on Trade in Services. Only a handful of members come close to meeting this standard.[57]

Equally important, in most of these areas the depth of China's commitments goes beyond those made by other countries. U.S. Trade Representative Charlene Barshefsky described China's commitment to liberalize its distribution system, for example, as "broader actually than any World Trade Organization member has made."[58] In financial services China also compares favorably because, unlike many other countries, China's commitment to national treatment is very broad, with practically no exceptions indicated in its schedule. China's commitment in telecommunications also is unusually strong.[59]

In part the depth of the market access commitments that were required from China as a condition for membership in the World Trade Organization reflects the general raising of the bar for new members. For example, all seven of the countries that acceded to the World Trade Organization between its establishment in 1995 and late 1999 agreed to bind all items in their tariff schedules.[60] Thus China's agreement to bind all rates at its new lower tariff levels is similar to the commitment made by other recent entrants. Although China's import tariffs on industrial products are low relative to comparable countries that are long-standing WTO members, they are only somewhat below those of most recent entrants.[61] For rules-based issues, however, China has accepted WTO-plus terms that go far beyond those agreed to even by other countries that have become members of the World Trade Organization since its founding in 1995.

## Rules-Based Issues

A country's accession protocol and working party report sets forth not only its market access commitments but also a number of provisions stipulating the rules under which the nation will conduct its trade. Like market access commitments, rules-based commitments are enforceable through the WTO dispute settlement process. China has agreed to comply with almost all rules provisions. For example, China has agreed to full compliance on entry with the Agreement on Trade-Related Investment Measures. That is somewhat faster than many countries committed to, but the ultimate character of China's commitment is identical to other states.

However, in two important areas—safeguards and antidumping—China was pressed to accept discriminatory treatment, that is, it is subject to WTO-plus requirements more onerous than those accepted by any other member of the World Trade Organization. And in several other areas of only slightly lesser importance, for example, subsidies, China very reluctantly accepted somewhat discriminatory treatment.

### Safeguards

Under certain conditions set forth in the WTO Agreement on Safeguards, a country may impose quantitative restrictions on imports. Since this is a major departure from the most basic WTO principle of eliminating all quantitative trade restrictions, the conditions that must be fulfilled before a country can impose import quotas are rather rigorous. Most important the country imposing the restriction must demonstrate that increased imports have caused or threaten to cause serious injury to domestic firms producing similar or competing products. The mere coincidence of increased imports and declining sales, employment, and profits of domestic producers is not sufficient. Under section 201 of U.S. trade law, which is the mechanism through which the United States implements the WTO Safeguards Agreement, not only must a causal link between rising imports and serious injury be demonstrated, it must also be shown that the increased level of imports is as important as any other cause of the serious injury to the domestic industry.[62]

Except under special circumstances, restrictions on imports imposed under a safeguard measure must be applied on a most favored nation basis, that is, proportionately on all suppliers. Thus an import restriction imposed under the WTO general safeguard provision can not be imposed only on goods originating in a single country.

The transparency requirements for imposing a safeguard measure are quite demanding. Under the WTO agreement a safeguard measure normally cannot be taken until after the relevant governmental authority has conducted an investigation to determine whether serious injury or the threat of serious injury to the domestic industry exists. Reasonable public notice must be given to all interested parties, including importers and exporters. They must be given an opportunity to present their views, rebut the evidence presented by others, and so forth. The findings and conclusions of the investigation must be made public.

Again except under special circumstances, if a country invoking the WTO safeguard clause elects to use a quota to control the level of its imports, the quota can not be set so low that it would reduce total imports of a good below the average level over the prior three years. The conditions that must be met to impose a safeguard beyond four years are somewhat more stringent than those already outlined, and under no circumstances can a safeguard measure be imposed for more than eight years. Once an import quota is imposed, it must be progressively liberalized over time, that is, the quota quantity must be increased each year.

When the safeguard clause is invoked the exporting country has a right to retaliate, under certain conditions. A country imposing a safeguard may offer exporting countries compensation for the restriction of their exports. If compensation is not offered, the countries subject to the safeguard may withdraw substantially equivalent concessions to the trade of the member applying the safeguard measure. If a country imposes a safeguard after its imports have increased absolutely, the exporting countries may withdraw substantially equivalent trade concessions only if the restrictions remain in effect for more than three years. If a country imposes the safeguard in response to an increase in imports only relative to domestic production (that is, imports do not increase by an absolute amount) and offers no compensation, the exporting countries may withdraw substantially equivalent concessions immediately.

In contrast, under the terms of the transitional product-specific safeguard clause in China's protocol of accession to the World Trade Organization, it will be fairly easy for the United States and other countries to impose restrictions on goods imported from China.[63] And China's ability to respond, by withdrawing substantially equivalent trade concessions, is more circumscribed. A comparison of the two safeguard mechanisms supports these conclusions.[64] The injury standard in the transitional product-specific safeguard is low—market disruption, rather than serious injury. This standard permits action more easily than the serious injury standard required in the regular WTO safeguard. Market disruption in U.S. trade law is defined to exist whenever "imports are increasing rapidly, either absolutely or relatively" so as to "be a significant cause of material injury, or threat of material injury to the domestic industry." According to U.S. Trade Representative Charlene Barshefsky, the transitional product-specific safeguard "permits us to act based on the lowest showing of injury."[65]

A WTO member may impose a quota or other restrictive arrangement solely against goods originating in China, even when imports of the same product from other countries have increased. The U.S. Trade Representative General Counsel refers to this as the "China-specific" feature of the transitional safeguard.[66] This is a major exception to the nondiscrimination principle that is at the core of the World Trade Organization and its predecessor organization, the General Agreement on Tariffs and Trade.

The transparency requirements of the transitional product-specific safeguard are less demanding than those set forth in the WTO Agreement on Safeguards. Invoking the transitional product-specific safeguard begins not with an investigation of the merits of an industry's claim that it is suffering from increased imports but with a request by the government in the importing country for consultations with the Chinese government. If the Chinese government agrees that its exports have caused or threaten to cause market disruption, it may voluntarily restrain exports to the country in question. Again, this action would be contrary to the Safeguards Agreement, which prohibits voluntary restraint agreements. If the Chinese side does not "take such action as to prevent or remedy the market disruption" and the United States or other WTO member plans to restrict imports, the members must provide reasonable notice and allow interested parties to rebut the views expressed by others. Sixty days after the initial request for consultations the country may unilaterally impose restrictions on imports from China of the good in question. In other words the actions available under the transitional product-specific safeguard clause include a voluntary export restraint by China or the unilateral imposition by the importing country of increased tariffs or even quotas.

China's ability to retaliate when this clause is invoked is more restricted than under the WTO safeguard. If the restraint on the sale of Chinese goods in the United States or another market is based on a relative increase in imports, China may not retaliate for two years. Under the normal WTO safeguard the exporting country can withdraw equivalent concessions immediately if the safeguard has been imposed in response to a relative increase in exports. In place of the absolute eight-year time limit on safeguard measures imposed under the WTO Agreement on Safeguards, the transitional product-specific safeguard may be applied to imports from China "only for such period of time as may be necessary to prevent or remedy the market disruption."[67] In effect there is no specific time limit. Once a restrictive quota has been imposed against Chinese imports, there is no requirement for progressive liberalization of the quota over time.

Finally, the transitional product-specific safeguard contains an unusual special provision to deal with market disruption as a result of trade diversion. After one WTO member invokes the transitional product-specific safeguard to limit imports of a good from China, diversion could arise if Chinese firms redirected their exports of that product to other markets where a product-specific safeguard was not in effect. Under the terms of

China's accession, after one country has imposed a safeguard measure, any other member may request consultations with China if it anticipates that the application of a safeguard elsewhere will lead to increased imports of the good from China. China must respond within thirty days and, if China is unwilling to restrict its exports, that country may impose restrictions unilaterally starting sixty days from the initial request for consultation. These restrictions can remain in effect for up to thirty days after the first country to impose the safeguard removes it. The effort of Chinese negotiators to require that importing countries demonstrate that trade diversion is a significant cause of material injury to their industry before placing limits on imports from China was rejected by members of the working party.[68] Thus in the case of a transitional safeguard imposed on China as a result of trade diversion, there is no requirement for any investigation to determine if market disruption exists.

China has agreed to allow WTO members to apply the terms of this transitional product-specific safeguard, which are far more onerous than those that have been imposed on any other country as a condition for WTO membership, for a period of twelve years from the time of its accession.[69] Only then will China be subject to the less onerous provisions of the WTO Safeguard Agreement.

Thus in a worst-case scenario China could face a quantitative restriction on its exports of a product for twelve years with no liberalization over time on the restriction. These restrictions would start in one country but likely quickly cascade to all significant markets. They could be imposed even if the increased inflow of Chinese goods were only displacing goods from other countries and when only the country initially imposing the safeguard had carried out an investigation establishing the existence or threat of material injury to the domestic industry.

Besides this transitional product-specific safeguard, China also agreed to allow the United States and other WTO members to utilize, until December 31, 2008, a special textile safeguard.[70] The safeguard is substantially the same as the safeguard provision that was originally part of the 1997 bilateral textile agreement between China and the United States.[71] Bilateral agreements on textiles between China and the United States and some other advanced industrial countries are founded on the WTO Agreement on Textiles and Clothing (ATC), the successor to the Multifiber Arrangement. In a major departure from the principles of the World Trade Organization, the ATC allows countries to impose quotas on textiles and apparel imports. Under the terms of the ATC, countries imposing restrictions are required to phase them out in several stages, beginning January 1, 1995. They must entirely phase out such restrictions by December 31, 2004. As chapter 4 discusses, the phaseout of the restrictive trade arrangements for textiles and clothing has the potential to greatly increase China's share of world trade in these products. But the Chinese have agreed to let WTO members use a special textile safeguard until the end of 2008.

This textile safeguard, if fully implemented, would allow WTO members to limit the growth of Chinese textile and apparel imports to 7.5 percent per year.[72] The conditions under which restrictions can be imposed are relatively easy to meet, and Chinese exporters have limited opportunity to retaliate. As with the transitional product-specific safeguard, the injury threshold that must be demonstrated is very low—only the existence or the threat of market disruption. The test is not whether there is serious injury to the domestic industry in the United States or in another country proposing quotas on imports but material injury or the threat of it. Under U.S. trade law this is defined as imports increasingly rapidly, either absolutely or relatively. Restrictions can be imposed even when total imports are not growing, but products from China are displacing those of other suppliers. Moreover, even in this case, when imports from China have only increased relatively, China cannot retaliate against the restriction. Finally restraints on textile and apparel imports automatically take effect immediately, whereas under the usual WTO textile safeguard procedures restrictions usually cannot be imposed until after consultation with the exporting country that would be directly affected by the proposed restrictions. If consultations fail to result in a mutually satisfactory solution, the quota restrictions stay on until the end of the year or, if the case arises in the last quarter of any year, for twelve months. When the restriction ends, the country imposing the restrictions is then free to start the process all over again.

This process can be used to restrict textile and apparel imports from China until the end of 2008. Thus although the countries that maintained textile and apparel quotas on China before its entry in principle have agreed to phase out these quotas, they may, on a case-by-case basis, continue to impose restrictions on these imports from China for four years beyond the time that the restrictions have been phased out completely for all other supplier countries. And countries that previously have not maintained quotas on Chinese textile and apparel products under the terms of the ATC now are free to impose them under the terms on which China has entered the World Trade Organization.

China's exports of textile and apparel products also could be subject to restrictions under the terms of the transitional product-specific safeguard.[73] Indeed there are two reasons that it is likely that the transitional product-specific rather than the textile safeguard will be used to restrict the inflow of Chinese textile and apparel products. First, the transitional product-specific safeguard is available for twelve years after China's entry into the World Trade Organization, while the textile safeguard expires at the end of 2008. Second, there is no requirement to liberalize the transitional product-specific safeguard over time. Once an import quota is fixed, it could remain in effect at the same level until the transitional product specific safeguard expires twelve years after entry. By contrast the duration of a textile safeguard against China is generally limited to a year. Although it may be renewed, on each occasion the quantitative limit must be increased 7.5 percent.

### Antidumping

China also agreed to accept discriminatory WTO-plus terms in its protocol of accession in a second important area—antidumping. A country can impose antidumping duties on imports if it can show that a firm is selling a product abroad at less than its "normal value" and that there is "material injury" or the threat of that to the domestic industry that is caused by dumped imports. WTO rules define normal value as the price at which the good is sold in the home country or in a third country. As in the case of safeguards, the country imposing the sanction must show that material injury or threat of material injury to its domestic industry was caused by dumped imports, not other factors.

Under the provisions of U.S. trade law, China has for many years been treated as a nonmarket economy in antidumping cases. That means that the U.S. Department of Commerce does not determine whether or not a product is being dumped in the U.S. market by comparing the price of a good imported from China with the price of the same good sold in China or in a third market. The presumption is that since China is in a transition from a planned to a market-based economy, not all of its domestic prices fully reflect supply and demand. For example, if some inputs are subsidized heavily by the Chinese government, domestic prices of goods utilizing that input will not reflect the true cost of production. In that situation, comparisons of the prices of Chinese goods at home with prices of the same goods sold abroad would not necessarily indicate whether or not a good is being sold at less than "normal value." Thus U.S. producers could be forced to compete unfairly with a Chinese producer that had access to subsidized inputs.

When an American firm files a dumping case against a good from China the U.S. Department of Commerce establishes the normal value of the good by one of two possible nonmarket economy methods. In the first the department asks the Chinese producers to supply information on the quantities of each of the inputs that they utilize to produce the good. The department then constructs the cost of producing the good by using input prices of a third country where the prices of factor inputs are market determined. The department then adds to this estimate of direct production costs reasonable amounts for administration, selling and other costs, and profit. The sum of these items is considered normal value. This is usually called the factors of production or constructed value method. Alternatively, when the input data are not available from the Chinese producer, the U.S. Department of Commerce can simply use as a standard for "normal value" the cost of production of the good in a third country. This is usually called the surrogate country approach.

The use of the nonmarket economy methodology, whether the factors of production approach or the surrogate country approach, disadvantages China for several reasons. First, countries that are selected as surrogates or whose prices are used in the constructed value approach sometimes have labor costs that are much higher than those prevailing in China.[74] Particularly for labor-intensive goods, that gives rise to the distinct possibility of a finding by the U.S. Department of Commerce that a good is being sold in the United States at less than "normal value" when in reality the price is well above the actual Chinese cost of production plus appropriate markups for selling costs and profit. In effect, the likelihood is that the application of the nonmarket economy methodology means that the "Chinese producers' comparative advantage over its world-wide competitors is lost."[75]

Second, firms in market economies sometimes sell their products for less than average total cost. In a downturn, for example, a firm may be willing to sell its goods for a price that covers only its marginal cost of production. If this firm sold its products at home and abroad at the same price, it could not be subject to antidumping duties, even though those sales occurred at a loss. By contrast the U.S. Department of Commerce always includes profit when calculating normal value in the nonmarket economy methodologies. How profits are calculated means that "constructed value calculations usually involve very high (antidumping) margins."[76] Thus even if wages in the country whose prices are being used were not higher than in China, the inclusion of profits in the calculation of normal value disadvantages Chinese firms subject to antidumping investigations in the United States.

The third reason the protocol disadvantages China is that it does not define market economy conditions. Thus each WTO member has broad discretion in setting or even changing the conditions under which it applies nonmarket economic provisions in antidumping cases against Chinese firms. Finally, under U.S. law the decision of the U.S. Department of Commerce to designate a trading partner as a nonmarket economy is not subject to judicial review.[77]

China has agreed to allow the United States and other WTO members to use the nonmarket economy methodology in dumping cases for fifteen years from the time of its accession.

The bilateral agreement with the United States and China's WTO accession package does allow for the possibility of suspending the nonmarket economy methodology on a case-by-case basis. Chinese firms charged with dumping can petition for a review of the appropriateness of the nonmarket economy methodology on the grounds that the sector of the economy in which they operate has become sufficiently market oriented that it should no longer be subject to the special methodology. But this option has been open to Chinese firms for a decade, and "to date no industry in China has been able to obtain such treatment."[78]

In the early 1990s the U.S. Department of Commerce allowed what was referred to as the "bubbles of capitalism" approach in dumping cases involving nonmarket economies, including China. This approach acknowledged that a firm subject to a charge of dumping might be operating in a market environment, even if the industry of which it was a part still had significant nonmarket elements. By 1992 the Commerce Department abandoned this approach in favor of a much more stringent "market-oriented industry" approach. Since then a firm subject to an antidumping case cannot escape the use of the nonmarket economy methodology unless it demonstrates that its entire industry operates in a competitive environment. Under the "bubbles of capitalism" approach the firm had only to demonstrate that it operated in a market environment.

That difference, which may seem somewhat obscure, could be important, especially for private firms in China. Although they may not benefit from any state-provided subsidies, these private firms frequently would not be able to demonstrate that all state-owned firms in their industry operate in a purely market environment. Thus these private firms would be unable to make the case that they should not be subject to the nonmarket economy methodology in antidumping cases.

### Subsidies

China should be concerned about the prospect of its firms facing investigations on subsidies and exposure to countervailing duties if there is a finding that a subsidy exists for two reasons. First, China gives firms access to credit from state-owned banks at interest rates that are fixed by the state and which also carry other conditions that may differ from those that would prevail in a market-oriented financial system. Second, in China restructurings of the debt owed by state-owned companies to state-owned banks are a major component of the effort to make the state-owned manufacturing sector more competitive. To address the accumulation of massive nonperforming loans in state-owned banks in the 1990s, the government in 1998 created four asset management companies that assumed RMB 1.4 trillion in loans from the banks. The State Economic and Trade Commission authorized the asset management companies to swap RMB 460 billion of this amount into equity. After the swap the asset management company becomes an equity owner of the firm, and the original loan obligation of the firm is eliminated.[79]

Several aspects of China's commitments on subsidies make it more likely that other WTO members will prevail in an investigation of subsidies not specifically related to exports and that Chinese exporters will face countervailing duties. The WTO Agreement on Subsidies and Countervailing Measures is a detailed, complex document. It outlines the definition of a subsidy and the remedies that a member may take against subsidies that are deemed "actionable," meaning that a member could impose countervailing duties, regardless of whether any subsidy was conferred on the good at the export stage. To take action against a subsidy provided to an industry in another state, a member must demonstrate that the government or a public body is making a financial contribution to the industry and that this contribution confers a specific benefit to the industry. Consistent with long-standing practice in the United States, government assistance that is deemed generally available and widely and evenly distributed is not an actionable subsidy.[80] China, however, in its accession protocol agreed that subsidies that are widely available to state-owned companies are actionable by foreign governments if "state-owned enterprises are the predominant recipients of such subsidies or state-owned enterprises receive disproportionately large amounts of such subsidies."[81]

Second, because of its delayed WTO entry, China will not be able to take advantage of one provision that applies to some subsidies provided by transition economy members, that is, those that are "in transformation from a centrally-planned into a market, free-enterprise economy."[82] During a seven-year period from the founding of the World Trade Organization, transition economies were allowed to forgive government-held debt and make grants to cover debt repayment to help privatization and restructuring of state-owned enterprises. For transition economies these subsidies were not subject to the "serious prejudice" rule, which in effect allows other member states to presume rather than demonstrate that such subsidies cause adverse effects.[83] Transition economies that have joined the World Trade Organization after its founding in 1995 were eligible for such treatment. Bulgaria, when it became a member at the end of 1996, for example, was allowed to invoke the transition economy provisions on subsidies, meaning that debt equity swaps and other forms of debt forgiveness were not actionable subsidies.[84] China will not be able to take advantage of the transition economy provision of the Agreement on Subsidies and Countervailing Measures because the provision expired seven years after the entry into force of the Uruguay Round Treaty, that is, at the end of 2001.

The third noteworthy aspect of China's commitment on subsidies is closely related to the second. China agreed not to take advantage of several provisions of the Agreement on Subsidies and Countervailing Measures that are available to developing countries. Developing countries, for example, are allowed to forgive debts and subsidize social costs when they are linked to a program of privatization. China agreed to forgo this provision, meaning subsidies related to privatization will be actionable. This is especially significant because, unlike the transition economy provisions on debt forgiveness that have expired, the debt forgiveness provision for developing countries is available without time limit. Similarly China agreed to forgo other developing country provisions that raise the threshold for challenging a developing country's subsidies in the WTO dispute settlement process.[85]

Fourth, in article 20 of its protocol China agreed that in antidumping cases WTO members may use what is referred to as an "alternative benchmark" when measuring the value of government-provided subsidies. That means WTO members may "use methodologies for identifying and measuring the subsidy benefit which take into account the possibility that prevailing terms and conditions in China may not always be available as appropriate benchmarks."[86] That provision, which is analogous to the alternative nonmarket economy methodology used in antidumping cases, will facilitate action against Chinese industries that are charged with receiving soft loans or equity infusions in countervailing duty cases.[87]

In the United States and the EU the potential adverse effects of countervailing duties on Chinese firms have not been felt but could become important in the future. The U.S. Department of Commerce, for example, does not apply the U.S. countervailing duty law to countries that have been designated as nonmarket economies. It takes the view that when prices and costs of inputs are set by central planners, it makes little sense to try to identify separate subsidies resulting from government grants, loans, or other funding mechanisms usually considered under the WTO Agreement on Subsidies.[88] However, once the U.S. Department of Commerce determines that a Chinese industry is sufficiently market oriented that it is no longer subject to the special nonmarket economy methodology used in antidumping cases, firms in that industry will then be subject to countervailing duty investigations. Thus the use of alternative benchmarks in determining whether or not a Chinese firm is receiving a government subsidy could become significant, either after the U.S. Department of Commerce or the EU determines that a Chinese industry is market oriented or fifteen years after China's accession, when the use of the nonmarket economy methodology in antidumping cases expires. The Chinese agreement to allow the use of alternative benchmarks in countervailing duty cases has no time limit.

Besides the subsidy provisions just analyzed, which apply to nonagricultural goods, China also agreed to several limitations on its domestic subsidies for agriculture. The WTO Agricultural Agreement limits the ability of member governments to provide domestic agricultural support. The goal is to avoid overstimulation of agricultural production, which would distort world agricultural markets. Each member must agree to bind and reduce these subsidies, which are measured according to the WTO's aggregate measure of support (AMS) methodology. Domestic food aid for the needy, direct payments to farmers for not growing certain crops, income insurance, and other safety net programs, referred to as Green Box subsidies, are not included in the calculation of AMS. If a country's agricultural subsidies fall below certain minimum levels it need make no AMS commitment, but it is prohibited from raising support beyond these de minimis levels.[89]

China's Ministry of Foreign Trade has acknowledged that domestic agricultural support in 1999 was RMB 50 billion, an amount equal to approximately 3.5 percent of the value of agricultural output.[90] Although China's domestic agricultural subsidies are relatively low, in 2001 they became a chief source of disagreement in the multilateral negotiations in Geneva. China sought to reserve the right to increase domestic agricultural support subsidies to an amount equal to 10 percent of the value of agricultural output, the de minimis level allowed for developing countries.[91] The United States and some other members of the working party sought to hold China to the 5 percent limit that applies to developed countries.

China's motivation in seeking greater flexibility was fairly clear. Agriculture will be the sector most adversely affected by China's WTO accession. China does not have the administrative capacity to provide domestic food aid, income insurance, safety net support payments, or payments for not producing certain agricultural goods, all of which would be excluded from China's AMS. These subsidies must be provided based on the characteristics of individual households. But China has more than 240 million rural households, and its rural administrative infrastructure is not sufficiently developed to assess the need for and deliver the needed transfer payments for such a large number of households. Its only viable instrument to support farm income is price supports. The World Trade Organization considers price supports trade distorting and includes them in its AMS calculation.

The final compromise on agricultural subsidies had several elements.[92] First, China is allowed to extend subsidies up to 8.5 percent of the value of agricultural output—more than the developed country limit initially proposed by the working party but less than the developing country limit that China desired. Besides limiting the aggregate amount of domestic support for agriculture, China also agreed to limit its subsidy of any single agricultural product to no more than 8.5 percent of the value of that crop. This product-specific restriction is responsive to the concern of the United States and other members of the working party that if China were to concentrate subsidies on one or a few specialty fruit or vegetable crops, that could have a substantial negative effect on world prices, even if China stayed within its overall subsidy limit. Second, China also agreed that it would not take advantage of the normal provision that allows developing countries to exempt from inclusion in their AMS agricultural investment subsidies and subsidies for inputs, such as fertilizer, if they are generally available to low-income or resource poor farmers. China has agreed to forgo recourse to this exemption.

### Agricultural Export Subsidies

Besides China's market access commitments in agriculture and its commitment to limit domestic subsidies, another important component of China's WTO promises on agriculture relates to subsidies of agricultural exports. U.S. trade negotiators believe that in the past these subsidies allowed China to increase its share of world markets for corn, rice, and cotton, resulting in lower exports of these commodities from the United States and perhaps other WTO members. In the base period used for negotiation in the Uruguay Round, China's agricultural export subsidies were $500 million, the ninth largest of any country.[93] By value the largest Chinese agricultural export subsidies were for oil cakes, coarse grains (corn and barley), vegetables, and poultry. In the Uruguay Round negotiations China in 1994 offered to reduce the value of its agricultural export subsidies by 24 percent and the quantities of subsided exports by 14 percent. These reductions, which were required of all developing country members, were to be phased in over ten years.[94] Since China did not become a member of the World Trade Organization at its formal establishment in 1995, that offer was never accepted.

After the signing of the bilateral agreement between China and the United States in November 1999, U.S. trade officials repeatedly said that China had committed to eliminate all subsidies of agricultural exports on entry. However, the published text of the bilateral agreement contains no such commitment; indeed in retrospect it seems that the subject was not discussed in the bilateral negotiations leading up to the November 1999 agreement.[95] The claim was the understanding of the U.S. and other trade negotiators, based on verbal comments of the Chinese delegation, at a meeting of the working party in 1999. When China in May 2000 notified the World Trade Organization of all of its subsidy programs in preparation for the June meeting of the working party, this verbal pledge had vanished. China offered only to reduce agricultural export subsidies by 35 percent over six years starting from its date of entry. The initial level of subsidies was $545 million; the commitment for the sixth year was $350 million. China's written proposal for entry in May 2000 was comparable to its Uruguay Round offer in that the end point was similar—$355 million in remaining subsidies in 2005 under the Uruguay Round offer; $350 million in subsidies remaining in 2006 under its offer in 2000.

In the end China did commit to eliminate agricultural export subsidies on entry—far exceeding the agricultural export subsidy commitments made by GATT members at the founding of the World Trade Organization. Neither the United States nor the EU, for example, agreed to eliminate agricultural export subsidies. Developed countries agreed to reduce the value of their agricultural export subsidies by 36 percent and developing countries agreed to a 24 percent reduction by 2005. The least developed countries were exempt.[96] Further reductions, beyond those mentioned, will depend on the outcome of the next round of multilateral WTO negotiations. After the failure of the Seattle WTO ministerial meeting to agree on an agenda for the next round of talks, the willingness of the Chinese government to agree to eliminate agricultural export subsidies is somewhat surprising. In effect, China made a concession that may surpass what the members of the World Trade Organization will agree to in the next round of multilateral trade negotiations.

### Sanitary and Phytosanitary Standards

Besides its commitments to reduce tariffs on agricultural commodities, to introduce a tariff-rate quota system for grains, soybean oil, and cotton, limit domestic agricultural subsidies, and eliminate agricultural export subsidies on entry, China agreed to comply with the provisions of the WTO Agreement on Sanitary and Phytosanitary Standards. This means that all measures to protect human, animal, and plant life and health from pests and diseases will be based on scientific standards and will not be a disguised restriction on trade. Even before entering the World Trade Organization China had already reached related bilateral agreements with the United States covering citrus, meat, wheat, and leaf tobacco.[97] Although they are not part of China's WTO agreement, each of these bilateral agreements embodies WTO principles on sanitary and phytosanitary standards.

The bilateral agricultural agreement with the United States commits China to remove long-standing health and safety barriers to the import of several U.S. agricultural products. China had long banned the import of U.S. citrus fruit originating in Arizona, California, Florida, and Texas, ostensibly for fear that imports from these regions might be contaminated with Mediterranean and Mexican fruit flies. Under the agreement the Chinese government will allow imports in accordance with the standards and principles of internationally accepted pest risk assessment. China essentially has agreed to import citrus fruit that is certified by the Animal and Plant Health Inspection Service of the U.S. Department of Agriculture to be free of fruit fly infestation.[98] Similarly China has agreed to import beef, pork, and poultry from packing plants approved by the U.S. Department of Agriculture Food Safety Inspection Service. In effect the Chinese government has recognized that the United States has a sound system of epidemiological disease control and an effective program to control chemical residues in meat.

China had banned for more than two decades wheat originating in seven states in the Pacific Northwest because of the presence of TCK smut, a wheat fungus, in earlier shipments. The extent to which TCK smut in imported wheat posed a potential threat to wheat production in China had been in dispute for years. In the 1992 bilateral market access agreement with the United States, China agreed to base its sanitary and phytosanitary standards on scientific methodology. Subsequently the Chinese side insisted that scientific evidence supported the ban on the import of wheat from the Pacific Northwest. The United States disputed this view, claiming that Chinese "import quarantine standards are often overly strict, unevenly applied, and not backed up by modern laboratory techniques."[99] The Chinese in 1999 agreed to accept shipments of wheat that have been certified by an accredited U.S. laboratory not to contain more than 30,000 TCK spores per 50 gram sample.

Finally, China banned the import of U.S. leaf tobacco starting in 1989 because of a fear of blue mold contamination. The mold is an airborne fungus that could spread rapidly and destroy China's domestic leaf tobacco production. China produces about a third of the world's leaf tobacco, making potential economic losses a serious consideration.[100] In 2001, after joint research, including a trip by Chinese scientists to the United States, China agreed that its ban on U.S. leaf tobacco did not withstand scientific scrutiny, since all leaf tobacco imported from the United States is cured and dried, a process that destroys any blue mold.

Starting in late 1999 China began to implement the bilateral agricultural agreement. The government sent delegations of specialists to review the standards applied by the U.S. Department of Agriculture in its certification programs and then issued rules to Chinese ports ending bans on imports of U.S. meat, citrus, and wheat.[101] The first shipments of U.S. wheat, oranges, and grapefruit were in March 2000; the first shipment of U.S. meat was in April 2000.[102] A bilateral agreement on blue mold was signed in February 2001, and Chinese imports were expected to begin after the issuance of new domestic regulations on leaf tobacco imports.

*Trading Rights*

In many member states of the World Trade Organization state trading companies conduct a large volume of international business. Frequently the companies enjoy a monopoly or near monopoly on the right to trade specific products, effectively limiting the availability of trading rights for other firms. The Uruguay Round Agreement does not prohibit the limitation of trading rights through the use of state trading companies. But it does require that their activities be fully transparent to ensure that they are not engaged in any discriminatory sales or purchase practices affecting imports or exports.[103] Transparency is achieved in part by requiring countries to submit an annual notification of their state trading activities.[104]

China is fully subject to these principles for the goods that will remain subject to state trading—imports of grain, vegetable oil, sugar, tobacco, crude oil, refined petroleum products, chemical fertilizer, and cotton and exports of tea, rice, corn, soy beans, tungsten ore and related tungsten products, coal, crude oil, refined petroleum products, silk, cotton, cotton yarn, woven cotton products, antimony, and silver.[105] China has agreed to provide detailed information on the transactions by state trading enterprises in these commodities, including domestic procurement prices, contract terms for delivery, and financing terms and conditions. Armed with this information interested external parties will be able to verify whether or not the Chinese government is influencing the quantity, values, or country of origin of goods purchased or sold.

But even for several of the goods that remain subject to state trading, the privileged position of state trading companies was eroded upon China's entry into the WTO or will be reduced according to a schedule. For example, as already discussed, private firms have gained important rights to import a share of grains, soybean oil, cotton, and other products that are covered by China's agricultural tariff-rate quota commitments. In its negotiations with the United States and the EU, China also agreed to apply a tariff-rate quota system to the import of chemical fertilizers. Under the terms of that agreement 10 percent of the 2.7 million metric-ton initial minimum access opportunity was given to nonstate trading companies on accession. The quantity of the minimum access opportunity is scheduled to rise by 6 percent per year, and the share of that available for import by nonstate trading companies will rise in equal steps to 49 percent over eight years. Similarly China agreed to allow nonstate companies the right to import crude oil and refined petroleum products. The import rights of nonstate companies for these products started at 4 million metric tons and 7.2 million metric tons, respectively, on accession and will grow at 15 percent per year for the next ten years.[106] Thus the monopoly power that state trading companies have for a few commodities that remain subject to state trading is being eroded.

Closely related, China has agreed to phase out entirely the system of designated trading.[107] As explained in chapter 2, under this system the right to import or export natural rubber, timber, plywood, wool, acrylic, and certain steel products has been restricted to a limited number of trading companies designated by the central government. There are two elements to the phaseout. First, the scope of products subject to designated trading is being reduced. For example, on entry only flat rolled steel is subject to designated trading. Historically the list of steel products subject to designated trading was much more extensive. Second, in a three-year transition period the Chinese government agreed to substantially liberalize designated trading by expanding the number of firms authorized to import and export these commodities. Trading rights for these commodities will no longer depend on previous levels of import and export volume, and the minimum capital requirement to trade these commodities will be reduced. At the end of three years the system of designated trading will be abolished, and all domestic and foreign enterprises will be allowed to trade these commodities.[108]

China has agreed to provide the right to import and export to all firms, foreign and domestic. Trading rights for foreign-invested firms will be phased in over three years.[109] Minority foreign-owned firms will gain the right to trade one year after accession; majority foreign-owned firms after two years; and wholly foreign-owned firms after three years. Foreign firms without any presence in China will be able to obtain trading rights in a nondiscriminatory and nondiscretionary way.[110] Finally, China agreed to reduce the minimum registered capital requirement for wholly Chinese-owned firms over a three-year period, from RMB 5 million in the first year, RMB 3 million in the second year, and RMB 1 million in the third year.[111] Three years after accession China will eliminate the minimum registered capital requirement and the system of examining and approving applications for trading rights. At that time all domestic firms will automatically enjoy trading rights. The liberalization of trading rights for foreign and domestic firms will greatly facilitate export sales to China.

## Trade Administration

Among the most basic obligations of WTO members is the requirement to promptly publish all laws, regulations, judicial decisions, and administrative rulings that affect trade. China accepted this commitment as early as 1992 in its bilateral Market Access Memorandum of Understanding with the United States.[112] Its WTO agreement reiterates this commitment. Another obligation, frequently referred to as uniform administration of the trade regime, is to ensure compliance with all WTO obligations at the provincial and local level, as well as by the national government. China has accepted this obligation and has agreed to provide a mechanism whereby foreign individuals and firms will be able to bring to the attention of the central government any case in which China's trade commitments are not being uniformly applied. The central government has agreed to address such cases.

China's commitment seems to exceed the usual transparency standard in two respects. Most important, it has agreed to provide a reasonable period of time for comment between the time that its laws, regulations, and other measures are published and the time they are implemented. Second, the scope of this requirement is not limited to laws, regulations, and measures affecting trade in goods but also includes those affecting trade in services, trade-related aspects of intellectual property, and the control or allocation of foreign exchange. The Uruguay Round Treaty is generally silent on foreign exchange arrangements and accession commitments rarely, if ever, refer to them.

## Judicial Review

WTO members agree to maintain judicial, arbitral, or administrative tribunals that are responsible for reviewing and potentially correcting any administrative action taken on a customs matter. These matters include the rates of duty, taxes, and other charges, as well as restrictions or prohibitions on the sale, distribution, transport, insurance, and so forth of imports or exports. Thus a party that believes a country has not fully implemented its WTO obligations may seek judicial remedy.

The Uruguay Round Treaty specifies that such tribunals must be independent of the agencies that are responsible for the administrative enforcement of a country's trade laws and that the relevant agencies must carry out the rulings of the tribunal. The treaty, however, provides a loophole to the requirement of independence. Arrangements that precede a country's membership in the World Trade Organization may continue if they "provide for an objective and impartial review of administrative action even though such procedures are not fully or formally independent of the agencies entrusted with administrative enforcement."[113]

China's protocol of accession is more demanding. It does not include the use of the loophole just described. It requires the establishment of tribunals that are independent of the agencies entrusted with administrative enforcement of China's WTO obligations. Further, the administrative actions subject to review by these independent tribunals go far beyond the trade and customs issues specified in the General Agreement on Tariffs and Trade. The coverage includes any administrative measure within the scope of the World Trade Organization including, but not limited to, China's commitments on trade-related aspects of intellectual property rights, services, balance-of-payments measures, and so forth. The scope of review seems unprecedentedly broad.

### Balance-of-Payments Measures

The Uruguay Round Treaty allows for an exception to the rule against import restrictions to allow governments to respond to balance-of-payments difficulties. Naturally such restrictions can be imposed only under narrowly delimited conditions. Detailed provisions require notification of the use of such measures, consultation by the member state with a special WTO Committee on Balance-of-Payments Restrictions, and the development of a plan for the phaseout of such restrictions. Members of the WTO also agree to give preference to what are referred to as price-based restrictions on imports, such as import surcharges or import deposit requirements, on the grounds that these measures are less disruptive and more transparent than quantitative restrictions, such as import quotas. However, if a balance-of-payments situation is critical, and there is reason to believe that price-based measures may not be effective, a member may impose quantitative restriction on imports through quotas and licensing restrictions.

China's commitments follow these general principles. The government has agreed to give preference to price-based measures but reserved the right to use quantitative restrictions. It has agreed to convert quantitative restrictions to price-based measures as soon as possible. Usually a member must notify the General Council of the World Trade Organization of the use of import restrictions for balance-of-payments purposes within thirty days of the introduction of such measures and must announce "as soon as possible" a plan for the removal of such restrictions. The working party asked China to promise to notify the General Council not later than the time it introduces such measures, and it wanted China to simultaneously announce a time schedule for progressive removal of the restrictions. China did not agree to these tougher notification requirements.[114]

### TRIPs and TRIMs

China has consented to uphold the provisions of trade-related aspects of intellectual property rights (TRIPs) beginning from its date of accession. That means it will comply with multilateral conventions, such as the Paris Convention for the Protection of Industrial Property and the Berne Convention for the Protection of Literary and Artistic Works, as well as agree to substantial additional protection of patents. China was not eligible for the one-year grace period for meeting the basic obligations of TRIPs, nor the additional four-year delay available to developing and transition economies before they come into full compliance with all provisions. These two benefits, which were provided for in the TRIPs agreement, had expired by the time China became a WTO member.[115] China's agreement is consistent with the bilateral agreements on intellectual property that it signed with United States in 1992 and 1995.

The Agreement on Trade-Related Investment Measures (TRIMs) precludes WTO members from imposing restrictions on investment that create trade restrictions or distortions. The measures that are precluded under the agreement are local content requirements, which typically require a wholly foreign-owned or joint venture manufacturing company to acquire a certain minimum amount or share of its inputs from local rather than international sources; trade balancing requirements, which typically demand that inputs purchased from abroad be offset with exports of locally produced product; and foreign exchange balancing requirements, which typically compel a wholly foreign-owned or joint venture company to meet its foreign exchange needs through exporting, rather than through converting domestic currency earnings to foreign exchange. China agreed to implement the provisions of the WTO agreement on TRIMs upon accession. Again since it had expired, China was ineligible for the five-year phaseout that was available to developing countries when the WTO was formally established in 1995.[116] China also agreed that it would no longer enforce provisions of existing contracts with foreign firms that are inconsistent with its TRIMs commitment.

*Forced Technology Transfer*

China has agreed that imports and approval of foreign investment in China will not be conditional on the transfer of foreign technology to China. Similarly imports and foreign investment approvals will not be conditioned on providing offsets or on conducting research and development in China. Historically China has made extensive use of offset arrangements in which its purchase of foreign goods is tied directly to the sale of goods produced in China. The sale of Boeing commercial aircraft, for example, has been accompanied by Boeing purchases of Chinese-produced aircraft parts and components, such as aircraft cargo doors and tail assemblies. In some cases Boeing has transferred technology and provided training of workers that facilitated Chinese production of the parts and components sold to Boeing. In principle these offsets can no longer be required as a condition for the sale of commercial jetliners. Boeing and Airbus of course will be free to offer offset arrangements and technology transfers as part of their marketing efforts in China.

*Government Procurement and Trade in Civil Aircraft*

The market access and equal treatment commitments made by WTO members do not apply to goods and services procured by government agencies.[117] But there is a separate agreement on government procurement negotiated in the Uruguay Round. This agreement requires governments to give foreign firms the same opportunity as domestic firms to bid for government contracts. The agreement achieves this objective by setting forth detailed provisions on tendering procedures, conditions on the qualification of suppliers eligible to bid, time limits for tendering, and so forth. All of these provisions are designed to ensure that foreign firms can compete on an equal basis with domestic firms.[118] The Agreement on Government Procurement, however, is plurilateral, meaning that each country's participation is voluntary. Participation is not a condition of membership in the World Trade Organization. At the end of 1999 only twenty-six countries, only about one-fifth of the members of the WTO, had signed the Agreement on Government Procurement.[119]

Nonetheless, members of the working party requested that China make a commitment to join the Agreement on Government Procurement and agree to start the process within two years of accession. The Chinese negotiators, while stating the government's intention to join eventually, were not willing to be bound by any specific date.[120] On the positive side, China did agree that state-owned companies, including state-owned trading companies, have to make purchasing decisions based on commercial considerations and provide foreign companies, including U.S. firms, with the same opportunity to compete as domestic firms. In other words purchases by Chinese state-owned companies, apart from purchases for the government's own use, are governed by normal WTO trade rules. Equally important, China agreed, effective on its date of entry into the World Trade Organization, that all public authorities, including those at the central, provincial, and local level, will apply the most favored nation principle of the Agreement on Government Procurement. Thus whenever a government body or authority procures goods or services from foreign suppliers, it must provide all potential foreign suppliers with an equal opportunity to compete for the business through bidding or another similar open process.

A second important plurilateral agreement covers trade in civilian aircraft. It seeks a comprehensive basis for free and fair trade in the aircraft sector.[121]

Although members of the working party asked China to consider joining, China declined to do so.[122]

### Price Controls

The World Trade Organization seeks to limit the use of price controls by members for the obvious reason that they are inconsistent with the market economy framework that the organizations is built on. Price controls are not forbidden, but when they are applied they must avoid, to the fullest practicable extent, prejudicial effects on imported goods. China has supplied a comprehensive list of the products, public utilities, and service charges that are subject to state pricing. It has agreed not to extend price controls beyond those already notified, to reduce and eliminate these controls over time, and not to use price controls to protect domestic industries and service providers.[123]

### Agreement on Technical Barriers to Trade (TBT)

The Agreement on Technical Barriers to Trade of the WTO seeks to prevent countries from using product standards, technical regulations, or conformity assessment procedures to protect a domestic industry. It grew out of the 1979 GATT Standards Code but differs in a few respects. It is broader. All WTO members are bound by the agreement, while the code was voluntary. And finally the provisions of the agreement are subject to the WTO multilateral dispute resolution mechanism, whereas the Standards Code was not enforceable under the GATT dispute settlement system.

China agreed to be bound by the provisions of the TBT agreement. It has committed, for example, to bring all of its standards, technical regulations, and conformity assessment procedures into conformity with the agreement at the time of its accession and to increase the use of international standards as the basis for its own standards, regulations, and procedures.

One important step the Chinese government took to ensure that uniform standards are applied to domestic goods and imports was to create a new State Bureau of Quality Supervision, Inspection, and Quarantine in April 2001. It was formed from the merger of the State Bureau of Quality and Technical Supervision, which had been responsible for testing and standards of domestic products, and the State Administration for Exit-Entry Inspection and Quarantine, responsible for the standards of traded goods.[124] Before the creation of the new agency Chinese trade negotiators had sought to maintain the two separate bureaucracies but allow each one to undertake assessments of imported and domestic products. Although China's WTO working party accepted this proposal, China went a step further by creating a single agency.[125]

### Tendering Requirements

Tendering, which is coordinated through the China National Tendering Center of Machinery and Electrical Equipment under the State Council, is a system for nongovernment purchase of scientific, medical, construction, and other equipment through a process of nontransparent negotiation rather than open bidding. The U.S. Trade Representative believes that the Chinese government uses tendering to discriminate against foreign firms by, in effect, depriving them of the opportunity to compete with domestic suppliers.[126]

Under the terms of its entry into the World Trade Organization, China has agreed to phase out the use of tendering for imports over four years. The use of tendering to purchase construction equipment, for example, will be phased out two years after China's accession. The phaseout for agricultural, scientific, and medical equipment will be four years after accession.[127]

*Transitional Review Mechanism*

All members of the World Trade Organization agree to a periodic examination of their trading rules and practices and their impact on the multilateral trading system. This trade policy review allows an examination of the adherence of each member to its WTO commitments. The frequency of each country's review is a function of its importance in the international trading system. The countries with the largest trade volume are reviewed every two years, those with intermediate-size trade volumes every four years, and the smallest traders every six years.[128] Given its rank in the international trading system, China will be subject to a review every four years. In addition, China has agreed to a transitional review mechanism in which it will be subject to an unprecedented annual review for the first eight years of membership. A final transitional review is scheduled for the tenth year, after which China will be subject to the ordinary trade policy review at the usual prevailing frequency, given its trade volume at the time. Not only is China's transitional review far more frequent, it appears that it will be more intrusive. It will involve sixteen subsidiary bodies of the World Trade Organization.[129] Each of these bodies will review China's compliance with its commitments in the area of that body's mandate. By comparison, the normal Trade Policy Review is conducted by the staff in the Trade Policy Review Division of the WTO Secretariat.[130]

## Summary

China's WTO commitments, on market access and on rules-based issues, far surpass those made by founding members of the World Trade Organization and, in some cases, go beyond those made by countries that have joined the organization since its founding in 1995. Its commitments to open its services markets are especially broad and will almost certainly lead to significantly increased foreign investment in telecommunications, financial services, distribution, and various other areas. Its commitments on rules-based issues are especially far reaching since they give firms in other WTO member countries unparalleled opportunities to restrict inflows of Chinese goods. These provisions include an unusually flexible transitional product-specific safeguard, which if invoked will give foreign firms protection from surges of Chinese imports, even when these products are being sold fairly, that is, without any evidence of dumping. This unusual safeguard, which diverges in several dimensions from the safeguard provision included in the Uruguay Round treaty, will be available for twelve years after China enters the World Trade Organization. And the provision to treat China in antidumping cases as a nonmarket economy for fifteen years after entry increases greatly the prospect that China will be found to be selling goods in foreign markets at less than normal value, allowing the imposition of antidumping margins against Chinese goods. In many antidumping cases in which the nonmarket economy methodology was used before China entered the World Trade Organization, the antidumping margins were so large that Chinese goods were essentially shut out of foreign markets. China also agreed to forgo the provision that makes debt forgiveness a nonactionable subsidy when it is linked to a privatization program and agreed to allow the use of alternative benchmarks in determining when soft loans or equity infusions constitute subsidies that can be offset with countervailing duties. These commitments raise the prospect that at some time in the future Chinese exporters will face countervailing duties in foreign markets. China's commitment to eliminate agricultural export subsidies on entry also seems without parallel. Indeed the launch of a new round of trade negotiations at the Doha WTO ministerial meeting in late 2001 was almost blocked by a few WTO members who feared that the round might lead to an agreement to eliminate agricultural export subsidies. China is already at zero.

# CHAPTER FOUR

# Implications of China's Entry

CHINA'S MEMBERSHIP IN the World Trade Organization has significant implications for its economic growth, domestic reforms, and integration into the global economy. As chapter 1 suggests, China's leadership undertook far-reaching WTO commitments as part of a strategy to increase economic efficiency and sustain high rates of growth. Will these commitments have the desired results?

## Downside Risks

Skeptics about China's entry into the World Trade Organization emphasize the high potential costs of adjusting to a more open trading system. They point to adjustment costs that under the best of circumstances could lead to worker unrest even more widespread than that of the late 1990s and, under less favorable circumstances, could lead to the collapse of the current regime. The adverse effects of WTO entry on output and employment are forecast to be particularly adverse in the motor vehicle industry, agriculture, and financial services, especially banking. Employment in the auto industry is expected to fall by 500,000 and in agriculture by 11 million. In banking the jobs of a substantial share of 1.7 million workers in the four largest state-owned banks are thought to be at risk.[1]

### Motor Vehicle Sector

Perhaps the most frequently cited example of a highly protected sector in which imports are forecast to grow significantly is motor vehicles. Since October 1997 China has imposed tariffs of 80 percent for passenger cars with engines less than three liters and 100 percent for those with engines of three liters or more.[2] Tariffs on imported buses and most types of trucks are somewhat lower, generally 40 to 70 percent. Import levies on vehicle parts average around 50 percent. Besides these high tariffs, when the state introduced an industrial policy for vehicles in February 1994, it simultaneously introduced new or more restrictive quotas on imports of automobiles, other vehicles, and parts. One goal of the policy was to increase the share of domestically produced vehicles to 90 percent of total consumption. This was to be accomplished in part through "restrictions on the total volume of imported cars, automobiles, and their key spare and component parts."[3]

As a result of these restrictions, imported passenger cars fell from a peak of 71,000 in 1993, the year before the auto sector was designated as a "pillar industry," to only 18,000 in 1998.[4] The total value of imported vehicles of all types and parts and accessories fell from a peak of $5.5 billion in 1993 to only $1.9 billion in 1998.[5] The combination of these tariff and nontariff barriers meant vehicle prices in China in the late 1990s were far above world levels. Thus before China's entry into the World Trade Organization it was possible to sell Buicks produced in the General Motors joint venture factory in Shanghai at a price about twice as high as the same vehicle sold in the United States.[6]

Under the terms of China's bilateral agreement with the United States, which in effect was incorporated in the accession documents, the domestic vehicle industry will be subject to greatly increased competition from imports. China will reduce tariffs to 25 percent for all automobiles by mid-year 2006, with proportionately larger cuts in the early years.[7] Tariffs on auto parts will be phased down to an average of only 10 percent, again with proportionately larger cuts in the early years. China will increase dramatically the quota limiting the import of cars, other vehicles, and vehicle parts. The initial import quota under the agreement is $6 billion for motor vehicles, with an additional $286 million separate quota for motorcycles.[8] The sum of the quotas for vehicles and motorcycles is $800 million more than the peak level of imports of these products in 1993, before the introduction of the industrial policy for the sector. It also is more than three times the level of imports in 1998, the year just before the conclusion of the bilateral agreement with the United States. China will raise the value of the quota for each category by 15 percent annually and eliminate all quotas on vehicles in 2005.

These market-opening moves will place much additional competitive pressure on the domestic vehicle industry, plagued for more than a decade with an uneconomic structure. By the mid-1980s China had established about 120 vehicle manufacturers. Although the Auto Industry Policy sought to consolidate the industry into a handful of major auto enterprises, local governments have successfully resisted closure of their small, mostly inefficient plants. In 2000 there were still about 120 companies. The 13 largest companies accounted for 92 percent of the 1.6 million vehicles of all types produced in 1998, implying average production of about 113,000 units. But the average production of the remaining companies was a mere 1,200 vehicles.[9] More than half the firms in the industry lost money in 1998.[10] Some, such as the Beijing Auto and Motorcycle Manufacturing Company, the Chinese partner in the Beijing Jeep factory, have been losing money for years. They first posted losses of RMB 1.4 million in 1994. By 1998 losses hit RMB 97 million.[11]

Only the largest auto producers, which are able to capture economies of scale, generate significant profits. Profits of the Shanghai Automotive Industry Corporation are likely to be significant since it is the majority owner of Shanghai Volkswagen, China's single most profitable joint venture company throughout the 1990s. The Shanghai Automotive Industry Corporation has partnered with General Motors in Shanghai General Motors, which surprisingly reported earning profits in its first year of production, 1999. First Auto Works in Changchun in northeast China and Tianjin Automotive also have generated large profits.

Other important types of vehicles are produced in industries characterized by an excessive number of firms. In a more market-oriented environment many of these industries would experience consolidation. For example, well over 100 motorcycle manufacturers are in China.[12] In the late 1990s motorcycle production in China was 9 to 10 million units annually, about 40 percent of world production.[13] The top six firms are large-scale producers, with production volumes ranging from 500,000 to 1.5 million units. Another dozen have production runs over 100,000 annually. But dozens of firms producer fewer than 10,000 units annually, well below the level needed to capture economies of scale.[14] Similarly more than 60 producers of wheel loaders exist in China. In the entire world outside of China there are only about a dozen significant producers in the wheel loader segment of the construction equipment industry.[15] Given the relatively small size of the wheel loader market in China, production levels of most plants are far below the level at which economies of scale can be realized, pushing up production costs.

The effect of WTO entry on the inefficient, small-scale producers of cars, motorcycles, and other vehicles is almost certain to be adverse. If China had a fully functioning market economy, many if not most of these firms would have disappeared some time ago, through mergers or bankruptcies. As prices of cars and other vehicles fall following China's entry into the World Trade Organization, the financial losses of these firms certainly will rise. Given the pressure on state banks to operate on more commercial terms, the rising burden of subsidizing these small-scale producers may well be the final straw that leads Chinese banks to curtail the flow of new credit to these firms, thus ensuring their demise. The Development Research Center of China's State Council forecasts that employment in the motor vehicle industry will fall by 498,000 following China's accession to the World Trade Organization.[16]

### Agriculture

A second sector where imports are almost certain to increase significantly as a result of China's WTO entry is agriculture. Even without the economic liberalization associated with accession, China's imports of certain agricultural commodities would grow substantially. World Bank economists estimate that even outside the World Trade Organization, China's imports as a share of world trade would become much larger for food grains, feed grains, oilseeds, meat and livestock, and even dairy products.[17] The trend of rising imports for these products is a consequence of China's acute shortage of arable land; it does not have a comparative advantage in the production of land-intensive crops such as grains.

Market opening in agriculture under China's WTO commitments, especially the tariff-rate quota system for grains and other major commodities such as cotton outlined in chapter 3, is potentially ample and probably will reinforce the trend of greater reliance on imports for land-intensive agricultural crops. The Development Research Center, for example, predicts that China's imports of wheat, feed grains, and planted fiber (cotton, hemp, and so on) in 2010 as a percentage of world trade will be 9, 6, and 13 percentage points higher, respectively, than would have been true if China had remained outside the World Trade Organization. Overall China's agricultural imports as a share of world total are forecast to more than double—from just over 5 percent in 1995 to more than 12 percent in 2010.[18]

The predicted employment implications of such expanded imports of agricultural products are substantial. The Development Research Center estimates that employment in the production of rice, wheat, and cotton will decline by 2.46 million, 5.40 million, and 4.98 million, respectively, as a result of China's WTO commitments. After taking into account modest projected employment gains of 16,000 in the production of grain crops other than rice and wheat and an additional 1.51 million farmers growing nongrain crops, cumulatively more than 11.3 million agricultural jobs will be lost as a result of accession.[19]

*Financial Services*

Perhaps the greatest challenge China will face in services is in the financial sector where, as described in chapter 3, China has agreed to a big increase in foreign presence in the banking, insurance, securities, and fund management industries. The challenge will be formidable in banking because of the weakness of domestic institutions, particularly the four large state-owned banks.[20] In a more liberalized interest rate environment that is likely to emerge as foreign banks are allowed to expand their domestic business to include both Chinese firms and Chinese households, the competitive advantage of foreign banks may be significant. They are likely to have far lower operating costs since they will concentrate on large firms and high-net-worth individuals in major cities, whereas the existing large state-owned banks have far-flung branch networks extending to China's smallest cities. China's largest state-owned banks must maintain hundreds of millions of accounts with relatively small balances, resulting in high operating costs. Foreign financial institutions have more experience in evaluating loan risk, which should give them an advantage over domestic banks in selecting the most creditworthy borrowers. Moreover, the government cannot require foreign banks to engage in policy lending in support of state objectives. For both these reasons their loan losses are likely to be much lower than those of domestic banks. Thus it is not unlikely that foreign banks could offer higher interest rates to depositors and charge lower interest rates to selected borrowers but still be more profitable than domestic banks.

Foreign banks have impressively expanded their presence in China since the Chinese government allowed the first foreign bank representative offices to open in the early years of reform. The first foreign branch banks were permitted beginning in 1981 in the special economic zones on the southeast coast.[21] By 1985, 17 foreign branch banks were operating.[22] In the early 1990s the Chinese began to permit foreign banks to operate in Shanghai and a few other major cities.[23] In 1999 central bank governor Dai Xianglong announced that geographic restraints on foreign banks were being lifted and that they could apply to open branches in any city. On the eve of China's entry into the World Trade Organization more than 150 foreign banks were operating in twenty-three cities.

China's central bank is concerned that as foreign banks are able to take deposits, first from companies and later from households, they might attract a growing share of deposits. If their deposit share were to grow rapidly, deposits in domestic banks might fall. Because these institutions have lent a large share of their deposits to borrowers who cannot repay, in a worst-case scenario the demand for significant withdrawals of funds could precipitate domestic bank failures. This would disrupt the payment system and impede the allocation of credit funds. The result would be much lower economic growth.

Although there is no doubt that China's entry into the World Trade Organization poses formidable challenges, focusing on only the most vulnerable sectors can be misleading. For one thing potential losses in the sensitive sectors are frequently overstated. China's domestic automobile industry is most unlikely to be wiped out by imports. Furthermore WTO membership should raise economic efficiency, contributing to more sustainable growth. Finally the worst-case focus on vulnerable sectors needs to be balanced by examining new export opportunities that WTO membership will create.

## The Vulnerable Sectors—A Contrarian View

How vulnerable are the sensitive sectors discussed at the outset of this chapter?

### Motor Vehicles

As tariffs are reduced and quotas liberalized, prices on the domestic market will fall, and imports of cars and other vehicles will increase. Price declines, however, will be far more modest than the tariff cuts might suggest. For larger cars, for example, the tariff will fall by three-quarters, from an initial 100 percent to 25 percent by midyear 2006. But that will translate into only a 37.5 percent decline in the price of large imported automobiles, a reduction of only about 5 percent per year.[24] For small cars the reduction is slightly smaller.

These reductions will put pressure on the more efficient car manufacturers, which are all joint ventures, but are hardly likely to drive them from the market. Shanghai Volkswagen, which was established in 1984 and has been the single largest producer of passenger cars in China for many years, in 1998 earned RMB 4.0 billion in profits on sales of RMB 26.3 billion.[25] Thus its profits as a percentage of sales were 15 percent, providing some leeway for price cutting while maintaining profitability. But Shanghai Volkswagen probably will be able to cut prices over time by much more than 15 percent, without suffering any decline in profitability. It established an impressive record in the 1990s for reducing costs as production levels and the share of parts and components acquired locally increased.[26] In 1993 Shanghai Volkswagen's Santana model sold for more than RMB 200,000. By 1999 Shanghai Volkswagen had cut the price on the same model to RMB 115,000.[27] Presumably Shanghai Volkswagen will be able to achieve similar cost savings with the Passat model, which was launched in mid-2000. Shanghai Volkswagen plans to begin producing the compact Polo model in 2002 to prevent a decline in its overall market share as the range of smaller, less expensive vehicles available from other joint venture car manufacturers expands.

Volkswagen's second joint venture, established in 1991 with First Auto Works in northeast China, produces the Jetta, Bora, and Audi A6. It too has been profitable, earning RMB 200 million on sales of RMB 4.9 billion in 1998.[28] Volkswagen's two joint ventures combined had total sales of 310,000 cars in 1999, giving them a combined share of one-half of China's car market.[29]

Another large-scale, relatively efficient producer of passenger cars is Tianjin Auto. It produces, under license from Toyota, the Japanese Daihatsu-designed Charade, a compact car marketed in China under the name Xiali. Production in the late 1990s was about 100,000 units annually, making it the second largest seller in China, after Santana. It sold for the equivalent of $9,400, which is probably no more and perhaps somewhat less than a similar-sized car produced abroad and then subject to a 25 percent import tariff and a 17 percent value-added tax as it is brought into China.

Tianjin Auto seems likely to continue its dominance of the compact car market. In May 2000 it entered into a joint venture with Toyota Motor Corporation, the world's third largest automaker, to produce a new small car that has been sold successfully in other markets. The joint venture, Tianjin Toyota Motor Corporation, will start production in 2002. Annual production capacity for the new vehicle is expected to be 30,000.[30] Tianjin Auto has reached a separate agreement with Toyota to upgrade the technology used in the production of the Charade. The new 1.3-liter Xiali 2000, which is based on the Toyota Platz, was launched in late 2000.[31] The projected new production capacity and the introduction of newer designs is likely to ensure that Tianjin Auto remains a major player in the small car market.[32]

In summary, although its car market historically has been highly protected, China's entry into the World Trade Organization is likely to have only modest effects on the larger joint venture car producers. There are two reasons. First tariff reductions will be phased in gradually. If the pace of cost reductions of the 1990s of the most successful joint venture manufacturers can be sustained for the first five years China is in the World Trade Organization, imports will gain little price advantage over domestically produced vehicles. Second the end point for the tariff is relatively high—25 percent—providing considerable protection to domestic producers after 2006. Their profit levels may be squeezed, but the falling cost of imports is not likely to drive the relatively efficient, large-scale joint venture producers that have emerged during the past decade from the market.

This does not mean imports of vehicles and parts will not rise as quotas rise and tariffs are cut. There presumably will be increased imports of luxury sedans and other specialty vehicles that are not produced in China. But most of the demand for conventional cars of varying sizes and models in the nonluxury segment of the market is likely to be met by existing producers or recently announced new joint ventures.

Indeed excess capacity could become a more important threat to the financial health of joint venture car producers than cheaper imports. Foreign firms historically have overestimated the size and growth of the market for cars in China. In 1994, when China's domestic sales were only 300,000 units, it was widely expected that the market would be 1.25 million cars by 2000.[33] But the market grew extremely slowly, and in 2000 only about 600,000 cars were sold, half the level forecast in 1994.[34]

Although the size of the market has been persistently overestimated, production capacity and announced new capacity have been expanding rapidly. Shanghai GM started production in 1999. In the same year Honda began to produce the Accord in a plant in Guangzhou it acquired from Peugeot, which had never able to produce a significant number of vehicles. Some existing joint venture firms have unutilized production capacity. The capacity of Shanghai GM, for example, is 100,000 units per year, roughly twice 1999 production. Several new joint ventures were approved in 1999 and 2000. Toyota and Ford, for example, have announced new joint ventures that will begin to produce cars in 2002 and 2003, respectively.[35] If all of the announced new plants are built, excess capacity in the industry could become so large that it will be a more important source of downward pressure on prices than tariff reductions on imports.

*Agriculture*

There is little doubt that the structural change of its labor force is one of the greatest challenges China faces. A predominantly rural society, employed primarily in agriculture, must be transformed to a much more urban society, employed primarily in manufacturing and services. The projected reduction in farm sector employment as a result of WTO membership, however, must be seen in a larger context. Since the beginning of the economic reform era official data show the share of employment in agriculture has fallen dramatically, from 71 percent of the work force in 1978 to only 50 percent in 1999. Some independent researchers believe that official data overstate the size of the agricultural labor force.[36] Given the slow growth of the total labor force and the rapidly declining share employed in agriculture, the official data show the absolute number of workers employed in agriculture peaked in 1991 at 390 million. Since then the number has fallen by an average of more than 4 million annually to reach 354 million at year-end 1999.[37] In comparison, the Development Research Center's projection of a loss of about 11 million farm jobs by 2010 is a slower rate of reduction than China achieved during the 1990s.

As chapter 1 notes, adjustment in the farm sector was well under way before China's accession to the World Trade Organization. Largely in response to relative price changes, farmers were moving out of land-intensive crops, such as grains and oilseeds, and into much more labor-intensive horticultural crops. Given its factor endowments China has a strong comparative advantage in the production of many fruits, vegetables, and flowers. Indeed China could become a major or even dominant supplier in world markets for walnuts, apples, citrus, strawberries, grapes, asparagus, processed tomatoes, and many other crops.[38]

*Banking*

Table 4-1 shows the growth in the number of foreign branch banks and their assets since 1991. The rapidly growing number of banks and a more than tenfold growth in their assets by 2000 might suggest that foreign banks are poised to capture a large share of banking business once the constraints under which they operate are lifted. For example, an analysis by a researcher in China's central bank projects that foreign banks will increase their share of the domestic currency market to 15 percent within five years of China's accession to the World Trade Organization.[39] The following analysis leads to a somewhat different conclusion.

Table 4-1. *Foreign Bank Presence in China, 1991–2000*

| Year | Number of institutions | Assets | |
|------|------------------------|--------|--|
| | | RMB billions | Percent of total financial assets in China |
| 1991 | 41/45 | 22.8 | n.a. |
| 1992 | 73/79 | 30.5 | n.a. |
| 1993 | 74/87 | 43.7 | n.a. |
| 1994 | 92/99 | 102.1 | 0.9 |
| 1995 | 120/135 | 159.8 | 1.2 |
| 1996 | 131/147 | 248.6 | 1.6 |
| 1997 | 142/161 | 314.0 | 1.9 |
| 1998 | 142/173 | 283.0 | 1.7 |
| 1999 | 154/177 | 263.1 | 1.5 |
| 2000 | 154/177 | 287.3 | 1.5 |

Sources: Nicholas R. Lardy, *China's Unfinished Economic Revolution* (Brookings, 1998), p. 224, and "China's Financial Sector: Evolution, Challenges, and Reform," unpublished paper prepared for the Asian Development Bank, August 1998, pp. 7–8; People's Bank of China, *China Financial Outlook 1994* (Beijing, 1994), pp. 101–02; Chinese Finance and Banking Society, *Almanac of China's Finance and Banking 1992* (Beijing, 1992), p. 57; *Almanac of China's Finance and Banking 1993*, pp. 602–36; *Almanac of China's Finance and Banking 1995*, pp. 661–80; *Almanac of China's Finance and Banking 1996*, pp. 42, 469; *Almanac of China's Finance and Banking 1997*, pp. 40, 499; *Almanac of China's Finance and Banking 1998*, pp. 39–40, 555; People's Bank of China, *China Financial Outlook 2000* (Beijing, 2000), p. 39; and Yang Shuang and Wang Baoqing, "Raise the Level of Central Bank Regulation and Supervision; Stress Paying Special Attention to the Work of Financial Supervision," *Jinrong shibao* (Financial News), January 16, 2001, pp. 1–2.

Note: Data on the number of institutions are as of year-end except for 1993, which is as of end of June. The number of institutions is the number of foreign branch banks followed by a number that also includes foreign-funded and joint venture banks and joint venture finance companies. The only systematic data on assets of foreign financial institutions cover the assets of the larger of these two universes. The data on the number of institutions and on assets exclude foreign insurance companies. Column three entries for 1997 and 1998 are estimated based on the assumption that total financial assets grew at a constant rate from year-end 1996 through year-end 1999.

n.a. Not available.

The restrictions described earlier have meant that foreign institutions have total assets that are quite small relative to those of domestic institutions. At their peak in 1997 the assets of foreign financial institutions were less than 2 percent of the total financial assets of all financial institutions in China.[40]

Moreover, in the aftermath of the Asian financial crisis, the volume of loans outstanding from foreign banks in China shrank in 1998. The shrinkage continued in 1999, despite the economic recovery in the region, presumably because of the bankruptcy of the Guangdong International Trust and Investment Corporation (GITIC) and the failure of several other Chinese borrowers to make timely payments to foreign banks. Thus even as their domestic-currency lending was expanding, the total assets of foreign financial institutions shrank by more than 15 percent between 1997 and 1999 before turning slightly upward. By year-end 2000, however, the assets of foreign banks and finance companies still accounted for only 1.5 percent of China's total financial assets.

Given the regulatory environment and trends already analyzed, how much might the role of foreign banks expand as they enter the domestic currency business? Will the opening of the domestic banking market to foreign banks create a banking crisis? A hypothetical scenario sheds light on these questions.

Assume that all foreign banks had been free to take domestic currency deposits from and make domestic currency loans to Chinese enterprises starting in 2000. That presumably would have reduced or perhaps eliminated the shortage of RMB for lending that has been of concern to foreign banks. But even after foreign banks are free to offer domestic currency banking services to Chinese enterprises, unless the central bank changes the regulation, they will still be subject to the restriction that their domestic currency liabilities not exceed 50 percent of their foreign currency liabilities. At the end of 1999 the share of deposits and other liabilities of foreign bank branches denominated in domestic currency was extremely small.[41] Thus if foreign banks had been authorized to take domestic currency deposits from Chinese companies starting in 2000, they could have taken deposits in an amount equal to almost 50 percent of their existing liabilities. That would have provided funds to expand their lending and other assets by about half. Thus total assets of foreign banks as a percentage of total financial assets in China could have jumped from about 1.5 percent in 1999 to 2.3 in 2000. That implies that foreign banks would increase their domestic currency deposits by about RMB 130 billion. But at year-end 1999 total deposits in Chinese banks and other financial institutions stood at RMB 10.9 trillion and had been increasing by an average of more than RMB 1.3 trillion annually in the three years ending in 1999.[42] In short, if allowed to enter the domestic currency business in 2000, foreign banks would have been able to expand their share of total assets sharply but from such a low base that it would not have posed a threat to domestic banks and other financial institutions. They would have suffered only a slight reduction in the inflows of deposits, not anything approaching a bank run.

In practice foreign banks might not even wish to expand their domestic currency deposits as rapidly as the hypothetical calculation suggests. The hypothetical calculation suggests that under the new regime lending by foreign banks would increase by almost half, or about RMB 100 billion. Under the assumed liberalization of the market for domestic currency banking services, all of the increased lending could be in domestic currency. But at year-end 1999 total domestic currency lending of foreign banks was only RMB 6.7 billion.[43] Foreign banks might not be able to increase their domestic currency lending fifteenfold in a short period for the simple reason that they might not be able to find a sufficient number of additional creditworthy borrowers. At year-end 1999 foreign bank lending was restricted entirely to wholly foreign-owned and joint venture companies in China. These firms have accounting records and other audited financial information required to satisfy foreign banks; most Chinese enterprises do not.

Thus once foreign banks are free to take domestic currency deposits and make domestic currency loans to Chinese firms, the growth of their domestic currency business likely will be constrained by the scarcity of creditworthy domestic borrowers and the rule that limits the buildup of domestic currency liabilities relative to foreign currency liabilities. Since foreign banks, like their domestic counterparts, have to pay interest on deposits, they will only be willing to take domestic currency deposits to the extent they can be used to support interest-bearing loans. Thus if foreign banks are unable to identify a sufficient number of creditworthy borrowers, they are likely to limit the expansion of their deposit-taking business as well. The net result is that commercial considerations in the short run may be a greater constraint than regulations limiting the expansion of foreign banks. Of course, over time more Chinese firms may adopt accounting and other standards that will make them more attractive borrowers, allowing foreign banks to expand their share of assets to the predicted 2.5 percent share.

As long as the regulation limiting the ratio of domestic to foreign currency deposits to 50 percent remains in place, once the predicted 2.5 percent foreign bank share of China's total financial assets is reached, further growth in the market share of foreign banks will depend on two factors: the share of total foreign currency lending by foreign banks and the relative rates of growth of lending in domestic and foreign currency. If foreign banks expand their share of total foreign currency lending, then they would be able to scale up their share of domestic currency lending as well. At year-end 2000 the foreign bank share of foreign-currency lending in China was more than one-fifth compared with just over a tenth at year-end 1999.[44] But the absolute amount of foreign currency lending fell significantly in

2000, while foreign bank dollar lending fell only modestly. The decline in the absolute amount of dollar lending by foreign banks suggests they have already taken the most attractive foreign currency borrowers and that their share of this market does not have a large additional upside.

Even if foreign banks succeed in enlarging their share of total foreign currency lending, that will not necessarily translate into a rising foreign bank share of total financial assets. Foreign currency lending might continue to grow more slowly than domestic currency lending, as it did in 2000. Thus the foreign currency base from which foreign banks would scale up their domestic currency lending might represent a smaller share of total financial assets. That could leave foreign banks with a market share a little below the previously estimated 2.5 percent.

So in the first five years after China enters the World Trade Organization the share of financial assets controlled by foreign banks is not likely to rise above 2 to 3 percent of China's total financial assets and might even be somewhat lower. This estimate implies only a most modest reduction in the flow of new domestic currency deposits going into domestic banks. The key point emerging from this analysis is that foreign institutions will not take a large share of the domestic currency deposits flowing into Chinese banks in the first few years after China enters the World Trade Organization.

If the above analysis is correct, the regulators may not have to confront a potential run on the deposits of domestic banks two years after China's entry into the World Trade Organization. The real challenge foreign banks pose to the stability of the domestic banking system will not arise until five years after China's entry. At that time foreign banks will begin to conduct business with Chinese households and enjoy the benefit of national treatment. Once national treatment is in place the central bank will no longer be able to restrict the ratio of domestic to foreign currency liabilities of foreign banks, and they will be able to expand their domestic business with no significant funding constraint.

At that point, however, the expansion of the business of foreign banks will still be constrained by two factors. First expansion still will be subject to their ability to identify desirable borrowers. Several foreign banks are likely to develop retail networks and emphasize lending for automobiles and mortgages, businesses that traditionally have been relatively low risk in most Asian markets. Hongkong and Shanghai Bank and Standard Chartered Bank, which had the largest number of branch banks in China in 2000, seem committed to develop this retail banking market. The Bank of

East Asia and possibly Citibank will join them. This approach may allow these banks to expand their lending more rapidly than other foreign banks.

Second foreign banks will have to meet the same prudential and regulatory requirements that are imposed on domestic banks. Most important, foreign banks will have to satisfy regulations on capital adequacy, which require that each bank maintain a minimum ratio of capital relative to loans and other assets. In applying this prudential regulation to foreign branch banks, China, like many other countries, considers only the capital of the branch in China, not the bank's global capital. Thus the ability of a foreign bank in China to expand its banking business depends on the willingness of the branch's head office to allow it to retain its earnings, which could then count toward the branch's capital, or to commit more capital to the branch. The constraint this decision will impose is suggested by a look at the position of foreign banks at year-end 1999. Their total capital was only $2.68 billion. Given the prevailing 8 percent capital adequacy ratio imposed by the People's Bank of China, banks could hold loans and other assets totaling $33.5 billion. But at year-end 1999 the total assets of foreign banks, including $21.47 billion in loans, were $31.70 billion.[45] Clearly, without additional capital the headroom for additional lending was limited.[46]

This critique of the downside risks China faces is not meant to imply that the challenges of adjusting to increased competition from foreign autos, agricultural products, and banks are insignificant. Indeed evidence from other countries suggests that the profitability of domestic banks is reduced by the simple entry of foreign banks, even if their share of bank assets remains small.[47] Thus Chinese banks are likely to face serious competitive pressure, even if foreign banks do not drain off a large-enough share of deposits to endanger the liquidity of domestic banks. The challenges to Chinese banks, however, are less daunting than sometimes portrayed. Although there will be real adjustment costs, they are unlikely to swamp the regime. Indeed the efficiency gained as a result of WTO membership will go a long way toward easing the adjustment burden.

## Efficiency Gains

Economic efficiency in China should improve as a result of China's accession to the World Trade Organization for two or three reasons. First of all trade liberalization will be accompanied by a reallocation of factors of production to sectors of the economy in which China has a stronger comparative advantage. These gains are sometimes called the static efficiency gains from improved allocative efficiency. Trade liberalization should also lead to great improvement in total factor productivity, because increased competition from foreign firms can be expected to stimulate improvements in efficiency by domestic firms and because trade liberalization will increase trade. Increased trade will allow China to import more capital goods that often will contain technology superior to that available domestically. The acquisition of more foreign technology through increased imports may be reinforced by increased inflows of foreign direct investment as a result of the investment liberalization that is part of China's WTO commitments. Thus the third possible source of efficiency gains is through increased inflows of capital that embody superior technology.

Implicit in this analysis is the view that while foreign direct investment inflows may increase following China's WTO membership, these inflows will not necessarily raise the rate of capital formation. This judgment is based on China's experience in the 1990s when large inflows of foreign direct investment did not raise China's overall rate of investment. China differs from most emerging market economies where capital inflows frequently result in a much higher rate of investment than could be achieved with domestic savings alone. In Thailand and Malaysia, for example, the inflow of foreign direct investment in the 1990s increased investment by about one-fifth.[48] China had very large gross capital inflows in the 1990s, but these were, on average, fully offset by capital outflows and additions to official foreign exchange reserves. Thus the inflows did not increase the share of investment. All three countries had investment rates slightly over 40 percent. China was unique in this group because its domestic savings were sufficient to fully finance its domestic investment.

Even if the rate of capital formation does not increase, the composition of foreign direct investment may evolve in ways that are conducive to increased productivity. Simply because China already has increased dramatically its share of the world export market for toys and footwear, foreign direct investment in these industries may moderate, even as investment inflows increase in telecommunications, distribution, and financial services. But more investment in telecommunications will make possible a much wider domestic availability of telephonic and other telecommunications services and reduce their costs, which by international standards are still high.[49] That will bring large productivity gains to other sectors of the economy. Similarly, increased foreign direct investment in wholesaling, retailing, and other distribution services should increase efficiency in the sector, bringing benefits to manufacturing firms, as well as lowering the cost of goods to consumers. Finally increased foreign direct investment in financial services could bring increased competitive pressure on domestic banks, insurance companies, and other financial institutions, leading them to allocate investment resources more efficiently. In short the productivity gains from changes in the composition of investment following China's accession to the World Trade Organization may be significant, even if rising foreign direct investment does not increase the share of capital formation significantly above the already high levels of the 1990s.

Empirical estimates of the effect of China's accession to the World Trade Organization on Chinese economic growth vary widely. At the high end China's Development Research Center believes that over time membership will affect economic growth positively. It estimates that membership will boost China's average annual growth rate by a full percentage point. One percentage point may not seem like much, but if it were achieved, by the year 2010 China's gross domestic product would be fully one-seventh larger than in a baseline scenario in which China did not become a WTO member.[50] The same study predicts large increases in trade as a result of the liberalization associated with accession. Exports and imports are each forecast to be one-fourth higher than if China remained outside the World Trade Organization.

At the other end of the spectrum, the U.S. International Trade Commission predicts more modest results. It estimated that the tariff reductions contained in China's April 1999 offer would raise China's gross domestic product in 2010 by 4 percent.[51] The commission estimated that exports by 2010 would be about 12 percent higher, and imports would be 14 percent higher as a result of WTO entry.[52] The commission has not disclosed its detailed estimates of the sector-by-sector effects, but the largest predicted reductions in output are in oilseeds and wheat, while the largest gains come in apparel, footwear, other light manufactures, and electronic equipment. The commission estimates of increased growth and trade are more modest in part because they are based only on China's scheduled tariff reductions. The Development Research Center's estimates also reflect the effects of phasing out nontariff barriers and the restrictions China faces on its sales of textile and apparel products in advanced industrial countries.

China's Development Research Center and the U.S. International Trade Commission use computable general equilibrium models to estimate the effects of trade liberalization on China's economic growth and foreign trade. Although these models are useful, they have limits. Most important, computable general equilibrium models assume that all firms are perfectly competitive. That means that Chinese firms, even before accession, are assumed to be using the optimum combination of inputs to produce their output. In economic terminology the assumption is that each firm is producing at a point on the production frontier so that its output is the maximum amount possible, given the quantity of inputs available. The precise production point on the frontier is determined by the relative prices of the factors of production. Trade liberalization, which lowers the price of imports and thus raises the relative price of exports, leads firms to increase their output of export goods and reduce the output of import goods. That adjustment in the structure of output, in turn, affects the relative prices of factors of production, to which firms smoothly adjust.

In reality, as chapter 1 makes clear, many Chinese firms, particularly state-owned firms, do not behave consistently with the assumptions of profit-maximizing behavior. For various reasons they produce at points well within the production frontier and generate profits far below the level that could be achieved. However, increased competition from foreign firms, induced by reducing barriers to imports and liberalizing restrictions on foreign direct investment, should change the underlying behavior of Chinese firms. To the extent that happens, the economic gains China will accrue from WTO accession will exceed the predictions of the general equilibrium models. Thus the quantitative predictions just summarized should be regarded as a lower-bound estimate of the gains China could accrue as a result of membership in the World Trade Organization.

## Structural Adjustment

The predicted increase in Chinese economic efficiency depends critically on economic restructuring. Unless the labor and capital utilized in more protected sectors of the economy are reduced and reallocated, the expansion of comparative advantage sectors will be stunted and opportunities for increased efficiency lost. The process must start with increased competition from imports forcing some inefficient firms to shrink or even go out of business. If China continues to subsidize inefficient producers of motor vehicles, motorcycles, wheel loaders, and other types of equipment or continues to protect inefficient agricultural producers, the efficiency gains of WTO membership will fall far short of what the studies postulate.

If China allows the market to work so that the least efficient producers shrink and perhaps even go out of business, where are China's best opportunities to expand production and thus employment?

### Textiles and Apparel

The Multifiber Arrangement and its successor arrangement, the Agreement on Textiles and Clothing (ATC), have long distorted world trade in textiles and apparel. These agreements, contrary to the general WTO prohibition on the use of quantitative restrictions, have allowed industrialized countries to impose quotas on imports of these products.[53] The Uruguay Round Trade Agreement gradually liberalizes these quantitative restrictions on the exports of WTO member states. They will be eliminated by the end of 2004, ten years after the creation of the World Trade Organization.

The phaseout of the restrictions takes two forms. WTO members maintaining such quantitative restrictions on imports of textile and apparel products are required to progressively eliminate them, a process referred to as "integration." Each country maintaining restrictions eliminated quotas on 16 percent of imports by volume in 1995; another 17 percent were eliminated in 1998. In 2002 an additional 18 percent are scheduled for elimination. The remaining quotas must be lifted at the end of 2004. The second mechanism of liberalization is an acceleration of the rates of growth of the quantities of permitted imports for those categories for which the quotas have not yet been eliminated.[54]

Under the terms of its accession, China will benefit from the phaseout of restrictions on trade in textiles and apparel.[55] This change will give China the opportunity to increase significantly its share of the world market, especially in apparel. As chapter 2 notes, even before becoming a WTO member, China's exports of textiles and apparel were growing rapidly. At its accession it already was the world's largest producer and exporter of textile and apparel products. Including re-exports through Hong Kong, it accounted for 12.5 percent of world exports of these products in 1996.[56] But compared with other labor-intensive products, such as footwear, its market share of world exports of textile and apparel has been restricted by quotas imposed by the United States and a few other industrial countries.[57] The United States, for example, under the 1997 bilateral U.S.-China agreement on textiles imposed quotas on 101 separate product categories. The bilateral agreement also limited the growth of quotas for all important products to only 1 percent per year.[58] China filled most of these quotas by 95 to 100 percent, indicating that they clearly restricted the growth of textile and apparel exports to the United States.[59]

Because China has a strong comparative advantage in labor-intensive products, several studies estimate that its share of the world export market for textile and apparel products will rise as the quotas constraining its exports are liberalized and then eliminated. China's Development Research Center, for example, predicts that China's world market share of these products will rise by about 1 percentage point while quotas are being phased out; then jump by about 4 percentage points in 2005, following the final elimination of the quotas; and then rise gradually over the balance of the decade.[60] For apparel alone China gains 10 percentage points of the world export market by 2010. The U.S. International Trade Commission estimates that China's share of the world apparel market will jump by about 6 percentage points in 2005 and 2006, immediately after the phaseout of the ATC restrictions.[61] Other estimates are much more robust. Will Martin, a World Bank economist, and his coauthors estimate that China's share of the world apparel market will jump by more than one-quarter after it enters the WTO and the restrictions are phased out, reaching 45 percent of world exports by the middle of the decade.[62]

Large and rapid increases in China's world market share in apparel are plausible because of the major role of foreign firms in the export of apparel from China. A significant share of apparel and textile exports are produced under processing contracts with foreign firms, and these firms are gearing up to shift additional production to China in anticipation of the phaseout of all quotas in 2004.[63] Hong Kong firms, because of their geographic proximity and high local production costs, are well motivated to move much of their remaining apparel production to China after 2004. Since they supplied 5.4 percent of the world market at the end of the 1990s, a shift of a large share of their production to China could account for most of the increase in China's share of the world apparel market predicted by the Development Research Center and the U.S. International Trade Commission studies.[64]

China's share of world textile exports, however, is not likely to increase significantly and may even shrink as the ATC restrictions are phased out. The studies of the Development Research Center, the U.S. International Trade Commission, and of Martin and his colleagues predict that China's share of world textile exports will stagnate. More interesting is that to become a much larger exporter of apparel China will become a large net importer of textile materials and products. In 1997 and 1998 China's imports of chemical fiber, wool, wool yarn, and woven wool fabric already were so large that China was a very slight net importer of textiles. In dramatic contrast China is a huge exporter of apparel, and imports are relatively small.[65] Martin predicts that by 2010 China will be a net importer of one-sixth of all textile products sold on world markets in order to be able to be a net supplier of more than two-fifths of the world market in apparel.[66]

This predicted pattern of net textile imports and net apparel exports is broadly consistent with China's comparative advantage. Moreover, it is an extension of China's evolving pattern of trade in these products in the past two decades. Production of apparel is far more labor intensive than textiles. Some types of textiles, notably continuous filament chemical fiber, which is produced in large-scale operations, are much more capital intensive than apparel. As a result, as China's textile and apparel exports expanded, the apparel share of these exports more than doubled, from about 30 percent in 1978 to more than 60 percent in 1995.[67] At the same time, as synthetics increasingly displaced cotton fabric, Chinese imports of chemical fiber and raw materials for making synthetic fiber shot up from a mere $183 million in 1975 to $3.73 billion by 1995.[68]

A comparison of the growth of exports of textiles and apparel on the one hand, with other labor-intensive manufactures, on the other, makes the ATC's restrictive role apparent. As chapter 2 notes, although exports of textiles and apparel expanded rapidly between 1980 and 1998, China was able to increase its share of world markets of footwear and toys even more rapidly. After China's accession the reverse is likely to be true, at least if trade is not distorted by the application of the safeguard mechanisms analyzed in chapter 3. China's share of the world market for clothing is forecast to rise dramatically. Exports of other labor-intensive manufactures will expand too. But since they begin from a much higher, largely already unrestricted base, the expansion will be somewhat less rapid. The Development Research Center, for example, forecasts that China's share of the world market for other light manufactures, mainly footwear and toys, will rise by less than 2 percentage points by 2010.[69] Of course, if WTO members make extensive use of the transitional product-specific safeguard or the special textile safeguard to protect their domestic textile and apparel industries, the expansion of China's exports could be thwarted. In that case gains in employment, which are forecast to be 5.4 million jobs in textiles and apparel, for example, would be lost.[70]

*Reduction of Other Trade Barriers Abroad*

Besides increased market access for textile and apparel, China will gain increased market access for other labor-intensive products in several important foreign markets as a result of accession. These increases are not considered in the general equilibrium models mentioned earlier. That is another reason for believing that those estimates provide a lower bound on the gains China will achieve from accession. Increased market access, mostly for labor-intensive products, will provide opportunities for higher levels of domestic employment in China, offsetting some of the reduced employment in industries such as automobiles and agriculture.

The most important countries that maintain WTO-inconsistent trade barriers against Chinese products are Taiwan, Mexico, and the European Union (EU). Of these three Taiwan is probably the most important. On the eve of both Taiwan and China becoming WTO members, Taiwan was banning the import of several thousand individual Chinese products, almost half of all the products listed in its tariff schedule.[71] In contrast, China consistently has treated Taiwanese goods to tariff and other terms at least as favorable as those afforded to goods from alternative foreign sources of supply. That asymmetry was an important factor in the large deficit that China incurred in trade with Taiwan. The deficit expanded from $1.9 billion in 1990 to more than $15.6 billion in 1999.[72] Although it may take some time, Taiwan almost certainly will lift these import bans.

Mexico, before China's accession to the World Trade Organization, maintained quantitative restrictions or tariffs as high as 1,000 percent on about 1,400 Chinese products, mostly labor-intensive manufactures such as textiles, garments, footwear, and toys.[73] The Mexican government imposed these restrictions in 1993, after a dumping investigation. Although Mexico had been a member of the General Agreement on Tariffs and Trade since 1986, the investigation was not carried out in accordance with the GATT Antidumping Agreement. Mexico was the last member of the working party to conclude a bilateral trade agreement with China. The delay was largely because of the difficulty the two sides had in agreeing to the length of time Mexico would have to phase out all of the quotas and other restrictions that had been imposed on Chinese goods in violation of WTO rules. Mexico also sought the right to use the special textile safeguard analyzed in chapter 2 for fifteen years after China's accession, rather than the four-year period agreed to by other members of the working party.[74] A compromise was not worked out until September 2001. The final deal gave Mexico six years to phase out WTO inconsistent restrictions on Chinese goods and Mexico gave up its desire to use the special textile safeguard after 2008.[75]

As part of its bilateral agreement with China, the EU has agreed to phase out WTO-inconsistent quotas on certain types of footwear, tableware, and kitchenware. The quotas on these products increased by 5 percent on accession in late 2001 and an additional 5 percent in 2002. They will go up by 10 percent in 2003 and 15 percent in 2004, and finally will be phased out entirely in 2005.[76] Argentina, Hungary, Poland, Thailand, and Turkey also will phase out WTO-inconsistent quotas and high tariffs imposed mostly on Chinese apparel, footwear, toys, and other labor-intensive goods. Argentina, for example, will eliminate quotas on textiles, clothing, footwear, and toys by July 31, 2002, and phase out import duties in excess of 35 percent on the same products over six years.[77]

A potentially important market to which China already has gained greater access is India. India, under the terms of its commitments in the Uruguay Round of trade negotiations, was required to phase out in April 2001 long-standing restrictions on the import of 743 consumer products, most of which are labor intensive.[78] Although China has had some success in increasing its sales to India, export volumes have remained modest, only about $1.2 billion in 1999.[79] If China had remained outside of the World Trade Organization, India could have continued to impose WTO-inconsistent restrictions on imports from China.

The reduction of import barriers in the EU, Taiwan, Mexico, and several smaller countries will create new opportunities to expand Chinese exports of labor-intensive products, generating significant employment opportunities in China.

More important than these specific cases, China's WTO agreement does impose some restrictions on the conditions under which other countries can use the nonmarket economy methodology in antidumping cases directed against Chinese goods. Member countries, for example, must establish and publish in advance the criteria they use for determining whether or not market economy conditions prevail and the methodology used in comparing prices.[80] They are required to make their best efforts to ensure that price comparisons are made with market economies that are at a level of economic development comparable to China and that the country is a significant producer of the product in question. These and other provisions set forth in the working party report will reduce the likelihood that other countries will be able to impose unjustified antidumping duties.

Certainly if these provisions had been effect in the 1990s, Mexico would have had to follow quite different procedures in its antidumping cases against Chinese goods.

## Risks to the Domestic Banking System

Even though foreign banks are not likely to pose an immediate direct threat to domestic banks, China's WTO membership indirectly could generate more pressure on the financial system. The reason is that the character of China's adjustment to opening to the international economy is likely to differ somewhat from other countries entering the World Trade Organization. Before entry in most countries there is a significant distortion of the domestic price structure, reflecting protection provided by the country's trade regime. Relative prices of goods in protected sectors tend to be higher in the home market than in the world market. The reduction of tariff and nontariff barriers typically leads to a convergence of the relative domestic price structure toward the international level, at least for most traded goods. As relative prices change in the domestic market there is a restructuring of output. Output in industries facing stiffer competition from now lower-priced imports tends to shrink as the least efficient firms are forced out of business. Relative prices of goods in which the country has a comparative advantage rise, however, stimulating greater output. Restructuring is facilitated by the reallocation of factors of production through markets for land, labor, and capital.

In China, however, the story may be somewhat different. As chapter 2 makes clear, even before entry into the World Trade Organization, China's tariff revenues relative to the value of imports were extremely low, compared with other developing countries. Indeed 60 percent of all imports entered China entirely free of duties in the first half of 2000. Moreover nontariff barriers in the form of quotas and licensing requirements were largely phased out during the 1990s. Finally, as chapter 1 shows, most transactions on the domestic goods market took place at market-determined rather than government-dictated prices. Thus, when China entered the World Trade Organization, the convergence between domestic and international prices already was advanced. Yet by most accounts industrial restructuring had lagged somewhat.

This paradox is explained partly by the nature of China's financial system. Adjustment is inhibited not by high tariff and nontariff barriers but by the ability of some money-losing firms, which would shrink and perhaps even go out of business in a market economy, to finance their losses by borrowing additional funds from the banking system. They are able to compete with imports not because of high tariffs or nontariff barriers that insulate them from foreign competition, but through an ability to sell their output year after year at a price below the cost of production. In some cases they continue to produce, even when the market for their products is limited and a disproportionate share of output ends up as unsold inventory.

Interestingly this state of affairs does not seem to have greatly inhibited the growth of Chinese exports. Normally one would expect that the flow of plentiful funds into money-losing enterprises would starve comparative advantage sectors of the economy of financial resources, limiting their ability to expand output and exploit international market opportunities. This effect has been mitigated somewhat because China's export sector has been financed in part by foreign capital. As chapter 1 discusses, the share of exports originating in foreign-funded enterprises grew extremely rapidly since the mid-1980s, reaching almost one-half by 2000. Chinese-owned firms that are engaged in export processing have increased their exports rapidly. Foreign firms frequently supply the parts and components and sometimes even the machinery required for the production of goods for foreign markets under processing contracts. In effect foreign firms supply both the fixed and working capital of many Chinese firms engaged in export processing. Thus the export sector has been financed in part by foreign companies—directly for foreign-funded enterprises and indirectly for much export processing by Chinese firms.

As the price of imported goods, such as autos, now falls as China implements its scheduled cuts of tariffs and nontariff barriers, China's leadership faces a clear choice. It can accelerate structural reform, which would simultaneously free up the human and financial resources to allow the expansion of comparative advantage sectors. Structural reform should include ending policy lending by banks, thus allowing them to focus their lending on firms where rates of return are sufficiently high that they will be able to service their borrowing. Or the leadership can delay structural reform and require banks to continue their policy lending to firms whose losses probably will be rising.

The cost of the latter strategy would be high. It would saddle the banks with even more nonperforming loans, increasing the ultimate fiscal burden of rebuilding the financial system.[81] And it would inhibit the flow of resources into sectors that have an opportunity to expand exports, thus depriving China of some share of the increased efficiency that would otherwise be expected as a result of WTO membership. Thus the pace of China's adjustment to further opening up to the outside world and the further reform of China's financial system are profoundly interrelated. If the government requires the banks to lend substantial new funds to inefficient companies in order to stretch out significantly the process of adjusting to increased international competition, it would undermine the long-term goal of creating a commercialized banking and financial system. It also would create more doubt about the sustainability of China's domestic fiscal situation.

Put alternatively, one could argue that whether or not China's WTO commitments result in improved efficiency depends on the further transformation of the financial system. If state-owned banks can transform themselves to operate on a commercial basis, China's leadership may well be successful in using its WTO commitments as a lever to advance domestic economic reforms. If transformation is delayed and banks continue to channel disproportionate amounts of funds to inefficient state-owned companies, the leverage of WTO commitments on domestic economic reform will be largely lost.

In the favorable scenario China's entry into the World Trade Organization is likely to give indigenous firms greater impetus to become competitive in world markets. Increased foreign competition will help stimulate greater efficiency, and a more efficient banking system will provide the financial backing allowing many more purely domestic firms to become important players in the export market.

Although foreign-invested firms have helped greatly to generate exports, a number of domestic firms have already established their competitive position in comparison with foreign firms. Initially this action was in China's domestic market, but increasingly Chinese firms are active in the global market. In the first half of the 1990s, for example, foreign firms dominated China's domestic personal computer market.[82] In 1994 Compaq, IBM, Hewlett-Packard, and Digital Equipment, in that order, were the market leaders. But Legend, a domestic firm that got its start in the mid-1980s as a distributor of foreign computers and did not begin making its own PCs until 1990, was already beginning to take market share away from foreign firms. By 1997 Legend, which introduced numerous desirable features as well as cut prices, held the top spot decisively, with sales 40 percent greater than those of second-ranked IBM.[83] In the ensuing years Legend expanded its market share, while the market share of the former leaders—IBM, Hewlett-Packard, and Compaq—declined.[84] By the third quarter of 2000 the combined market share of all foreign computer companies had fallen to less than 15 percent, while Legend supplied 31 percent of the market.[85]

Similarly before 1995 foreign joint venture firms such as Alcatel's Shanghai Bell and Siemens' Beijing International Switching Systems Corporation, along with pure foreign suppliers such as Lucent, were the dominant firms, supplying more than 90 percent of the telephone switching equipment for China's rapidly growing telecommunications sector.[86] Beginning in the mid-1990s, however, domestic firms, notably Great Dragon and Huawei Technologies, began to be significant competitors. By 1998 Huawei's share of the domestic market was 18 percent, and by 2000 it rose to 35 percent.[87] It also began competing internationally, opening forty offices internationally. Its export sales accounted for about 10 percent of total sales of $2.65 billion in 2000; a share the firm envisages will increase to 40 percent within five years.[88] In 2001 Huawei invested $500 million in a production facility in Mexico to support its international expansion.[89]

A similar pattern emerged in the white goods sector—home appliances such as refrigerators, freezers, washing machines, microwave ovens, and so forth. In the early 1980s imported foreign brands dominated China's small domestic home appliance market. But as household incomes rose and the market for consumer durables grew, domestic manufacturers were established. Haier, a Qingdao based firm, was founded in 1984 and quickly became a major manufacturer of refrigerators, freezers, air conditioners, and other consumer durables. By the end of the 1990s it was China's number one producer of home electrical appliances. Beginning in 1992 Haier also began to compete on international markets. By the end of the decade it was exporting to eighty-seven countries and had five manufacturing plants around the world. In the United States it had captured more than one-fifth of the market for small refrigerators, commonly used in hotel and student rooms, and had invested in a $30 million factory in South Carolina to enter the U.S. market for large upright refrigerators. Its global exports in 1999 were $140 million and doubled to $280 million in 2000.[90]

Konka, China's leading manufacturer of televisions, also has broken into international markets. Initially it was an original equipment manufacturer, meaning its products were marketed internationally under other brand names. By 1997 it began exporting Konka-branded televisions, usually through established chain stores such as Sears. In 1999 it sold 600,000 sets on overseas markets. It has also launched a manufacturing joint venture in India. It anticipates that by 2005 half of its sales will be international.[91]

Another example is Galanz, which produced 12 million microwave ovens in 2000, making it not only China's but the world's leading producer. It is an OEM for several foreign brands and exported microwaves valued at $200 million in 2000.[92]

The success of these firms has contributed to an explosion in Chinese exports of consumer durable goods. In 1999 the value of exports of refrigerators, washing machines, air conditioners, and vacuum cleaners alone was almost $6.5 billion, more than seven times the $872 million in exports of all household electrical appliances in 1990.[93]

## Summary

China's membership in the World Trade Organization creates the potential for impressive gains in economic efficiency. Indeed the gains are likely to be greater than those predicted in most published quantitative estimates, since those studies do not capture fully the likely effect of more foreign competition on domestic firms. No doubt many jobs will be lost in a few sectors. But prospects for generating employment are bountiful as China benefits from the phaseout of arrangements restricting world trade in apparel, and as Taiwan, Mexico, the EU, and other markets phase out and eliminate the WTO-inconsistent trade barriers they have maintained against a broad array of Chinese goods. The implied pace of structural transformation of the labor force that will be required, especially the reduction in employment in agriculture, does not seem much greater than the rate China already has attained during the past decade or more. China will bear the social costs of this transformation more easily, however, if it accelerates the development of unemployment insurance programs and other elements of a social safety net.

Efficiency gains are likely to be reflected in the emergence of more indigenous firms that are successful in competing with foreign goods. These firms will act first in China's domestic market and eventually in the global marketplace. Foreign-invested firms, which have been the most aggressive in exploiting the tariff and other incentives of the export processing regime, have been disproportionate contributors to export growth, especially in the 1990s. The disadvantage of China's pre-WTO trade regime was that its high protective barriers, combined with the deep exemptions associated with export processing, led China to discriminate "against industries that rely more heavily on domestic value-added, rather than imported intermediate inputs."[94] Under China's WTO liberalization the mix of exports is likely to shift in favor of goods that use import goods indirectly, rather than directly. These goods probably will have a higher domestic value-added content than goods produced under export processing arrangements.

Reaping these gains, will, however, depend very much on accelerated reform of the domestic banking system. Two adverse consequences will occur if a significant number of state-owned firms are insulated from foreign competition by an ability to sell their output at less than the cost of production while financing the losses by ever-increased borrowing from state-owned banks. First, the resources necessary to finance an expansion of comparative advantage sectors, particularly those relying more heavily on domestic rather than imported components, will be insufficient. Thus the several sources of efficiency gains that would otherwise follow from WTO membership could be largely lost. Second, such a strategy would leave Chinese banks wholly unprepared for the real competition with foreign banks, which starts five years from accession to the World Trade Organization.

Beyond these efficiency gains, China will reap other benefits from WTO membership. Perhaps the most important is that China will be able to use the WTO dispute settlement process to protect its economic interests. The most obvious area is antidumping. China has been the object of more antidumping cases than any other country. But, as is true of Mexico, arbitrary antidumping margins have sometimes been applied against Chinese goods. In the past China has been helpless to challenge these cases. As a WTO member China can use the WTO dispute settlement process against countries that do not apply fair procedures.[95] Moreover China will be able to use the dispute settlement process to challenge the way the nonmarket economy methodology has been applied by another member. If the methodology is not applied in a nondiscriminatory manner on all nonmarket economies, the decisionmaking process is not transparent, or fails to consider significant facts presented by the Chinese side, China might well have grounds to initiate a dispute settlement case.[96]

# CHAPTER FIVE

# China, the World Economy, and U.S. Policy

THE IMPLICATIONS OF China's membership in the World Trade Organization for the world economy, the international trading system, and the United States are immense. China's economy and international trade are so large that the expansion of economic output and trade resulting from its membership is likely to perceptibly affect the growth of global trade and thus the pace of expansion of global output. No other country that has become a WTO member in recent years has been large enough to affect global trade and output so positively because of the trade and investment liberalization required. China will be influential in future rounds of WTO trade negotiations. As the only major trading nation that is not an advanced industrial economy, China will almost certainly bring a distinct perspective to the negotiations and exert its power on matters important to its trade. Finally, China's membership poses momentous opportunities and challenges for the United States and other countries.

## The World Economy

A research team organized by the Development Research Center of China's State Council projects that the effect of China's entry, along with that of Taiwan, into the World Trade Organization will add 0.25 percentage point per year to the growth of world trade. In a model in which entry was assumed to have occurred in 1997, world trade was forecast to be about 2.7 percent higher by 2010 than it would be otherwise.

More rapid trade would lead world output to be almost 2 percent higher in 2010 than in the baseline scenario in which China, and thus Taiwan, remained outside the organization. Much of the predicted positive growth effect is felt in Asia because economies there have closer trade ties with China and Taiwan. Economic output in Japan, Hong Kong, Singapore, and Malaysia, for example, is forecast to be from 2.2 to 5.5 percent higher than in the case of nonaccession. But even the United States and the European Union (EU) are projected to have slightly faster growth as a result of the combined effect of China's and Taiwan's membership. By 2010 their output is expected to be boosted by 0.8 and 1.2 percent, respectively.[1]

As chapter 4 notes, models used by the Development Research Center assume that even before WTO membership Chinese companies were operating as fully efficient firms in a competitive environment. Since this assumption is unrealistic, if domestic economic reform is successful in the wake of WTO entry, the efficiency gains and ultimately the pace of growth and foreign trade may be much larger than those models suggest. If so, the effects on world trade and output would be greater than estimated.

The redistribution of world trade will be as important as the overall expansionary effect of China's membership. China's exports of labor-intensive manufactures are expected to expand more rapidly than exports in general, partly because the phaseout of restrictions on textiles and apparel in developed market economies will lower prices and thus increase demand for those products. But China's export of these and other products likely will grow much more rapidly than the growth of world demand for these products because China will displace labor-intensive exports from other developing countries, for example, India and Mexico. This will be most obvious in apparel, where countries with higher costs have retained a significant share of the world market because the system of quotas has limited the erosion of those shares by lower-cost production in China.

A few countries with resource and labor endowments and an export structure similar to China are likely to lose world market share to China and thus grow more slowly. The Development Research Center, for example, predicts that output growth in South Asia will be 0.01 percent per year lower as a result of China's entry, putting its output in 2010 at 0.16 percent below where it would be if China did not enter.[2] If foreign direct investment inflows into China increase significantly following accession, the adverse regional effects of China's WTO entry could easily extend to parts of Southeast Asia. Even in the 1990s it appeared that multinational corporations redirected to China some of the direct investment that might have gone to Southeast Asia. At the beginning of the decade direct investment flows to China composed only 18 percent of flows to Asian developing countries, while ASEAN countries received 61 percent. By the end of the decade the proportions were reversed. China received 61 percent of the flows and the ASEAN countries only 17 percent.[3] The relocation of

Japanese electronics manufacturing is emblematic of this trend. Toshiba, Japan's third largest television set producer, in early 2001 announced that it would move all of its conventional television production to China. Toshiba is following its competitors in moving offshore. But the earlier moves, for example, of Mitsubishi Electric and JVC, were to Southeast Asia.[4] The combination of the opening of new sectors to foreign investment in China, the apparent faltering of ASEAN trade liberalization, and the failure of some states in the region to follow up on needed domestic reforms in the wake of the Asian financial crisis, could accelerate the trend of the 1990s.

## Implications for the International Trading System

Critics raise two fundamental concerns about China's membership in the World Trade Organization. They argue that China is uninterested in or incapable of meeting its far-reaching WTO obligations.[5] And they claim that in the next round of multilateral trade negotiations China might seek to reshape the World Trade Organization to serve its own narrow interests. These are serious charges.

### Compliance

Predicting China's future compliance with its WTO obligations is difficult. Several approaches are necessary. One can start by examining China's compliance with past trade agreements, particularly those dealing with market access and protection of intellectual property. One can also examine the preparations, beyond the general trade reforms discussed in chapter 2, that the authorities have made to come into compliance with the terms of accession. Did the authorities take steps in advance to come into compliance with their obligations? Finally and most difficult to evaluate, are there important structural impediments that, despite the best intentions of the leadership, could lead to a massive failure to comply?

Has China failed to live up to prior trade agreements? That was frequently asserted during the debate in 2000 surrounding the vote in the U.S. Congress to give China permanent normal trade relations status and in the run-up to the conclusion of the multilateral negotiation process in Geneva for China's WTO entry.[6] Compliance is a complex subject, but a brief review of the record does not support the charge of China's systematic noncompliance.

In October 1992 China and the United States signed a bilateral agreement on market access.[7] The key provisions required China to reduce nontariff barriers imposed on many imported products and to increase the transparency of its trading system. Most important, the agreement required China to phase out, over five years, 90 percent of the quotas and licensing requirements then imposed on imports.[8] As chapter 2 notes, when the agreement was signed, these requirements covered less than one-fifth of all imports.

The Chinese did lift the licensing and quota limitations on imports according to the agreed schedule.[9] The U.S. Trade Representative, however, noted that other nontariff barriers remained and that some new nontariff barriers, such as the automatic registration system discussed in chapter 2, were introduced in 1994.

Contrary to the suggestion of the U.S. Trade Representative, the new barriers do not seem to have undermined the trade-liberalizing effect of eliminating quotas and license requirements. That judgment is supported not only by the earlier analysis of trends in imports of steel, the most important item subject first to quota and license restrictions and subsequently to the automatic registration system, but also by a more systematic examination of the pattern of Chinese imports. This analysis shows that imports from the United States of the products for which restrictions were phased out rose much more rapidly than China's overall imports (table 5-1). For example, by 1995 China's imports of goods that had been liberalized at year-end 1992 were $83.5 million, almost ten times 1992 imports of $8.7 million. Imports of these goods in 1995 constituted a six-times larger share of China's total imports than they did in 1992. By 1995 China's imports from the United States of all goods for which quotas and licenses had been phased out by the end of 1994 composed 3.2 percent of China's total imports, compared with 1.8 percent in 1992. Despite the overlapping and redundant forms of trade protection discussed earlier, through 1995 Chinese imports from the United States of those products for which quotas and licenses were eliminated rose at 42 percent per year. That is well over twice the 18 percent annual growth of China's total imports during the same period.

China also largely fulfilled its commitment in the market access agreement to increase the transparency of its trade regime. The Ministry of Foreign Trade published in its annual almanac, beginning in 1992, the texts of important trade laws and internal regulations related to foreign

Table 5-1. *China's Imports of U.S. Goods Covered under the 1992 U.S.-China Bilateral Market Access Agreement*

| Goods liberalized in | Value and quantity of imports in | | |
|---|---|---|---|
| | *1992* | *1994* | *1995* |
| *1992* | | | |
| Millions of U.S. dollars | 8.7 | 64.7 | 83.5 |
| Percent of China's total imports | 0.01 | 0.06 | 0.06 |
| *1992 and 1993* | | | |
| Millions of U.S. dollars | 172.9 | 1,017.3 | 1,091.9 |
| Percent of China's total imports | 0.21 | 0.88 | 0.83 |
| *1992, 1993, and 1994* | | | |
| Millions of U.S. dollars | 1,471.7 | 2,645.7 | 4,183.0 |
| Percent of China's total imports | 1.83 | 2.29 | 3.17 |

Sources: General Administration of Customs of the People's Republic of China, *China Customs Statistics Yearbook 1992* (Beijing, 1993); *China Customs Statistics Yearbook 1994* (Beijing, 1995); and *China Customs Statistics Yearbook 1995* (Beijing, 1996).

Note: Owing to changes in the classification system for Chinese imports beginning in 1996, the analysis cannot be extended beyond 1995.

trade that had been promulgated in earlier years but never made public.[10] The ministry also began publishing a gazette that included the same types of laws but on a much more timely basis than in its annual almanac.[11] The U.S. Trade Representative has noted that as a result of the implementation of the market access agreement, and the process of negotiation for membership in the World Trade Organization, that "China's trade regime has become significantly more transparent in recent years."[12]

The Chinese government, however, has not openly published various forms of administrative guidance on the conduct of foreign trade. Moreover, the Ministry of Foreign Trade has not disclosed systematically the quantitative limits on import products subject to quotas.[13] Overall, despite much improvement in transparency, the U.S. Trade Representative notes, "Businesses sometimes encounter difficulties in learning which regulations or rules apply to their operations in China."[14] In short, China's record in implementing the 1992 market access agreement is mixed. Quantitative restrictions were removed on schedule, leading to proportionately larger increases in imports of previously restricted goods, but at least in the view of some foreign firms doing business with and in China, the nation fell short of fully meeting its commitment to increased transparency.

In the U.S.-China bilateral trade agreement of 1979 the two countries agreed to provide reciprocal protection for trademarks, patents, industrial property, and copyrights.[15] This rather loose commitment, while appropriate as China was just emerging from its self-imposed isolation of the Cultural Revolution, was less satisfactory as violations of intellectual property became widespread in the 1980s. This led the U.S. Trade Representative to threaten trade sanctions against China in 1991.[16] China in response in 1992 signed an agreement promising to improve further the protection provided to intellectual property.[17]

In the 1992 bilateral agreement China agreed to modify its domestic legal structure to comply with standards of the conventions of the World Intellectual Property Organization (WIPO). In the ensuing years China promulgated several important domestic laws and joined almost every international convention dealing with intellectual property issues, particularly those covering patents, copyrights, and trademarks.[18]

Although China complied with the bilateral agreement in a manner comparable to most other developing countries, intellectual property violations had expanded by the mid-1990s. There were two problems. First many of the new domestic laws were not enforced. Most of the WIPO conventions lack enforcement provisions. Chinese laws, which were modeled on these conventions, similarly lacked enforcement provisions. Second the digital revolution dramatically reduced the cost of pirating sound recordings, movies, computer software, and so forth. Given the favorable economics of pirated digital production, worldwide violation of intellectual property soared. By the mid-1990s China had emerged as a major global center of pirated compact disk production. And, for the first time, a significant portion of the pirated output was exported to international markets. As a result, foreign companies, including those from the United States, were not only losing sales in China but also in third countries, such as Canada, Europe, and the United States. The U.S. Trade Representative launched a formal investigation in June of 1994, which led to the threat of trade sanctions against more than $1 billion of Chinese products entering the U.S. market.[19] That led to the second bilateral agreement on intellectual property, which was signed on February 26, 1995.[20]

The 1995 agreement focused on closing factories producing pirated products and prohibiting the export of such products from China. Initially implementation of this agreement lagged, so the U.S. Trade Representative started a second investigation that galvanized the Chinese authorities to take decisive action. By June 1996 the U. S. Trade Representative confirmed that fifteen pirate CD factories, with an annual production capacity estimated between 30 and 50 million units, had been shut, their equipment largely destroyed, and their business licenses revoked.

Moreover, China's General Administration of Customs had launched vigorous border enforcement and had confiscated large quantities of CDs, video compact disks, and laser disks that were destined for international markets. The Chinese authorities also took steps to prevent the importation of any new CD presses to prevent the culprits involved in piracy from reestablishing their operations. Finally the Chinese agreed to take several steps, such as using SID codes, title verification, and inspections to ensure that legitimate CD factories and publishing houses have valid licenses for each foreign title they produce.[21]

As a result of the initial steps taken and the depth of the commitments made by China in the 1995 agreement, the U.S. Trade Representative in June 1996 suspended the pending imposition of prohibitory tariffs on a broad range of Chinese goods entering the United States.[22]

In the ensuing years China implemented provisions of the agreement reducing the flow of pirated products from China to the international market. In March 2000 the U.S. Trade Representative reported that while China in 1995–96 was the world's largest exporter of pirated CDs and CD-ROMs, the total number of pirate factories closed had risen to more than seventy and that "China no longer exports pirated CDs and CD-ROMs."[23] By the end of 2000 the number of closed pirated factories was more than one hundred.[24] Nonetheless imported pirated intellectual property continues to be widely available in China, and the estimate of the losses suffered by foreign firms in China's domestic market has risen. Most of this pirated product initially originated in production lines in Hong Kong and Macau, but by the late 1990s Thailand and Malaysia had become the primary sources.[25]

The lesson is that China's record in protecting intellectual property, like that of many emerging market economies, is mixed. It has promulgated a body of domestic intellectual property laws that meets international standards, and it did close the large-scale factories that were major sources of supply of pirated product in third countries. But pirated intellectual property still is widely available in China. Enforcement of domestic intellectual property laws clearly lags, partly because China's enforcement agencies lack sufficient resources, the courts lack trained personnel, and some provisions of the domestic legal structure remain imperfect.[26]

More fundamentally, throughout the world effective protection of intellectual property invariably follows the emergence of significant domestic constituencies that demand enforcement of intellectual property laws to protect their own economic interests. When the value of domestically produced intellectual property is small, external pressure alone is rarely sufficient to induce vigorous and sustained enforcement. But the rapidly rising value of China's output of books, newspapers, magazines, audio products, e-publications, software, and other copyright material presages rising domestic demand for the protection of intellectual property.[27]

An examination of other bilateral trade agreements produces the same conclusion as analysis of the market access and intellectual property rights agreements—China's record is mixed. By and large China complies, but it frequently takes ample time and effort to do so, and full compliance with every detail of an agreement is sometimes not achieved.

### Preparations to Meet WTO Obligations

Critics argue that China is uninterested in or incapable of meeting its far-reaching obligations.[28] These critics have failed to note that even before WTO membership China's leaders began a far-reaching campaign to inform government officials and enterprise managers of the scope and implications of China's WTO obligations. The Ministry of Personnel organized special WTO classes at the Central Party School in Beijing for the leading party and government officials from every ministry and equivalent administrative unit, and from each province throughout the country. The Ministry of Foreign Trade organized courses for many provincial officials who deal with trade issues. A few jurisdictions, notably Shanghai, established special WTO consultation centers that research the implications of China's WTO accession for particular regions and sectors and provide advisory services to businesses seeking to adjust to increased international competition. The Chinese academic and think tank worlds have produced numerous descriptive studies of the workings and general principles of the WTO system and a few analytical studies of the implications of membership for the economy as a whole and for specific sectors.[29]

Besides these educational efforts, China began to implement some of its WTO obligations even before it became a member. This was feasible partly because of a substantial lag between the time the bilateral WTO agreement with the United States was completed in the fall of 1999 and China's WTO entry. Most of China's market access commitments were fixed in the bilateral agreement. The implementation of some obligations in advance in effect spread the domestic adjustment process out over a longer period, increasing the prospect that the economic and political system will

be able to absorb the adjustment costs within the phase-in periods specified in China's commitments.

Cumulatively the many examples of early implementation do not prove
that China will abide by all of its WTO commitments. Presumably China
took some steps out of a sense of economic self-interest. Not all of the
obligations that it will have to meet will completely share this characteristic. Thus how strictly China complies with its obligations will become
clear only over a long period. But the record to date suggests that the
government is making a substantial effort to comply with a broad range
of its obligations and that it believes that further economic liberalization
and opening up are essential to meeting long-term economic goals.

As chapter 2 details, China cut its tariffs dramatically over time. This
served two of the leadership's interests. First, opening up the economy
placed more competitive pressure on domestic firms. Second, it demonstrated that China was responsive to the expectation of the members of
the WTO working party that China make a large down payment toward
catching up with the tariff cuts that other countries had made in the Uruguay Round of trade negotiations. Between the time China first expressed
interest in becoming a member of GATT in the mid-1980s and the time it
completed major bilateral trade deals with members of the WTO working
party in the late 1990s, China cut its average statutory tariff rate from 43
percent to 17 percent. The government continued to cut tariffs after it
completed bilateral agreements with the United States and the EU, even
though it legally was not required to do so until after WTO entry (box 2-1).
These cuts in 2001 included the tariff reductions on imported cars, parts,
and accessories that were promised in China's bilateral 1999 agreement
with the United States.[30] If China had not intended to complete its multilateral WTO negotiations, there would have been no reason to implement
this scheduled reduction, which when it was agreed to, assumed China
would enter the World Trade Organization in 2000.[31]

China began to implement its commitments in telecommunications even
before it entered. An important early liberalization in telecommunications
was AT&T's investment in 2000 in a 25 percent stake in Shanghai Symphony Telecommunications Company, which will provide broadband value-
added telecommunications services in the Pudong district in Shanghai.[32]
China Netcom Corporation, a major telecommunications carrier running
China's first broadband Internet backbone linking seventeen cities, also
jumped the gun. In early 2001 it raised $325 million in a private equity
placement, giving foreign firms a big stake in the company. The foreign

investors included News Corp., Goldman Sachs, and MSD Capital, a personal investment company owned by Dell Computer founder Michael Dell.[33] Similarly AOL Time Warner and Legend, China's largest personal computer maker and the operator of a major Internet portal, in 2001 formed a joint venture to develop interactive services in the Internet market.[34] As chapter 3 notes, China was not required to allow foreign ownership in companies like Shanghai Symphony Telecommunications and Netcom or to allow foreign investment in Internet service and content providers until after it entered the World Trade Organization.

China Telecom, the dominant fixed-line service provider, is considering offering a stake to potential strategic foreign investors, in advance of a stock market listing in New York or Hong Kong.[35] As shown earlier in table 3-1, under the terms of China's WTO agreement, China is not obligated to provide any opportunities for foreign participation in fixed-line telecommunications services until three years after accession. Initially the listing of China Telecom was scheduled for 2001, but it was postponed, pending decisions on how to restructure the company. Even if the sale of an ownership stake to a strategic investor does not occur until three years after entry, the discussion that started in 2000 reflects a sea change in attitudes in what traditionally has been one of China's most protected and insular sectors.

China started to implement its commitment to the Information Technology Agreement (ITA) ahead of the promised schedule. In its November 15, 1999, bilateral agreement with the United States and in its accession agreement China promised to eliminate all tariffs on these products according to a schedule—the higher the initial tariff, the longer China has to eliminate the tariff.[36] But in January 2000 China cut tariffs on eighteen products subject to the ITA. It was not obligated to make any cuts in tariffs on ITA products until it became a WTO member. Moreover, it made generous cuts on some products for which it does not have to eliminate tariffs until 2004 or 2005. China does not have to cut the tariff on flight data recorders to zero, for example, until January 1, 2004. But the Customs Administration cut the 18 percent tariff to 1 percent at the beginning of 2000. In July 2000 early implementation of the ITA commitment again occurred when the Chinese software industry, a principal user of information technology products, was given the right to import all information technology equipment, technology, accessories, and parts on a duty-free basis.[37]

China is implementing some of its audiovisual commitments ahead of schedule. In July 2000 the Ministry of Culture and the State Administration of Radio, Film, and Television issued regulations allowing foreign investment in film distribution and cinema theater services, which it was not required to do until it became a member of the World Trade Organization. Moreover, it has gone further and will allow foreign investment in film production companies, an area not even covered by China's WTO agreement.[38]

China is selectively opening its construction sector to foreign participation more rapidly than scheduled in its WTO commitments. Beijing Municipality announced in mid-2000 that all large-scale construction projects in the municipality would be decided by international competitive bids, with foreign and domestic construction companies receiving equal treatment.[39] Thus the city opened up to wholly foreign-owned construction companies before accession, whereas China's WTO commitment was to allow joint venture construction companies to operate in China on accession, and wholly foreign-owned construction companies beginning three years after accession.

China is fulfilling commitments to liberalize the retail sector ahead of schedule. In its November 15, 1999, bilateral agreement with the United States and in its protocol of accession, China agreed to open additional cities to foreign retailing on a schedule, beginning when it entered the WTO. But in late 1999 it issued regulations opening up all provincial capitals to foreign retailing, a step it could have postponed, under the terms of its WTO agreement, until two years after entry.[40] The new regulations also allow for majority foreign ownership with approval of the State Council. China was not obligated to allow any majority foreign-owned retail establishments until two years after accession.

China has begun to open up its tourist industry to foreign firms ahead of the schedule established in its WTO commitments. In its bilateral agreement with the United States in November 1999 and in its protocol China agreed to allow, starting on the date of accession, joint venture travel agencies and tour operators to provide tourism services in Beijing, Shanghai, Guangzhou, Xian, and designated holiday resorts. The groundwork for this commitment was laid in late 1998 when the State Council approved the establishment of joint venture travel agencies on an experimental basis.[41] In April 1999 Vice Minister of Foreign Trade Chen Xinhua announced that foreign travel agencies could establish joint venture travel agencies in China.[42]

China has opened up retailing and wholesaling of petroleum products far more rapidly than agreed to in its WTO commitments. In its bilateral agreement with the United States of November 15, 1999, and in its protocol China agreed to allow joint ventures to engage in the retail distribution of refined petroleum products no later than January 1, 2003. But major foreign oil companies, such as BP (eventually merging and becoming BP Amoco) and Esso, have operated gasoline stations in southern Guangdong Province since the early 1980s.[43] By mid-2000 foreign oil companies, in partnership with Chinese companies such as Sinopec and the China National Petroleum Corporation, already were operating nearly 300 filling stations, and the number was poised to grow dramatically well before 2003. Exxon, for example, has operated a string of filling stations in Guangdong Province since the mid-1990s, and Shell operates filling stations in Tianjin, Guangzhou, Wuhan, and Beijing.[44] Shell in 2000 announced that in partnership with Sinopec it would operate a network of 500 stations in Jiangsu Province.[45] Also before entry ExxonMobil and BP Amoco each received approval to invest with Sinopec to build an additional 500 stations in Guangdong and Zhejiang provinces, respectively.[46]

China has announced a pilot program to open one or two cities to foreign wholesale distribution of refined petroleum products in 2001.[47] Under the terms of its WTO accession China is not required to begin liberalizing wholesale distribution of processed oil until January 1, 2005.[48] Chinese officials envision the pilot project as helping domestic companies prepare for full-fledged competition in the domestic market five years after WTO entry.

It seems that China will ease restrictions on the operations of foreign law firms more rapidly than it committed to under its protocol. In the summer of 2000 Vice Minister of Justice Duan Zhengkun, announced that the "one firm, one office" rule limiting the expansion of foreign law firms would be abolished "soon."[49] As chapter 3 says, according to the terms of its protocol of accession, China was not required to ease this rule until one year after accession. Since a large share of the work of foreign law firms is advising companies on joint venture investments, permitting offices in more than one city is important. It means that foreign law firms will no longer have to choose between operating in Beijing, where all large-scale projects must be approved, or in Shanghai, China's emerging finance and banking center. For the first time they will be able to maintain offices in both or any other combination of cities that facilitates their ability to serve their clients.

China liberalized trading rights in advance of scheduled obligations. In July 2001 China granted all foreign-invested firms, regardless of the foreign ownership share, the right to export any product. Under its WTO commitments some foreign-invested firms were not scheduled to receive this right until three years after accession.[50]

China began to open other business and distribution services in advance of the date required under its WTO obligations. General Electric, for example, in 2000 formed a wholly foreign-owned company to purchase products for export to GE companies and affiliates on a worldwide basis. It provides what are known as commission agents' services but only to GE-affiliated companies. The company also is providing consulting services to Chinese companies to assist them in meeting quality and technical standards specified by GE end users.[51] China was not obligated to permit commission agents' services until one year after entry into the WTO, and entry was limited to joint ventures. It does not have to allow wholly foreign-owned companies in this field until three years after entry. Under its WTO agreement China was not obligated to allow foreign companies to enter the technical consulting service business except as joint ventures. But the GE firm, up and running in 2000, is wholly foreign owned.

As China prepared to enter the World Trade Organization it took or was contemplating other liberalizing steps not set forth in its accession commitments. Zhou Xiaochuan, chairman of the Chinese Securities Regulatory Commission, announced in 2000 that China was preparing to allow qualified foreign institutional investors to invest in the A share market.[52] The State Council is considering allowing foreign insurance companies to invest part of their premium income in the domestic A share market—long forbidden to foreign investors.[53] And China is preparing to license the first joint venture fund management companies, which will be able to invest in the domestic A share market. These examples represent cautious steps toward capital account convertibility, a topic not even mentioned in China's protocol of accession.

Besides the film production companies already mentioned, sectors previously seen as too sensitive to allow foreign investment began to open up. The natural gas sector, for example, relaxed barriers. The State Development Planning Commission announced in 2000 that it would seek foreign participation in a gas pipeline running from the Xinjiang Autonomous Region in China's northwest to Shanghai. The opening includes not just the opportunity to make a financial investment in the project but also to explore for gas, bid for construction and management of the pipeline, and, perhaps most important, build the downstream urban distribution network for the gas. Previously these activities were under the control of state-owned monopolies. Surprisingly, there are to be no limits on the foreign share, meaning that consortiums of foreign firms, without any participation by domestic companies, will be able to bid on the project.[54] Foreign firms, including ExxonMobil, Royal Dutch/Shell, and BP Amoco, invested $1.8 billion in shares of Sinopec when it was listed in 2000. Finally the Singapore Investment Corporation, the American International Group's Asian Infrastructure Fund, and other investors injected $460 million in China National Offshore Oil Corporation Ltd. in advance of that firm's international public stock offering in early 2001. Several international oil corporations, such as BP Amoco and Royal Dutch/Shell, took strategic stakes when the firm listed in February 2001.[55] Most of the petroleum companies at the same time concluded separate agreements with the three Chinese oil majors to cooperate in oil and gas exploration and marketing and distribution of petroleum products.[56]

### Structural Impediments to Compliance

One of the most important structural impediments to China's compliance with its WTO obligations is its legal system. In the spring of 2000 Chinese negotiators presented to the working party a list of 177 domestic laws dealing with customs administration, foreign investment administration, intellectual property, and services that required revisions to be consistent with its new international obligations.[57] Although many of the required changes were minor, some were not, and in any case drafting and approving all the necessary amendments will be a lengthy process.

China did amend a few of the most important laws in advance of its entry. The National People's Congress Standing Committee, for example, in 2000 passed amendments to the laws governing Sino-foreign cooperative joint ventures and foreign-funded enterprises. The amendments, which took effect October 31, 2000, dropped the original provisions requiring these firms to be responsible for balancing their foreign exchange needs and to give priority to domestic sources of raw materials and other required inputs. The amendments eliminated provisions limiting the access of these firms to the domestic market.[58] At the same meeting the Standing Committee passed similar changes to the Law on Chinese-Foreign Equity Joint Ventures. At its annual legislative session in the spring of 2001 the National People's Congress gave final approval of amendments to that law. Parallel changes were made to the Foreign Exchange Law, allowing foreign-funded firms to use the domestic currency earned in local sales to purchase foreign exchange.[59] All of these changes were required to make these laws consistent with China's TRIMs obligations, summarized in chapter 3.

Before WTO entry China revised several laws dealing with intellectual property to make them consistent with international standards and its WTO obligations. The Patent Law, for example, was changed to allow judicial review of all decisions of China's patent office. Previously there was no possibility for appeal. Now when a foreign or domestic firm believes that a patent has been awarded incorrectly, the decision can be appealed to the courts.[60] China also amended its Copyright, Trademark, and Customs laws to make them consistent with its TRIPs obligations.[61]

The State Council promulgated new telecommunications regulations in the fall of 2000.[62] Although many provisions on licensing and other matters of great interest to foreign firms are left to the anticipated Telecommunications Law and related administrative regulations, the regulations issued in 2000 clearly allow foreign investment in telecommunications operating companies, establish interconnection rights for new market entrants, and require cost-based pricing. As chapter 3 notes, China agreed to all of these terms, which are essential for foreign telecommunications firms, in its November 1999 bilateral agreement with the United States.[63]

In the interim, before all of the necessary amendments to existing laws can be made, the vice president of China's Supreme Court announced that when domestic law and WTO requirements still conflict, the latter will prevail.[64]

Another structural feature of the Chinese economic system frequently cited as a potential impediment to China's compliance with WTO obligations is the independent power of provincial and local governments. Are they so powerful on economic issues that they can thwart implementation of the WTO agreement, which was negotiated by the central government in Beijing? The most frequently cited evidence for this possibility is the ability of local governments to effectively exclude from their own markets products made in other administrative jurisdictions in China.

Some provinces and municipalities, for example, have imposed high taxes, fees, and other obstacles to licensing motor vehicles made in other localities, including imported and joint venture vehicles. In Shanghai, for example, the license fee for a locally produced Santana was RMB 20,000, while for a vehicle made elsewhere the fee was RMB 98,000.[65] Other localities retaliated with differentiated taxes and fees favoring their local producers. This explains why in the 1990s Santana taxis were pervasive in Shanghai but rare in some other major municipalities. Small Xiali taxis were common in Tianjin and Beijing, but almost unseen in Shanghai. If Shanghai Municipality can protect locally produced Santanas from competition from other domestically produced vehicles, what hope is there that vehicles imported from abroad will penetrate the local Shanghai market? In short the usual assumption is that a country entering the World Trade Organization will have an economy that, by virtue of substantial interregional trade flows, is well integrated. If local protectionism is rampant, it will be more difficult to accommodate greatly increased inflows of foreign goods.

Evaluating the prospect that local governments will impede implementation of the WTO agreement is complex. First of all provincial and local governments are not always an illiberal force on foreign trade and investment issues. They sometimes have sanctioned foreign investment, even when it stretched or explicitly violated national laws and regulations. Guangdong Province granted foreign firms the right to distribute refined petroleum products at the retail level in the early 1980s. Almost two decades later the national government, in its bilateral negotiations with the United States, agreed to allow retail distribution of refined petroleum products by joint venture companies starting no later than 2003. Similarly in the 1990s several local governments authorized foreign retailers to expand their operations far beyond the restrictive parameters established by the national regulations. Largely for this reason Carrefour was able to become China's second largest retailer only five years after it opened its first store.

Second despite anecdotal evidence that local governments have engaged in restrictive trade practices, the Chinese economy in the reform period has become far more integrated economically.[66] Barry Naughton, who has done the most comprehensive study of this subject, has shown that interprovincial trade between 1987 and 1992 grew more rapidly than gross domestic product or foreign trade, suggesting that the Chinese economy was becoming more, not less, integrated. By 1992 interprovincial trade was high, averaging about 70 percent of provincial gross domestic product. As a percentage of value added in the goods-producing sector, interprovincial trade in China was a little more than twice as high as trade within the EU.[67] Moreover, Naughton has demonstrated that interprovincial trade in China is dominated by intraindustry trade, as is typical of trade among market economies, rather than one-way transfers of raw materials, as might be expected under a system of central planning or interregional trade in the early stage of economic development. Finally interprovincial integration has likely increased since 1992 because on average the share of gross domestic product invested in transportation and communication in 1993–1998 was more than twice the share invested in 1981–92.[68] In light of this evidence generalizations about barriers to trade and lack of economic integration probably are not warranted.

Third the central government has launched a determined effort to overcome the most glaring case of local protectionism—automobiles. In the summer of 2000 Zeng Peiyan, the head of the State Development Planning Commission, announced that abolishing illegal fees and other forms of local protection of the automobile industry was part of a ten-point economic reform agenda.[69] By the spring of 2001 the State Council issued formal regulations banning regional blockades and other forms of local protectionism of all commodities.[70] It remains to be seen whether the central government is able to enforce these new regulations.

Another development favorable for the prospects for China's compliance with WTO obligations is the evolution of Chinese industrial policy. In the mid-1990s China launched a formidable industrial policy initiative.[71] The "Outline of State Industrial Policies for the 1990s" was a broad policy document that sought to enhance the role of the market in resource allocation while maintaining the state's preeminence in macroeconomic policy. It was short on specifics in most areas, instead advancing general goals such as stimulating agricultural development, expanding foreign trade, developing pillar industries, and promoting "rational competition." The document promoted the idea that in many industries firms should be consolidated into a few industrial groups to take advantage of economies of scale. The drafters of the policy were clearly influenced by the historical pattern of industrial development in Japan, which later was emulated in South Korea.

Almost simultaneously, the government released an industrial policy for the vehicle sector and announced it was drafting industrial policies for the transport, telecommunications, construction, electronics, machine building, and petrochemical industries.[72]

Many of the main provisions of the industrial policy for the vehicle sector were clearly inconsistent with the provisions of the WTO agreement, especially the Agreement on Trade-Related Investment Measures (TRIMs). Most important, the policy set the goal that domestically produced vehicles would meet more than 90 percent of the demand for all vehicles and half of the demand for sedans, clearly violating the requirement that WTO members provide national treatment for imports. Second the state fixed annually the total number and specific mix of imported cars at the same time it set the state plan for automobile production. That clearly was inconsistent with article 11, section 1, of the GATT 1994, which obliges members to eliminate quantitative restrictions on imports. Third the policy contained several provisions to promote localization of parts and component production, clearly violating article 2 of the TRIMs agreement, which requires that imports and domestic goods compete on a level playing field and precludes any local content requirement. Article 31 of the Auto Industry Policy, for example, requires joint ventures to "give priority to" locally made parts and components. This policy reinforced this general injunction by stipulating successively lower tariffs on imported car parts and components when a manufacturer achieves 40, 60, and 80 percent local content levels. Article 31 of the Chinese auto policy requires foreign exchange balancing, also violating the provisions of article 11, section 1, of GATT 1994. Again the requirement that joint ventures balance their foreign exchange was reinforced by a state policy of providing funds on a favorable basis to firms that export a certain share of their output. The auto policy also limited the number of foreign firms that would be able to enter the vehicle industry and imposed a 50 percent ceiling on the foreign ownership share in the joint venture structures foreign firms were required to use to participate in the domestic auto industry.

For many years after negotiations for its entry into the General Agreement on Tariffs and Trade began in 1987 Chinese trade officials argued in multilateral negotiations in Geneva that China should enter the world trading system as a "developing country." That designation might have allowed China to retain, during a phase-in period, some the features of the auto policy just summarized. Developing countries, for example, are allowed up to five years to come into compliance with the TRIMs agreement. The members of the Working Party on China's Accession to the World Trade Organization, led by the United States, firmly rejected this approach. Rather than give China the broad benefits that come with the formal classification as a developing country, the working party sought to negotiate phase-in periods for various standards on a case-by-case basis. Chinese negotiators, up until the end, asserted the principle that China should be treated as a developing country, but eventually they understood that the working party would not budge on its demand that China comply fully with TRIMs, effective on the date of accession. The only solution was to begin to adjust the auto policy of 1994.

Thus by the time China entered the World Trade Organization it had modified or abandoned most of the principal features of its industrial policy for the auto industry. The Chinese government, agreed to lift, two years after accession, the long-standing constraint limiting each automotive joint venture to produce only a single category or type of vehicle. That will allow joint venture producers to select the categories, types, and models they produce.[73] Shanghai Volkswagen announced shortly after the bilateral agreement between the EU and China was signed that it would launch new models, besides its Santana, Santana 2000, and Passat cars, after China entered the World Trade Organization.[74] Shanghai General Motors moved even faster, announcing in July 2000 a new smaller car, the Buick Sail, with a smaller engine than its initially approved car.[75] The first models rolled off the assembly line in December, and regular production began in the spring of 2001.[76] That also effectively ended the limitation in the auto industrial policy of allowing no more than two joint ventures producing vehicles with similar-sized engines. The new Buick model, with a 2.49-liter engine, was at least the third joint venture car in the same engine size range.[77] In its negotiations with the EU, China agreed to raise the 50 percent ceiling on foreign ownership of automobile engine manufacturing facilities to 100 percent.[78]

In effect, the Chinese government has completely abandoned the idea of nurturing a purely indigenous automobile industry. Based on the trends analyzed in chapter 4, it is likely that the Chinese car market will be heavily dominated for the foreseeable future by joint ventures rather than local companies.

Even more important than abandoning the goal of an indigenous automobile industry, the Asian financial crisis emboldened economic reformers in China to criticize directly the supposed merits of the Japanese and Korean models of industrial organization. These had provided the intellectual underpinning for the policy of fostering large industrial conglomerates in China. Support for mergers to create what the Chinese called industrial "groups" was strong through most of 1997, and the government orchestrated several important mergers.[79] By year-end 1997, as the Asian financial crisis revealed the structural problems of Korean-style conglomerates, criticism of the strategy of government-directed, top-down mergers emerged in public. Critics, including the research arm of the State Planning Commission and Wu Jinglian, one of China's leading economic reformers, argued that mergers should be market driven. They decried the government's objective of creating corporations that would be listed on the Fortune Global 500.[80]

The evolution of China's approach to industrial policy is perhaps most fully reflected in the policies adopted for the software and integrated circuit industries.[81] In marked contrast with the protectionist approach taken to stimulate the development of an indigenous auto industry in 1994, the policy toward computer software and integrated circuits adopted in 2000 presumes that the domestic market is open, competitive, and internationally oriented. For example, all of the imported equipment and technology that enterprises in both industries need is exempt from import duties and value-added taxes. The State Council document explicitly states that joint ventures and wholly foreign-owned manufacturing companies will play leading roles in the development of the integrated circuit industry. Indeed, in marked contrast with the 1994 auto policy, there are no preferences for indigenous firms. These policies, combined with zero tariffs on the import of software and integrated circuits, will ensure that these industries will operate at international prices.[82]

Although most of the sectoral industrial policies drafted in the mid-1990s were never promulgated, and the policy on software and integrated circuits promulgated six years later had an entirely different orientation, the proclivity for industrial policies inconsistent with WTO principles persists in a few industrial ministries. In the fall of 2000, for example, the Ministry of Information Industry announced an industrial policy to support ten domestic firms in the cellular telephone industry. The policy bans new foreign investment in this sector and requires existing joint venture firms to export 60 percent of their product and attain 50 percent domestic content by the end of 2001. The government will set the quantity of handsets foreign manufacturers will be allowed to sell on the domestic market based on their export performance and their local content in manufacturing.[83] All of these provisions violate the TRIMs agreement.[84] And there are still times when local governments, worried that bankruptcies would increase unemployment, orchestrate the merger of failing companies with somewhat stronger firms in the same industry.

What conclusions should one draw about China's likely compliance with WTO obligations from this brief summary of some of the conflicting evidence? As the experience with the protection of intellectual property suggests, commitments to general principles may not lead to the result anticipated by Western firms and governments. China is more likely to comply with detailed and concrete commitments than vague principles. This certainly was the perspective of negotiators in China's working party. China's WTO commitments are spelled out in great detail, as reflected in a protocol and working party report of unprecedented length. This bodes well for compliance.

Three factors, however, suggest that compliance may be somewhat problematic. First China has made WTO-plus commitments that surpass those made by other countries entering the World Trade Organization. The expectations of the international community are high. Second the less than fully developed state of domestic institutions, especially the legal system supporting the market, increases the prospect that China will fall short of full compliance. China has only begun the process of amending domestic laws to make its legal system consistent with WTO obligations.[85] More important, it will take years to achieve fair, uniform, and impartial implementation of these laws and to ensure that judgments are enforced.[86] Thus China could become the object of a large number of WTO dispute settlement cases.

Third China is entering a period of major transition in leadership, and relatively little is known about the attitudes on globalization and the World Trade Organization of those individuals who are expected to assume the top leadership positions in the party and the government in the fall of 2002 and the spring of 2003, respectively. Premier Zhu Rongji and President Jiang Zemin seem to have personally driven China's decision to make the far-reaching commitments necessary to become a WTO member. The views of Hu Jintao, who is widely expected to succeed Jiang Zemin, are much less well known. Although he has said that globalization is an inevitable trend, he seems not to have spoken publicly in any detail on WTO-related issues. Although he has traveled in Asia, the Middle East, and Africa, he did not make his first trip to western Europe until the fall of 2001 and has not traveled to the United States. He seldom meets with business leaders from advanced industrial economies. Wen Jiabao, the putative successor to Premier Zhu, is not quite as insular. But his views on foreign trade and investment issues are largely unknown. The rise of top leaders possibly less committed to China's greater integration into the global economy coincides with the growing importance of domestic interest groups in policy formulation and implementation. Sectorally and regionally based interest groups were important long before China entered the World Trade Organization. But as increased openness imposes economic hardship on those employed in formerly protected segments of the domestic economy, these groups could easily become an even larger factor in China's domestic politics. The combination of a less cosmopolitan top leadership, possibly less committed to globalization, and a system of policy implementation in which interest groups are acquiring an expanding role underlines the risk that China's implementation of its WTO commitments could fall short of Western expectations.

### China's Future Role in the World Trade Organization

Critics of China's WTO accession have raised fears that once it is a member China might disrupt the organization's work or try to reshape the institution to serve its interests. The *Wall Street Journal* editorialized, "The worry has been that Beijing would get inside the WTO and then mess up the organization by not respecting the letter or the spirit of its rules. The concern is not unreasonable."[87]

This hypothetical worry is difficult to evaluate, but one can gain some initial insight by examining China's role in the United Nations and other major international bodies. When China was admitted to the United Nations in late 1971, some feared that China immediately would seek to join all other important international organizations affiliated with the United Nations and use its memberships to disrupt the status quo. Critics feared that China would use its veto power to paralyze the UN Security Council. Reality turned out to be somewhat different. China only gradually joined all of the important international intergovernmental organizations of the UN system, including the World Bank and the International Monetary Fund. Moreover, as Sam Kim's analysis has shown, Beijing's orientation "became distinctively *system-maintaining*. Accordingly, Beijing became more interested in what the U.N. system could do for China's modernization and less interested in what China could do to reform the United Nations."[88] In the Security Council China has exerted substantial leverage but, except for an incident in 1981, has rarely used its veto power.[89] In Kim's words, "The disruptive impact of Chinese participation that was so widely and wrongly predicted and feared . . . has not come to pass . . . within the world organization it is a satisfied conservative system maintainer, not a liberal system reformer nor a revolutionary system transformer."[90]

Although China has expressed little interest in leading fundamental reform at the United Nations and has acted judiciously in the use of its veto power in the Security Council, it certainly has used the United Nations to protect its interests. For example, China in 1998, acting in parallel with Russia, made it clear that it would not support UN intervention in Kosovo. China feared UN-sanctioned military action in what it regarded as a domestic Yugoslav affair could set a precedent constraining its actions toward Taiwan. As a result Western intervention was orchestrated under NATO auspices without UN authorization.

Its experience in the United Nations suggests China will not seek to lead a fundamental transformation of the World Trade Organization. Rather, like most nations, it will try to use the institution to advance its interests. There is little doubt that China's leaders believe that the opportunity to participate in shaping the rules of the international trading system is one of the benefits of WTO membership.[91] But Chinese leaders have not been specific about how they believe the world trading system should evolve. Shi Guangsheng, the minister of foreign trade, and other officials have articulated the view that the WTO decisionmaking process is dominated by a few states, acting behind the scenes, and that the views and interests of developing countries are not adequately considered.[92] Minister Shi reiterated forcefully at the abortive Seattle WTO ministerial conference in December 1999 the well-known Chinese view that the next WTO round should have limited objectives and that any expansion of the scope of the WTO beyond trade issues should be based on consensus.[93] In September 1999 China joined other developing countries in the Group of 77, for example, to "firmly oppose [both] any linkage between trade and labor standards" and "the use of environmental standards as a new form of protectionism."[94] Like many developing countries, China fears that these issues could be used by developed countries to restrict access to their markets. Since some advocates of labor rights in the West believe that the World Trade Organization should allow countries to impose restrictions on the import of products from countries that do not meet certain labor standards, China's fear certainly seems to have some merit.[95]

Similarly since China has been subject to more antidumping actions than any other country, it may well take the lead in insisting on reforms of WTO antidumping procedures.[96] China, like many developing countries, believes that antidumping has been used systematically by developed market economies to limit access to their markets.

A third area in which China is likely to seek fundamental reform is the WTO's approach to domestic agricultural subsidies. In the final negotiations on agricultural subsidies Chinese trade negotiators found it difficult to understand how the members of the working party could demand that China limit its agricultural subsidies to 8.5 percent of the value of agricultural output when, for example, the U.S. government provides subsidies to its farmers that are almost equal to net income that farmers earn from the sale of agricultural commodities.[97] The United States is able to subsidize at a nearly 100 percent rate because most of its subsidies take the form of direct payments to farmers rather than price subsidies. In the rules established in the Uruguay Round trade negotiations direct subsidies to farmers were classified as "green box" measures, meaning that they are not included in the aggregate measure of support (AMS) and thus are not subject to any limitation. The United States and other developed countries, which largely controlled the Uruguay Round negotiations, wrote the rules so that their preferred form of subsidies was not limited. Most developing countries lack the administrative capacity to provide direct subsidies, which must be tailored to individual farm household characteristics. Thus they rely on indirect or price subsidies. China still has 240 million farm families and does not have sufficient government staff at the village level who could determine the direct subsidy to each household based, for example, on each household's income or other characteristics.

These Chinese views on labor and environmental standards, antidumping, and agricultural subsidies are part of a general theme China espouses that the World Trade Organization should place a higher priority on the interests of developing countries "so that they can benefit more from the multilateral trade system."[98]

China is likely over time to seek changes in the WTO's informal governance structures. Unlike the highly bureaucratic processes that dominate decisionmaking at the United Nations and many of its affiliated agencies, the World Trade Organization, like its predecessor the General Agreement on Tariffs and Trade, is a more low-key organization. Informality prevails partly because of the organization's small budget and low staffing levels. Supporters of the organization point out that the WTO's entire budget is less than the travel expenditures of the World Bank. The WTO's informal decisionmaking in recent years has been dominated by the so-called quad countries—the United States, Japan, the EU, and Canada. This group effectively has set the agenda for meetings. As the Chinese government becomes more familiar with WTO issues it is likely to insist that much of the decisionmaking now said to go on in the "green room" be opened up to allow greater participation by all members.

## Implications for the United States

U.S. trade negotiators led the discussion on China's entry into the World Trade Organization. This perhaps was natural given the large economic stake of the United States in the creation of more open markets globally.

China was a focus because of its rapidly increasing role as a global trader and, as chapter 3 says, because beginning in 1991 the terms of its entry were seen as providing a template for WTO membership for several formerly centrally planned economies. Moreover, as the United States became far and away China's largest export market, the resulting expanding bilateral deficit with China came to preoccupy U.S. policymakers.

### Trade Expansion

Trade between China and the United States has grown rapidly since trade relations resumed in 1978. Bilateral trade turnover (the sum of exports and imports) grew from $1 billion in 1978 to $116 billion in 2000. However, bilateral trade flows became increasingly imbalanced in the 1990s (figure 5-1). By 2000 the U.S. bilateral deficit reached $84 billion and for the first time on an annual basis exceeded the bilateral deficit with Japan. The growing imbalance frequently is cited as evidence of the closed nature of China's economy. China, it is said, has an "economic vision [that] is fundamentally not free-market oriented, but mercantilist."[99] Some fear China will displace Japan as our most troublesome trading partner.[100]

The argument that the U.S. trade deficit with China derives from the latter's relatively closed domestic market is fundamentally flawed for several reasons. Perhaps most important the U.S. global trade deficit, which reached an all-time record of $435 billion in 2000, primarily reflects the extraordinarily low rate of savings in the United States.[101] Because of meager domestic savings, borrowing from abroad must finance a large fraction of U.S. domestic investment. But the rest of the world would be unable to lend to the United States if it did not have a trade surplus with the United States. Policies that open specific markets abroad for U.S. firms, of course, could lead to more U.S. exports to those individual markets. But at least in the short run the U.S. global trade deficit would be unaffected. In short the U.S. global trade deficit is the mirror image of its low savings rate relative to its rate of investment. Until the U.S. savings rate rises or the rate of investment falls, no amount of trade liberalization abroad will reduce significantly the global U.S. trade deficit. Selective trade liberalization abroad only affects the country-by-country distribution of the U.S. global trade deficit, not its overall size.

Most of the growing U.S. deficit with China stems from China's rapid displacement of alternative foreign sources of supply, primarily of labor-intensive manufactures. That results from the migration of labor-intensive manufacturing to China from other locations in Asia, notably Hong Kong,

Figure 5-1. *U.S.-China Trade, 1979–2000*

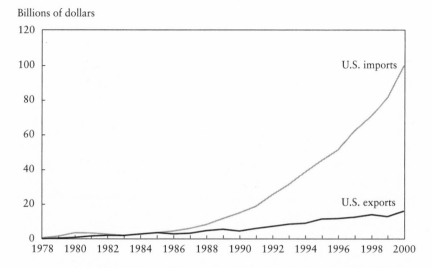

Billions of dollars

Sources: Census Bureau, *Statistical Abstract of the United States 2000* (U.S. Department of Commerce, 1998) p. 794; *Statistical Abstract of the United States 1998*, p. 801; *Statistical Abstract of the United States 1995*, p. 819; *Statistical Abstract of the United States 1992*, p. 800; *Statistical Abstract of the United States 1990*, p. 808; *Statistical Abstract of the United States 1987*, p. 794; *Statistical Abstract of the United States 1984*, p. 836; *Statistical Abstract of the United States 1982–83*, p. 838; Census Bureau, *FT 900: U.S. International Trade in Goods & Services*, December 2000, exhibit 14, p. 19 (www.census.gov/foreign-trade/ [February 21, 2001]).

Taiwan, and Korea. In the 1980s and 1990s, as wages in these countries rose and China liberalized its foreign direct investment environment, Asian entrepreneurs moved a growing share of their labor-intensive production to China. Thus a very large share of U.S. imports from China are produced in joint venture or wholly foreign-owned factories.[102] In contrast the U.S. deficit with Japan is primarily the result of the import of much more capital-intensive goods, produced in Japanese-owned factories, which displace production not in third countries but primarily in the United States.

The two largest categories of goods the United States imports from China, accounting for more than a quarter of all U.S. imports, are baby carriages, toys, games, and sporting goods, followed closely by footwear. Goods in these categories are extremely labor intensive and produced predominantly in foreign-invested enterprises or under processing contracts in which foreign firms supply Chinese firms with a significant portion of the inputs needed to produce the final good.

Figure 5-2. *Sources of U.S. Footwear Imports, 1985–99*

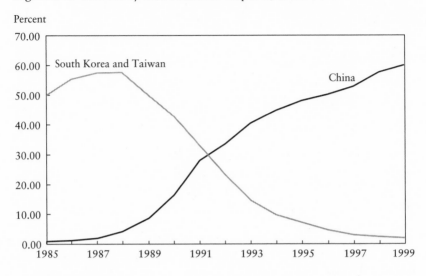

Percent

Sources: U.S. Department of Commerce, International Trade Administration, "U.S. Trade by Commodity with World," "U.S. Trade by Commodity with China," "U.S. Trade by Commodity with Taiwan," "U.S. Trade by Commodity with Korea, South" (www.wwwita.doc.gov/td/industry/oteal [February 2000]); U.S. International Trade Commission, Interactive Tariff and Trade Dataweb (www.dataweb.usitc.gov [February 2000]); Census Bureau, "Highlights of U.S. Export and Import Trade," Report FT 990, December 1988 (U.S. Department of Commerce, 1989), pp. B-14–B-15, table 5; "Highlights of U.S. Export and Import Trade," Report FT 990, December 1987, pp. C-14–C15, table 5; "Highlights of U.S. Export and Import Trade," Report FT 990, December 1986, pp. C-14–C-15, table 5; and "Highlights of U.S. Export and Import Trade," Report FT 990, December 1985, pp. C-14–C-15, table 5.

The rapid growth of U.S. imports of these two categories of goods from China largely reflects the displacement of alternative sources of supply in Asia, notably Hong Kong, Taiwan, and South Korea. For example, from 1986 through 1988 almost 60 percent of U.S. footwear imports were from Taiwan and South Korea; China was the source of only 2 percent of U.S. footwear imports (figure 5-2). By 1999 the relative importance of the two sources of supply had reversed completely. The share of U.S. footwear imports originating in Taiwan and South Korea was only 2 percent, and the share originating in China was 60 percent.

The story is identical for toys and sporting goods (figure 5-3). Hong Kong, South Korea, and Taiwan supplied just over 60 percent of U.S. imports in 1985; China was the source of only 6 percent of U.S. imports. By the late 1990s these shares were exactly reversed. China supplied just over 60 percent of U.S. imports; Hong Kong, South Korea, and Taiwan supplied only 6 percent.

Figure 5-3. *Sources of U.S. Imports of Toys, Games, and Sporting Goods, 1985–99*

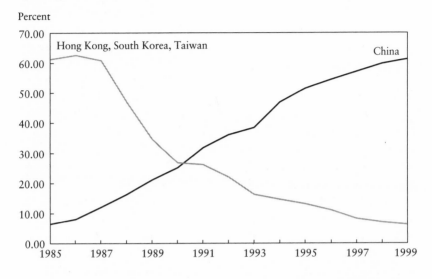

Percent

Sources: See figure 5-2; and U.S. Department of Commerce, International Trade Administration, "U.S. Trade by Commodity with Hong Kong."

The final flaw in the argument that the ever-growing bilateral trade imbalance reflects a fundamentally closed Chinese economy is that exports of U.S. firms to China have grown extremely rapidly since China's reform and opening up began in the late 1970s.[103] Because this growth initially was from a very low base, China did not become a predominant market for most U.S. exporters in the 1980s. U.S. exports to China almost quadrupled between 1990 and 2000. But since the base for the growth in the 1990s was much larger, by 2000 China had become the eighth largest international market for U.S. firms. Moreover from 1990 to 2000 exports of U.S. businesses to China grew more rapidly than to any other large export market.[104] The contrast with Japan is striking. Exports to Japan grew only 20 percent between 1990 and 2000, partly because sales to Japan by U.S. firms reached a peak in absolute terms in 1996 and then fell through 1999. The U.S. deficit with Japan rose in the 1990s in large part because U.S. exports fell for part of the decade; the deficit with China rose despite fast and sustained growth of U.S. exports to China throughout the decade. The main reason for the bilateral deficit with China is the huge buildup of foreign direct investment in labor-intensive export industries in China, which has led to an explosion of U.S. imports from China.

China's accession to the World Trade Organization is not likely to fundamentally change the pattern of bilateral trade between China and the United States. Accession will positively affect the growth of U.S. exports to China. The bilateral deficit with China, however, will expand because of the continuation of the displacement effect that has been evident since the mid-1980s when foreign firms began moving to China in large numbers. Thus, even as the U.S. trade deficit with China continues to expand, bilateral trade between the United States and several other Asian countries likely will be characterized by smaller deficits or growing surpluses. But the global U.S. trade deficit is likely to change little.

The U.S. International Trade Commission estimates that Chinese tariff reductions will raise total U.S. exports to China by $2.7 billion, about 10 percent. But the commission predicts imports from China will rise by $4.4 billion, about 7 percent. Thus the bilateral trade imbalance is increased.[105] Interestingly the commission model suggests that as a result of China's accession U.S. global imports will rise only $1.1 billion, one-quarter of increased imports from China. That is because while imports from China will rise, U.S. imports from other countries will fall by enough to offset most of what otherwise would be a more rapidly rising global trade deficit. The reason is the displacement effect already described—Chinese goods will displace higher-cost alternative suppliers. The commission's model shows that U.S. trade balances with Japan, Korea, Taiwan, Hong Kong, ASEAN, and South Asia will improve. A small increase in global U.S. exports is expected. The commission predicts that the result of China's accession would be to leave the U.S. global trade balance "unaffected."[106]

Overall the expected increase in U.S. global trade is so small that the commission predicts that the effect of China's accession on the growth of the U.S. economy will be imperceptible. The effects of China's accession, however, will be significant for some sectors of the U.S. economy, especially agriculture, where huge increases are expected in U.S. exports of wheat and other grains, oilseeds, and cotton.

The commission's forecasts are based only on the tariff reductions that are part of China's accession agreement and do not consider the reductions in nontariff barriers or the opening up of several sectors previously closed to foreign investment. The commission, however, estimated the effect of removing nontariff barriers for twenty-five products for which these barriers are known to be relatively high. It found that the predicted increases in U.S. global exports were half again as great when these nontariff barriers were eliminated, compared with the scenario in which they remained in place, and only tariff reductions occurred.[107]

Even when lowered trade barriers mean more exports of specific products to China, overstating the benefits to U.S. producers is possible. There seems little doubt, for example, that exports recorded by the U.S. Customs of U.S. citrus to China will grow impressively. Following the conclusion of the bilateral agricultural agreement between China and the United States in the fall of 1999, Sunkist expected to sell $500 million worth of oranges, grapefruit, lemons, and other citrus fruit to China between 2000 and 2004.[108] The firm's sales to Hong Kong, however, are likely to fall considerably. Despite China's virtual ban on imports of U.S. citrus, U.S. oranges and other citrus were widely available from vendors on street corners in major cities in China throughout the 1990s. The source was oranges sold to Hong Kong and Macau and then smuggled into China. The value of oranges smuggled into China from Hong Kong in 1998 was a minimum of $43.5 million and more likely several times that amount. Almost all of the smuggled fruit originated in the United States.[109] Smuggling was even more rampant for cigarettes and 35mm color film. The minimum amount of smuggling in 1998 of these products was $172 million and $129 million, although the shares of smuggled cigarettes and film originating in the United States were much less than for oranges.[110] A similar pattern applied for U.S. meat and poultry. Hong Kong was the fourth largest foreign market for U.S. pork in 1999, according to U.S. trade data. But more than half of the product sold to Hong Kong subsequently made its way to China.[111] The ability of U.S. producers of citrus, cigarettes, color film, poultry, and meat to ship their products directly to China, rather than indirectly through Hong Kong, presumably will eliminate the costs of smuggling. Combined with lower tariffs this change should result in much lower prices for Chinese consumers, and that should increase sales. But U.S. sales of these products to Hong Kong are likely to decline significantly, offsetting some of the gain in direct sales to China.

### U.S. Interests

The United States has a big stake in China's further domestic economic reforms and deepening integration into the global economy. Most obviously accession serves U.S. economic interests. China's commitment to liberalize the terms under which foreign firms can invest in telecommunications, distribution, and financial services creates enormous opportunities since in these areas U.S. firms are very competitive globally. China in the 1990s already was the most rapidly growing large foreign market for U.S. goods and services. China's WTO commitments have increased the access of U.S. firms to this market and increased the prospect that the bilateral trade relationship will remain robust. More liberal access for agricultural products and automobiles could be especially important for the United States. In short China can continue to contribute to the dramatic growth of U.S. trade, which doubled to $2.5 trillion in the eight years ending in 2000. Trade expansion was an important source of the record growth of output and employment in the United States during the 1990s. Equally important, the availability of lower-cost imports allowed this growth to occur with an unusually low rate of price inflation. The United States has and will benefit from the shift of production within Asia, since growing imports of these goods help to hold down prices in the United States.

China's deeper integration into the global economy may make China a more constructive participant in a new round of global trade liberalization. China's leadership already has recognized the economic advantages of globalization. Premier Zhu Rongji at an ASEAN meeting in the fall of 2000 went so far as to suggest the formation of a free trade area between China and the Association of Southeast Asian Nations, something that would have been unthinkable a few years ago.[112] Subsequently China's minister of finance, Xiang Huaicheng, indicated China would also be open to pursuing greater economic integration among the members of ASEAN, Korea, Japan, and China, the grouping referred to as ASEAN plus three.[113]

Deeper integration and the concomitant acceleration of domestic economic reform will make it more likely that China will be able to meet the expectations of its population of 1.3 billion for improved living standards. An economically failing China, by contrast, could impose heavy costs on the United States and the rest of the world.[114]

The implications of rising living standards based on a more market-oriented economy are favorable to U.S. long-term interest in the development of a more pluralistic political system in China. As was true of Taiwan from the 1950s onward, a rapidly modernizing economy is likely to generate gradually growing pressure for political change, away from one-party, authoritarian rule. In Taiwan it took almost four decades of rapid economic growth between the time popular elections for county and city officials were introduced in 1950 and the time martial law was lifted in 1987 and opposition parties were legalized in 1989. Another decade elapsed before the first national popular election for president took place. Although China has been conducting popular elections at the village level for more than a decade, given its still relatively low level of per capita income, at least another decade or two of sustained economic growth probably will be required before a more pluralistic political system emerges.[115]

Finally, China's entry into the World Trade Organization will lead to stronger trade and investment ties between China and Taiwan that may contribute to a gradual reduction of tensions between the two. Given the strong interest of the United States in the peaceful resolution of the Taiwan Strait issue, this is an important potential benefit of China's deepening integration into the global economy. Even before each one became a member of the World Trade Organization, bilateral economic links between China and Taiwan were growing quickly. During the 1990s, as China became a more and more important part of the production chain for many Taiwanese firms, more than two-fifths of all Taiwanese foreign direct investment was in the mainland.[116] And trade ties have burgeoned. By 1999 a quarter of Taiwan's exports went to the mainland, making that market almost as important as the United States.[117]

Membership of China and Taiwan in the World Trade Organization will accelerate these linkages for several reasons. Membership eventually will lead to an end of Taiwan's long-standing ban on direct shipping and air travel between Taiwan and the mainland.[118] Because shipping, civil air, and postal links are not covered in the Uruguay Round Trade Agreement establishing the World Trade Organization, Taiwan does not have to establish such links as a result of its own WTO accession. But the bans, especially on direct shipping, are seen as incompatible with the most basic WTO principle—most-favored-nation status. Since the authorities on Taiwan allow many countries to ship goods and fly civil aircraft directly to and from Taiwan, pressure is growing to extend the same basic privileges to China. These pressures stem not only from Taiwanese companies that are anxious to reduce barriers to business ties with the mainland but also from foreign firms. American multinationals, such as Dell Computer, have criticized the reluctance of the Taiwanese authorities to allow direct trade and transport ties with the mainland.[119] Direct shipping ties will boost trade for the simple reason that they will reduce the cost of transport. When trade between Taiwan and the mainland goes through a third area such as Hong Kong or Japan, it adds to the cost. A Taiwan business group estimated that the transshipment of goods by way of a third country added an extra $1.51 billion to annual transport costs of bilateral trade.[120] These extra costs, which amount to a little more than 5 percent of the value of two-way trade, will disappear with the establishment of direct shipping links.

Taiwan will have to eliminate important nontariff barriers on Chinese goods, notably the ban on the import of 5,691 goods from China, 44 percent of all of the lines in its tariff schedule. The elimination of these bans should help reduce Taiwan's trade surplus with China, which stood at $15.6 billion in 1999.[121]

President Chen Shui-bian faces increasing pressure to ease many restrictions on investment in China that have been in place as part of the "go slow, be patient" policy that Taiwan's then-ruling Nationalist Party adopted in 1996 to discourage direct investment in the mainland. Chen's government had continued the policies of not permitting investments in some sectors, such as notebook computers and chips, and also prohibiting direct investment projects with a value above $50 million. Many Taiwan firms skirted these constraints by investing indirectly, through companies established in the Caribbean or Hong Kong for that purpose. But, because of their high profile, it was difficult for Taiwan firms to avoid the ban on investment projects exceeding $50 million and the ban on investment in infrastructure projects or in critical products such as notebook computers and semiconductors. In August 2001 President Chen endorsed a recommendation from an advisory committee to lift these investment bans.[122]

All of these developments—the opening of direct trade, the elimination of Taiwan's bans on the import of a broad range of Chinese products, and liberalization by the Taiwanese government of restrictions on the outflow of foreign direct investment to China—will contribute to closer bilateral economic relations.

## U.S. Policy

Given U.S. trade and investment interests, the linkage between economic and political change that has been demonstrated in Taiwan, and the potential contribution of growing economic ties between China and Taiwan to the peaceful resolution of the Taiwan Strait issue, what are the implications for U.S. economic policy toward China? U.S. policies that have given rise to the perception in China that the United States seeks to delay or even block China's emergence as a major economic power must be abandoned. That means the United States should drop the economic sanctions that remain in place as a legacy of the Tiananmen crisis of 1989.[123] These include the practice of the U.S. executive director voting against or abstaining on many World Bank loans to China and the withholding of some U.S. Export-Import Bank China-related loans and credit guarantees. For many years the United States has been the only country in the world still imposing such sanctions. U.S. abstention on China loans at the World Bank does not block loans to China, and under a waiver program some loans from the U.S. Export-Import Bank to China have gone forward. Thus these sanctions are largely symbolic. They send an incorrect message, however, that the United States seeks to block the emergence of China as a major economic power. Except for the ban on sales of military equipment, these sanctions should be dropped at the earliest opportunity.

The United States ought not to remain the only advanced industrial country that has no systematic technical assistance program to help the Chinese government develop the capacity to meet its WTO obligations. Australia, Canada, the EU, and many of the individual members of the EU are providing such assistance. It ranges from helping to build administrative capacity by training officials of the Ministry of Foreign Trade, the General Administration of Customs, and other organizations to providing WTO-related legal assistance. The EU-China Legal and Judicial Cooperation Program, for example, is the largest international judicial cooperative effort operating in China.[124] The World Bank, the International Monetary Fund, the Asian Development Bank, and the United Nations Development Program have each launched programs with similar goals. The Ford Foundation and other private U.S. groups have funded some WTO-related legal training programs. But the U.S. Congress has never funded the rule of law program for China that was announced with great fanfare by President Bill Clinton in 1997 at the time of his summit meeting in Washington with President Jiang Zemin. The absence of any official U.S. government program of technical assistance on WTO-related issues feeds the impression in China that the United States is more interested in imposing tough conditions on China's WTO entry than in assisting China's historic economic transformation.

The legislation providing the U.S. president with the authority to extend permanent normal trade relations to China reinforces that view. That bill authorized increased funding so that many U.S. government agencies could hire additional staff to monitor China's compliance with WTO commitments. Funds were appropriated to increase staffing in the departments of Agriculture, Commerce, and State, as well as the Office of the U.S. Trade Representative.

The United States should be extraordinarily judicious in exploiting the three highly protectionist measures that U.S. negotiators insisted China agree to as a condition for WTO membership. As chapter 3 explains, under the transitional product-specific safeguard the United States may impose onerous unilateral restrictions on any Chinese import under conditions that are easier to meet than for any other WTO member. The restrictions can be directed solely against goods from China. Under the normal WTO rules, if the conditions for a safeguard can be met, any restriction must be imposed proportionately on all supplying countries. Using the transitional product-specific safeguard would violate the most fundamental WTO principle of equal treatment for all countries, so the United States should invoke it against China only under the most extraordinary circumstances.

Similarly the United States should make modest use of the special textile safeguard that allows it to impose unilateral restrictions on the import of Chinese textiles and apparel for four years after the current system of quotas is phased out completely at the end of 2004. Beginning in 2005 and through 2008 China will be the only member of the World Trade Organization potentially subject to quota restrictions on its textile and apparel products. Limiting China's ability to expand apparel exports could severely limit its ability to meet its WTO obligations.

Perhaps the single most important external determinant of China's success in meeting the multifaceted challenge of opening its market more extensively will be the reaction of developed market economies, particularly the United States, the EU, and Japan, to increased imports of labor-intensive goods from China. As China opens further, it will face increasing imports and rising domestic unemployment in agriculture and in certain capital-intensive industries, where its products will face drastically increased international competition. The one area in which China has a real opportunity to expand output and exports, and thus employment, is labor-intensive manufacturing.

Textiles and particularly apparel are the sectors with the greatest potential to generate jobs to offset job losses elsewhere in the economy. The two industries are the most important. In 1998 their combined employment was more than 5 million and accounted for more than 10 percent of employment in manufacturing. They accounted for almost 10 percent of industrial output, more than half of which was exported, in turn accounting for more than a fifth of all Chinese exports.[125] These two sectors have benefited from substantial foreign involvement. As early as 1994, 30 percent of all textile and apparel product exports were processed, a form of exporting that invariably involves foreign-invested plants in China or processing contracts between domestic and foreign firms.[126]

Most studies, which chapter 4 reviews, forecast that China's textile and apparel exports could grow dramatically as the restrictive Agreement on Textiles and Clothing is phased out and eliminated at the end of 2004. This expansion would greatly affect employment, especially in apparel, which is more labor intensive and has the potential for the fastest export growth. The Development Research Center projects that employment in the apparel and textile industries could be 28 percent and 8 percent higher, respectively, by 2010 as a result of China's entry into the World Trade Organization, creating 5.4 million new jobs.[127] No other sector offers nearly as much potential for employment growth. In part this is because Chinese exports of other labor-intensive manufactures have been subject to many fewer restrictions in developed market economies, and they have grown much more rapidly during the past two decades. And because of the initially high absolute level of employment in textiles and apparel, no other sector has the potential to offer as many new jobs. Even after the cutbacks in the textile industry described in chapter 1, the textile and apparel industries combined employed almost twice as many workers as any other manufacturing industry.

These projections, however, are driven by market economy assumptions, notably that trade is determined by comparative advantage. If the United States or other major advanced industrial countries invoke the textile and apparel safeguard discussed in chapter 3 or block expanded exports of these goods by invoking the provisions of the transitional product-specific safeguard, the large increases forecast in output, exports, and employment in the textile and apparel industries in China will not materialize. If either safeguard is widely invoked against these goods, China might gain some modest additional share of the world apparel market but far less than would prevail in an open trading environment. That would exacerbate the challenge China faces in generating new jobs for workers displaced in sectors subject to increased international competition.

Similarly Chinese farmers are likely to accelerate the shift already under way toward producing labor-intensive fruit and vegetable crops. In the late 1990s farmers in Shandong and Hebei provinces in north China began to abandon traditional grain crops in favor of specialty vegetables and other agricultural products grown for the Japanese market. Japanese firms sell the seeds, and Chinese farmers use special techniques, for example, using natural rather than chemical fertilizers, to meet the demands of Japanese consumers. Chinese exports to Japan of vegetables and other specialized crops began to grow extremely rapidly. By 2000 China supplied 40 percent of Japan's imports of fresh vegetables.[128] But in response to pressure from farmers, the Japanese government in April 2001 imposed punitive tariffs on imports of shiitake mushrooms, green onions, and rushes used to make tatami mats. Chinese exports of these products that exceed specific amounts became subject to tariffs between 106 percent and 266 percent, rather than the 3 to 6 percent tariffs that had prevailed. If protectionist measures like this one are expanded in Japan and adopted by other developed countries, the process of adjustment in Chinese agriculture will be much more difficult.

If the textile and transitional product-specific safeguards are not invoked or are used with restraint, U.S. textile and apparel imports from China will rise significantly. The U.S. International Trade Commission estimates that as a result of the quotas on imports the prices of Chinese textiles and apparel in the U.S. market in 1996 were 11 and 37 percent, respectively, higher than they would have been in a quota-free environment.[129] These differentials are much higher for Chinese products than for textile and apparel from other U.S. trading partners, many of whom also face restrictions in the U.S. market. Because the acceleration of quota growth for China that began on its WTO entry is based on the extremely low base of only 1 percent annual growth, the commission believes that the price effect of the quotas will still be far reaching when the quotas are completely phased out at the end of 2004. Thus the commission estimates that prices of Chinese textiles, and particularly Chinese apparel, will fall sharply after 2004. As a result China's predicted share of the U.S. apparel market rises sharply, from about 10 percent in 2004 to more than 30 percent in 2006. The rise in its share of the U.S. textile market is much more modest, about 1 or 2 percentage points from a base of about 10 percent.[130]

China's greater share of the U.S. import market will come largely at the expense of the textile and apparel industries in third countries. The commission predicts that the combined world market share of apparel producers in Hong Kong, Taiwan, and South Korea will fall by 2 or 3 percentage points, and other suppliers whose apparel exports historically have been restricted will fall by a similar amount. Countries that are not subject to quotas are predicted to lose market share in the United States.

Table 5-2. *Effect of China's WTO Entry on the U.S. Textile and Apparel Industries*
Percent

| Item | Effect on textile industry | Effect on apparel industry |
|---|---|---|
| Production | −0.8 | −3.2 |
| Imports | 2.1 | 7.9 |
| Exports | −2.6 | −7.8 |
| Employment | −1.6 | −4.2 |

Source: Development Research Center, State Council of the People's Republic of China, *The Global and Domestic Impact of China Joining the World Trade Organization* (Washington: Washington Center for China Studies, 1998), pp. 57–59.

Although it is not identified separately in the commission's study, Mexico will probably be one of the largest losers of market share among the latter group. Based on the improved access firms in Mexico had to the U.S. market under the North American Free Trade Agreement starting in 1994, Mexico increased its share of the U.S. apparel market, partly at the expense of China, which lost market share.[131] By 2000 Mexican exports of apparel to the United States were two-fifths more than those of China.[132] As China's apparel quotas in the U.S. market are increased and then eliminated, Mexico probably will lose market share to apparel producers in China.[133]

The increases in U.S. imports from China that are at the expense of third countries obviously have no implications for employment in the U.S. textile and apparel industry. Unfortunately the commission's study does not predict the effect of the phaseout of quotas on the share of total consumption of textiles and apparel in the U.S. domestic market that is supplied by imports. Thus it cannot be used to address what will happen to U.S. employment in the textile and apparel industry when the quotas are phased out entirely in 2004. The study of the Development Research Center does provide an answer to this question. Its forecast for the effect of China's entry into the World Trade Organization on production, imports, exports, and employment in the United States is shown in table 5-2.

China's entry is anticipated to reduce U.S. production of textiles and apparel, compared with a scenario in which China is not a member. Imports of both products are anticipated to be higher, almost 8 percentage points higher for apparel. The U.S. textile and apparel industries lose in competition in third country markets, reducing U.S. exports of textiles and apparel by about 3 and 8 percent, respectively. As a consequence, employment is forecast to be lower in both industries than if China did not enter the World Trade Organization.

A closer examination suggests the predicted effects on U.S. employment will be modest. Apparel is the most sensitive sector since it is the most labor intensive. In the baseline scenario, without China's accession, the forecast is that employment in the U.S. apparel industry will continue its long-term decline, from about 825,000 in 1995 to about 630,000 in 2010. With accession the decline is slightly faster, with employment falling to about 600,000. In the baseline scenario employment falls about 24 percent, with accession about 27 percent. The entry minus 4.2 in table 5-2 indicates that with accession employment in the U.S. apparel industry in 2010 is expected to be 4.2 percentage points below where it would otherwise be. That translates into a loss of fewer than 30,000 U.S. jobs over a fifteen-year period. Extra job losses for the EU are under 30,000; those in Japan about 16,000.[134]

By two standards the estimated job losses in the United States are negligible. First for most of the 1990s the U.S. economy generated about 3 million new jobs annually, about 1,500 times the number of jobs estimated to be lost over many years in the apparel industry as a result of increased imports of Chinese clothing.

Second, employment in textiles and apparel has been plummeting as Mexico's exports to the United States have soared under the North American Free Trade Agreement. By July 2001 employment in apparel production had fallen by 400,000 compared with December 1993, immediately before NAFTA took effect.[135] The average annual reduction in employment in the apparel industry in the United States from the beginning of NAFTA through July 2001 was 53,000 employees. That is more than five times the annual job losses in the three years before NAFTA. The predicted cumulative loss of 30,000 jobs as a result of increased apparel imports from China over fifteen years pales in comparison. In short U.S. imports of apparel from China may surge as quotas are removed, but it is likely that much of this would reflect a displacement of Mexican apparel and would have an extremely modest adverse effect on employment compared with the precipitous decline evident since 1994.

The third protectionist provision included in China's terms of accession that should not be invoked except under the most extreme conditions is the nonmarket economy methodology in antidumping cases. The legal rationale for the special procedure is article 2.7 of the WTO Antidumping Agreement.[136] It refers to a supplementary provision to article 6 of GATT that states that "in the case of imports from a country which has a complete or substantially complete monopoly of its trade and where all domestic prices are fixed by the State, special difficulties may exist in determining price comparability." In such cases the importing country "may find it necessary to take into account the possibility that a strict comparison with domestic prices in such a country may not always be appropriate."[137]

China fit these parameters in the 1980s, but it no longer does. Chapter 1 presents evidence, especially in table 1-3, showing that the market, not the state, determines almost all domestic prices. Similarly chapter 2, including table 2-3, shows that the importance of state trading companies greatly diminished from the mid-1980s onward and that the Chinese government no longer can be accurately characterized as having a complete or substantially complete monopoly of the country's foreign trade.

The persistent and universal use by the United States of the nonmarket economy methodology in Chinese antidumping cases is anomalous. The EU, recognizing that China's economy had "fundamentally altered" leading "to the emergence of firms for which market-economy conditions prevail," since 1999 has determined whether or not to use the nonmarket economy methodology on a case-by-case basis.[138] When a Chinese exporting firm is able to demonstrate that it operates in a market environment, the EU antidumping investigation is based on Chinese prices rather than those of a surrogate country.[139] The Australian government has moved in this direction too. Since the use of the methodology invariably leads to higher antidumping margins, its use in all antidumping cases in the United States can be viewed as a protectionist practice.

Avoiding the use of the transitional product-specific and textile safeguards and using the nonmarket economy methodology in antidumping investigations only when the relevant firm cannot demonstrate that it operates in a market environment is important for the future of the international trading system. The safeguards should not be invoked under conditions that could be perceived as a response to pressures from adversely affected U.S. industries, unless it can be shown that increased imports are the source of serious injury. Neither should the United States continue to make widespread use of the nonmarket economy methodology in antidumping cases against Chinese firms. That would almost certainly undermine support for the WTO in China and perhaps even among other developing countries that are WTO members. That would reduce the prospects for the timely and successful conclusion of the new round of multilateral trade negotiations.

## Conclusion

Entry into the World Trade Organization is a seminal event in China's economic history and the history of the world trading system. It shows the commitment of China's leadership to accelerate domestic economic reform, pushing China more rapidly toward a market economy. Even before China's accession, the broad strategy was taking hold in some critical sectors. In telecommunications the government had made impressive progress in injecting competition into a traditionally insular and protected sector. The operating arm of China Telecom had been formally hived off from the regulator and broken into three independent telecommunications companies. The state created several new domestic telecommunications competitors. The state created China Netcom Corp. in 1999 to compete by providing Internet telephony, high-speed data network services, and other telecommunications services on its 8,490-kilometer fiber-optic backbone. Similarly in the fall of 2000 the state created China Railway Telecommunications Company (Railcom) to compete in basic telecommunications services, such as local and domestic long-distance service, satellite communication, data transmission, and Internet services. Since Railcom took over the communications system of the Ministry of Railroads, it began operations in 2001 with the country's second largest fixed-line network, including more than 40,000 kilometers of fiber-optic lines. Thus it should be able to provide serious competition to China Telecom, the successor to the traditional monopolist provider. State Power, China's largest power company, has applied for a telecoms license to offer local, long-distance, and mobile phone service. Like the Ministry of Railroads, State Power has its own telecoms system linking its grids and distribution networks, which could be used to develop a system to provide basic telecoms services.

Besides creating new competitors, the state changed the regulatory environment. The government created China Unicom in 1994 in an early attempt to inject competition into the wireless sector. But the would-be competitor was unable to achieve a market share of more than a few percentage points in the first five years of its existence because the traditional monopolist was unwilling to provide interconnection services to its subscribers. New regulations promulgated in late 1999 required China Telecom to provide interconnection services to allow it to compete more effectively with China Mobile, the wireless business carved out of the old structure. By January 2001 Unicom had captured a fifth of the cellular phone market, a dramatic increase in market share.[140]

The state facilitated the expansion of the new telecommunications firms by allowing them to sell equity stakes to foreign investors and enter strategic alliances with foreign telecommunications companies, even in advance of the schedule outlined in China's WTO commitments. China Netcom, for example, sold an important ownership stake to foreign investors and is expected to form a strategic alliance with a foreign telecommunications company that could help it expand its array of data networking services. Vodafone, the world's largest cellular operator, in 2000 took a small strategic stake in China Mobile (Hong Kong), with the expressed interest of increasing its participation over time.[141] The following year the two firms agreed to joint research and development projects to introduce global products and services in the mobile sector.[142] In 2000 AT&T became the first foreign firm to invest in a company providing Internet services in China. All of these moves were justified in China, at least in part, as necessary to create a more competitive and efficient domestic industry in advance of opening up the sector to foreign direct investment in telecommunications operating companies.

China's leadership used the WTO agreement to accelerate the pace of change in agriculture too. They recognize that China does not have a comparative advantage in land-intensive grain production.[143] They seem to have rejected Japan's approach of walling off its grain sector and then raising the prices of rice and wheat by amounts sufficient to stimulate domestic production enough to meet practically all consumption needs. They recognize that China's best prospect for sustaining the growth of farm incomes is not through ever-growing subsidies of inefficient production but through letting market incentives push farmers into growing less land-intensive agricultural crops or out of agriculture altogether.

That was a difficult policy choice since it meant lowering the relative price of basic grains even in advance of entering the WTO, reducing farm incomes in the transition. Thus China fought hard to keep the option of raising subsidies to agriculture above the limit imposed by the World Trade Organization on developed countries.[144] But China probably would not exercise this option on a sustained basis since the leadership believes that more market-driven pricing offers the best long-run prospect for efficiency of resource use and rising incomes. Similarly China's willingness to eliminate agricultural export subsidies on entry signals an important commitment to allow the market mechanism to work relatively unfettered in the domestic agricultural market. Terminating these subsidies also eliminates an important distortion of world trade in farm products.

China's entry is unique for the world trading system. The country seems almost certain in the next few years to overtake Canada, France, and the United Kingdom to become the fourth largest trading country in the world. Within a decade China's trade is likely to surpass that of Japan and Germany, making China the world's second largest trader. China's rising trade reflects its emergence as perhaps the world's preeminent manufacturer of labor-intensive goods. China's export-oriented manufacturing is not limited to toys, footwear, and apparel but encompasses information technology hardware, electronics, and consumer durables.

China's emergence as a global economic power poses a significant competitive challenge for other Asian countries that also export to third-country markets such as Japan, Europe, and the United States. China's strong investment linkages with Hong Kong, Taiwan, and, to a lesser extent, South Korea and Japan, suggest these countries can continue to benefit from China's growing economic role. Their domestic industries can thrive by producing products requiring higher levels of skill than China currently provides. Toshiba is a good example. As it eliminates production of conventional television sets in its Fukaya plant the factory's work force will shift to making higher-value products, such as projectors for liquid-crystal display televisions. Countries in Southeast Asia, some of which are dependent on the export market for their electronics products, may have a more difficult time adjusting.

Perhaps the main challenge will be to maintain open markets in advanced industrial countries. Japan's imposition in April 2001 of temporary duties as high as 266 percent on imports of Chinese leeks, shiitake mushrooms, and reeds used to make tatami mats is one inauspicious example. China's prospects of adjusting to more imports from the West will be dim if developed market economies impose restrictions on products for which they are unlikely to have a comparative advantage.

# Notes

## Notes to Chapter 1

1. The partners in the venture were a coal subsidiary of Occidental Petroleum, the China International Trust and Investment Corporation, and the China National Coal Development Corporation.

2. Kenneth Lieberthal and Michel Oksenberg, *Policy Making in China: Leaders, Structures, and Processes* (Princeton University Press, 1988), p. 365.

3. In the end the Chinese side purchased Occidental's share of the venture on quite favorable terms, allowing the company to recover a significant part of the $250 million it had written off. Dow Jones & Company, "Occidental Petroleum Sells Its 25% Interest in Chinese Coal Mine," *Wall Street Journal*, July 2, 1991, p. C8.

4. State Statistical Bureau, *Statistical Yearbook of China 1995* (Beijing: Statistical Publishing House, 1995), p. 542; *Statistical Yearbook of China 1997*, p. 593; and National Bureau of Statistics, *China Statistical Yearbook 1999* (Beijing: China Statistics Press, 1999), p. 582.

5. Mark Landler, "Selling Status, and Cell Phones," *New York Times*, November 24, 2000, pp. C1–C2.

6. Coca-Cola, Sprite, and Fanta, the leading Coke brands, had a combined 60.4 percent market share in 2000. The leading domestic brand, Jian Li Bao, had a market share of only 3.6 percent. Shen Gang, "Coke Secures Crown as Nation's Favourite Soda," *China Daily Business Weekly*, March 6, 2001, p. 20.

7. Jason Dean, "Coke Expects China Sales to Keep Soaring," Dow Jones Newswires, November 15, 2000 (http://interactive.wsj.com [November 15, 2000]).

8. "Starbucks in China," *Economist*, October 6, 2001, p. 62.

9. In 1999 Volkswagen sold 336,000 cars in China. Total market passenger car sales were 600,000, giving Volkswagen a 54 percent market share. Agence France-Presse, "WTO Hope Inspires Investment Surge," *South China Morning Post*, February 8, 2001 (http://china.scmp.com [February 7, 2001]); and David Murphy, "Chinese Car Makers Focus on Individual Buyers," Dow Jones Newswires, February 14, 2001 (http://interactive.wsj.com [February 15, 2001]).

10. James Kynge, "Carrefour May Get Off Lightly in China," *Financial Times*, July 24, 2001, p. 22.

11. "The Kodak Moment," *Business China*, vol. 26 (November 6, 2000), pp. 3–4; and Jia Hepeng, "Fears of Foreign Monopoly," *China Daily Business Weekly*, June 5–11, 2001, p. 9.

12. Approval of China's entry occurred on November 10, 2001, at the WTO Ministerial Conference in Doha, Qatar. The following day China formally signed the accord on entry and presented President Jiang Zemin's signature ratifying the terms of entry. The Standing Committee of China's National People's Congress in August 2000 had delegated to Jiang the authority to ratify the agreement. At this writing it appears that following the customary thirty-day waiting period China's formal WTO accession will be on December 11, 2001.

13. China's commitments are outlined in the Protocol of Accession of China and the Report of the Working Party on the Accession of China. The protocol includes nine annexes as well as China's schedule of tariff and services commitments. All of these are legally binding.

14. Jason Dean, "China Mobile Phone Users Doubled in '00 to 85 mln," Dow Jones Newswires, February 7, 2001 (http://interactive.wsj.com [February 8, 2001]); and Bloomberg News, "China Overtakes the U.S. as No. 1 Cell Phone Market," International Herald Tribune, August 15, 2001, p. 9.

15. John Thornhill, "Poor Showing Undervalues Region's Weight," Financial Times Supplement, FT 500: The World's Largest Companies, May 11, 2001, p. 53.

16. Dan Roberts, "A Dragon with Plenty of Good Connections," Financial Times Survey, FT Telecoms, September 20, 2000, pp. I, III; and James Kynge, "Many Obstacles Still Stacked against Foreign Operators," Financial Times Survey, FT Telecoms, September 20, 2000, p. III.

17. According to the EU account, the bilateral agreement, which was reached in June 2000, specified that five new licenses for life insurance and two for nonlife business "will be immediately provided to EU companies." "The Sino-EU Agreement on China's Accession to the WTO: Results of the Bilateral Negotiations" (www.europe.eu.int/comm/trade/bilateral/China/res.pdf [June 13, 2000]).

18. One was to be awarded before China's WTO entry, two after, according to Swiss Economics Minister Pascal Couchepin. "Swiss Insur/WTO: Cut in Watch Tariff to 12% from 25%," Dow Jones Newswires, September 26, 2000 (http://interactive.wsj.com [September 27, 2000]).

19. The link-ups were as follows: JP Morgan Fleming Asset Management with Huaan Fund Management based in Shanghai, Schroders with Huaxia Fund Management based in Beijing, and Invesco with Penghua Fund Management based in Shenzhen.

20. "Remarks by the President to the Business Council," February 24, 2000 (www.chinapntr.gov [September 21, 2000]).

21. Charlene Barshefsky, "China's WTO Accession: American Interests, Values and Strategy," Hearings before the House Committee on Ways and Means, 106 Cong. 2 sess. February 16, 2000 (www.fnsg.com).

22. "Beware Chinese Promises," Washington Post, October 16, 2000, p. A26.

23. "Statement of the International Brotherhood of Teamsters," Hearings before the House Committee on Ways and Means on the U.S.-China Bilateral Trade Agreement and China's Accession to the WTO, February 16, 2000.

24. National Bureau of Statistics, China Statistical Abstract 2001 (Beijing: China Statistics Press, 2001), p. 150.

25. China accounted for 0.6 percent of world trade in 1977 and 3.7 percent in 2000. Nicholas R. Lardy, China in the World Economy (Washington: Institute for

International Economics, 1994), p. 2; and World Trade Organization, *Annual Report 2001* (Geneva, 2001), pp. 12, 14. The WTO reports rankings separately for imports and exports. The rank of seventh is based on the combined volume of exports and imports.

26. A significant but unknown fraction of this foreign direct investment was Chinese in origin. To take advantage of tax and certain other preferences available to foreign-invested firms, Chinese companies and individuals moved funds illegally to Hong Kong and other locations and then brought them back into China as "foreign" capital. It is likely that the share of foreign direct investment accounted for by funds of this type has fallen over time as the government has reduced the number of preferences for foreign-invested companies.

27. World Bank, *World Development Report 1999/2000: Entering the 21st Century* (Washington, 1999), p. 38.

28. World Bank, *China Engaged: Integration with the Global Economy* (Washington, 1997), p. 26.

29. PetroChina is China's largest oil producer. Sinopec (China Petroleum and Chemical Corporation) is China's second largest oil company and its largest petroleum refiner and petrochemical producer. China Mobile (Hong Kong) is the largest mobile phone operator in China. Before May 14, 2000, China Mobile (Hong Kong) was named China Telecom (Hong Kong). The change in the name followed the legal restructuring of the parent, China Telecom, discussed in chapter 3, note 11. Joe Leahy and Richard McGregor, "Sinopec Joins List of Giant Chinese Privatisations," *Financial Times*, October 19, 2000, p. 20; and Rahul Jacob, "Giving Wings to the Tiger," *Financial Times Survey, China*, November 13, 2000, p. IV.

30. Susan L. Shirk, *How China Opened Its Door: The Political Success of the PRC's Foreign Trade and Investment Reforms* (Brookings, 1994); and Barry Naughton, "China's Trade Regime at the End of the 1990s: Achievements, Limitations, and Impact on the United States," in Ted Galen Carpenter and James A. Dorn, eds., *China's Future: Constructive Partner or Emerging Threat?* (Washington: Cato Institute, 2000), pp. 235–60.

31. Foreign-invested firms include wholly foreign-owned firms, equity joint ventures, and contractual joint ventures.

32. As chapter 2 explains, processed exports, including those produced by foreign-invested enterprises, grew from 27 percent of total exports in 1988 to 57 percent in the late 1990s (table 2-2). Value-added by foreign manufacturing firms (including those from Hong Kong, Macau, and Taiwan) in 2000 was RMB 533.3 billion of total manufacturing value-added of RMB 3,957 billion. National Bureau of Statistics, "Statistical Communiqué of the People's Republic of China on the 2000 National Economic and Social Development," February 28, 2001 (www.stats.gov.cn/english/gb/gb2000e.htm [August 26, 2001]).

33. Barry Naughton, "China's Emergence and Prospects as a Trading Nation," *Brookings Papers on Economic Activity*, no. 2, 1996, pp. 273–337.

34. China was the world's fifth largest exporter in 1999 if the European Union is considered as a single entity. World Trade Organization, *Annual Report 2000* (Geneva, 2000), pp. 20–21.

35. Naughton, "China's Trade Regime at the End of the 1990s," pp. 236, 242, 248.

36. Greg Mastel, The *Rise of the Chinese Economy: The Middle Kingdom Emerges* (Westview Press, 1997), pp. 125–37.

37. The only limitation is that if the imported good is subject to a quantitative restriction the importer has to have an import license or quota allocation before purchasing the foreign exchange.

38. Profit remission abroad, however, requires a prior vote by the board of directors of the firm to pay a dividend.

39. Beginning in 2001 the government allowed Chinese citizens to purchase foreign-currency denominated shares sold on China's B share market. Before that only foreigners could purchase B shares legally. But Chinese were only allowed to use foreign currency funds already deposited in their name in domestic banks to purchase such shares. They could not legally convert domestic currency into foreign exchange to finance purchases of B shares.

40. For a superb account of China's early approach to the General Agreement on Tariffs and Trade see Harold K. Jacobson and Michel Oksenberg, *China's Participation in the IMF, the World Bank, and GATT* (University of Michigan Press, 1990), chap. 4, pp. 83–105.

41. Between 1995 and 2000 ordinary imports, those unrelated to processing or foreign invested firms, grew 130 percent (18.2 percent per year) from $43.37 billion to $100.08 billion. The sum of processing imports (including inward processing or assembly, processing with imported materials, and imported equipment supplied by foreign firms to Chinese firms engaged in processing contracts and the imports of capital goods by foreign-funded firms, however, rose only 37 percent (6.5 percent per year) from $78.33 billion to $107.32 billion (see chapter 2, note 75, for definitions); and General Administration of Customs, *China's Customs Statistics*, no. 76 (December 1995), p. 13; and *China Customs Statistics*, no. 136 (December 2001), p. 15. In the first seven months of 2001, when total imports grew by 13.0 percent, ordinary imports grew by 22.6 percent compared with the same period in 2001 while processing imports (not including capital goods imported by foreign-invested firms or equipment provided to foreign firms for processing contracts) grew by only 1.3 percent. Tao Qiu, "Stable Increase in Foreign Trade Imports and Exports in the First Seven Months of the Year," *Guoji shangbao* (International Business Daily), August 14, 2001, p. 1.

42. National Bureau of Statistics, *China Statistical Yearbook 2000* (Beijing: China Statistics Press, 2000), p. 407; and "Globalization, Foreign Friends," *Economist*, January 8, 2000, p. 71.

43. Based on the data in table 2-2, domestic value-added in export processing in the late 1990s was 35 percent, up substantially from as recently as 1993 and 1994 when the domestic value-added share of processed exports was under 20 percent.

44. Thomas G. Rawski, "China's Move to Market: How Far? What Next?" in Ted Galen Carpenter and James A. Dorn, eds., *China's Future: Constructive Partner or Emerging Threat?* (Cato Institute, 2000), pp. 317–39.

45. Ibid., pp. 331–32.

46. "China to Crack Down on False Statistics," ChinaOnline, March 13, 2001 (www.chinaonline.com/topstories/000313/2/C00030906.asp [March 14, 2000]).

47. National Bureau of Statistics, *China Statistical Yearbook 1999*, pp. 67–68; and *China Statistical Abstract 2000* (Beijing: China Statistics Press, 2000), pp. 25–26.

48. Census Bureau, *Statistical Abstract of the United States 1998* (U.S. Department of Commerce, 1998), p. 451; and *Survey of Current Business*, vol. 80 (May 2000), National Data p. D-3.

49. Zhu Rongji, "China Releases Premier Zhu Rongji's Key-Note Work Report for the Whole Year," *China Daily*, March 16, 2000. (www.Chinadaily. com.cn.net/cover/storydb2000/03/16/mnzrjrep.html [March 16, 2000]).

50. National Bureau of Statistics, *China Statistical Yearbook 1999*, p. 67; and World Bank, *World Development Report 1999/2000: Entering the 21st Century*, p. 255.

51. Alwyn Young, "Gold into Base Metals: Productivity Growth in the People's Republic of China during the Reform Period," National Bureau of Economic Research Working Paper 7856, August 2000 (http://papers.nber.org/papers/ w7856.pdf [August 2001]).

52. Nicholas R. Lardy, *China's Unfinished Economic Revolution* (Brookings, 1998), pp. 31–33.

53. Ibid., p. 40.

54. Census Bureau, *Statistical Abstract of the United States 1996* (U.S. Department of Commerce, 1996), pp. 742, 744; *Statistical Abstract of the United States 1998*, p. 751; *Quarterly Financial Report of Manufacturing, Mining and Retailing Enterprises*, 1998, fourth quarter, p. 2; Bureau of Economic Analysis, "Fixed Reproducible Tangible Wealth," *Survey of Current Business*, vol. 78 (September 1998), p. 40, and "Fixed Reproducible Tangible Wealth," *Survey of Current Business*, vol. 80 (September 2000), p. 24.

55. National Bureau of Statistics, *China Statistical Yearbook 1999*, p. 421.

56. These calculations on the share of output, fixed assets, and working capital all are based on data in which the value of state-controlled shareholding companies is included in the scope of state owned.

57. Lardy, *China's Unfinished Economic Revolution*; and Pieter Bottelier, "WTO and the Reform of China's State Banks" (Washington: Center for Strategic and International Studies, June 2000).

58. Nicholas R. Lardy, "China and the Asian Contagion," *Foreign Affairs*, vol. 77 (July–August 1998), pp. 78–88.

59. "Financial Indicators: Cross-Border Investment," *Economist*, February 12, 2000, p. 105.

60. Bank for International Settlements, *Joint BIS-IMF-OECD-World Bank Statistics on External Debt* (www.bis.org/wnew.htm [June 21, 2000]).

61. These loans are not included in the data of the Bank for International Settlements on foreign bank claims on China. The data cited may understate the decline in lending in Hong Kong to Chinese related nonbanks. Such lending may have shrunk before September 1998, the first date for which data are available. Hong Kong Monetary Authority, "The Hong Kong Banking Sector's Exposure to ITICs (excluding GITIC) and Their Subsidiaries," press release, October 19, 1998 (www.info.gov.hk/hkma/eng/press [September 25, 2000]); and "Hong Kong Bank-

ing Sector's Exposure to Non-Bank Chinese Entities," press release, March 21, 2000 (www.info.gov.hk/hkma/eng/press [September 25, 2000]).

62. State Statistical Bureau, *Statistical Yearbook of China 1995*, pp. 578–79; *Statistical Yearbook of China 1997*, pp. 627–28; *Statistical Yearbook of China 1998* (Beijing: China Statistical Publishing House, 1998), pp. 92–93; and National Bureau of Statistics, *Statistical Yearbook of China 1999*, p. 100.

63. In August 1998 the Fourth Session of the Ninth National People's Congress Standing Committee approved the flotation of an additional RMB 100 billion in state bonds and an additional RMB 100 billion in state bank lending to increase investment, primarily in infrastructure.

64. World Bank, *China: Weathering the Storm and Learning the Lessons* (Washington, 1999), p. 18.

65. People's Bank of China and Ministry of Foreign Trade and Economic Cooperation, "Guidelines on Credit for Supporting Exports with Foreign Inputs," and People's Bank of China, State Development Planning Commission, Ministry of Finance, and Ministry of Foreign Trade and Economic Cooperation, "Provisional Regulations on Lending to Foreign Trading Enterprises through Special Administered Accounts," both cited in People's Bank of China, *China Financial Outlook 2000* (Beijing, 2000), pp. 14–15.

66. These are the losses of state-owned industrial companies that practice independent financial accounting. Lardy, *China's Unfinished Economic Revolution*, p. 35; and State Statistical Bureau, *China Statistical Yearbook 1998*, p. H61.

67. "Memorandum on the People-Run Economy," *Guoji shangbao* (International Business Daily), December 8, 2000, p. 8.

68. "PRC Private Enterprises Call for Protection," Xinhua, April 11, 2000, in Foreign Broadcast Information Service, *Daily Report: China* (hereafter FBIS-CHI) 2000-0411 (http://wnc.fedworld.gov); and Ramoncito de la Cruz, "Thriving Private Economy Overcoming Hurdles," Dow Jones Newswires, November 19, 2000 (http://interactive.wsj.com [November 20, 2000]).

69. Joseph Fewsmith, "China and the WTO: The Politics behind the Agreement," in *South Korea, China, and the Global Economy*, NBR Analysis, vol. 10, no. 5 (Seattle, Washington: National Bureau of Asian Research, December 1999), p. 29. Fewsmith believes the critical leadership decision to make the concessions paving the way for China's accession was made in early February 1999, after the receipt of three letters (dated November 6, 1998; February 8, 1999, and February 12, 1999) from President Bill Clinton expressing the hope that the WTO negotiations could be concluded during Premier Zhu Rongji's trip to the United States in the spring. The Chinese leadership appears to have made its basic decision before the visit by Federal Reserve Chairman Alan Greenspan, who arrived in Beijing on January 12, 1999. Premier Zhu Rongji reportedly told Greenspan that China was ready to make huge openings in telecommunications, banking, insurance, and agriculture in return for getting China into the World Trade Organization. David Sanger, "How U.S. and China Failed to Close Trade Deal," *New York Times*, April 10, 1999 (http://proquest.umi.com [February 16, 2001]). Similarly Yang Wang says the decision of China's top leadership to intervene and direct the WTO negotiations was taken in the "beginning

of 1999." Yang Wang, "China's Accession to the WTO: An Institutional Analysis," unpublished manuscript, June 22, 1999.

70. "China Won't Accept 'High Demands' in WTO Entry-Trade Min," Dow Jones Newswires, December 17, 1998 (http://interactive.wsj.com [December 17, 1998]).

71. Edward S. Steinfeld, "Beyond the Transition: China's Economy at Century's End," *Current History*, vol. 98 (September 1999), pp. 271–75.

72. James Kynge and Guy de Jonquieres, "China to Make Determined Effort for Entry into WTO," *Financial Times*, February 15, 1999, p. 3.

73. The White House, Office of the Press Secretary, "Joint Press Conference of the President and Premier Zhu Rongji of the People's Republic of China," April 8, 1999.

74. For a general analysis of the attitudes of the leadership on globalization see Thomas G. Moore, "China and Globalization," *Asian Perspective*, vol. 23, no. 4 (1999), pp. 65–95.

75. Long Yongtu, "Join the World Trade Organization; Fuse into the International Community Mainstream," *Guoji maoyi wenti* (Issues in International Trade), September 1999, pp. 1–10, in FBIS-CHI-1999-0929; and Gan Yuanzhi and Ye Fazhi, "Certain Issues about China's WTO Accession—Long Yongtu Speaks Frankly about the Thorny Issues," Ta Kung Pao, March 23, 2001, in FBIS-CHI-2001-0323.

76. Barry Naughton, "The Global Electronics Revolution and China's Technology Policy," in *Intellectual Property Rights in China: Evolving Business and Legal Frameworks*, NBR Analysis, vol. 10 (April 1999), p. 17.

77. Tariffs on ITA products will be phased out according to a schedule, depending on the MFN tariff rate prevailing in 1998. If the MFN rate exceeded 20 percent, the tariff must be eliminated by January 1, 2005; if it exceeded 15 percent but was less than or equal to 20 percent, the tariff must be eliminated by January 1, 2004; if it exceeded 10 percent but was less than or equal to 15 percent, the tariff must be eliminated by January 1, 2003; if it exceeded 5 percent but was less than or equal to 10 percent, it must be eliminated by January 1, 2002; if it exceeded 2 percent but was less than or equal to 5 percent, the tariff must be eliminated by January 2001; if the tariff was less than or equal to 2 percent, it must be eliminated by January 2000. "Agreement on Market Access between the People's Republic of China and the United States of America," November 15, 1999. Since the timing of these commitments did not slide as China's WTO entry was delayed, all ITA products with a tariff less than or equal to 5 percent had to be eliminated when China acceded to the WTO in December 2001. As chapter 3 notes, some of these cuts were made voluntarily in January 2000 and January 2001.

78. Long Yongtu, "PRC Trade Official Long Yongtu on China, Economic Globalization, WTO Entry," *People's Daily*, July 10, 2000 (www.peopledaily.com.cn [August 1, 2000]).

79. Author's estimate of unweighted average tariff is 9.7 percent. This estimate is based on an average rate of 8.9 percent for industrial goods and 15 percent for agricultural products. Agricultural products account for about 900 of the 7,100 lines in China's tariff schedule. World Trade Organization, "WTO Successfully

Concludes Negotiations on China's Entry," press release, September 17, 2001 (www.wto.org/english/news_e/pres01/pr243_e.htm [September 17, 2001]). General Accounting Office, *World Trade Organization: Status of China's Trade Commitments to the United States and Other Members* (May 2000), p. 17. The GAO estimated that the overall tariff average was 10.2 percent, but this only took into account China's bilateral tariff negotiations with the United States. Other countries, notably the EU, subsequently negotiated for lower tariffs on their priority products.

80. Zhang Shuguang, Zhang Yansheng, and Wan Zhongxin, *Measuring the Cost of Protection in China* (Washington: Institute for International Economics, 1998), p. 29.

81. For example, the study of the Institute of International Economics, cited in note 80, was based on statutory tariff levels prevailing in 1994.

82. There were 237 tariff lines subject to both import quotas and licensing and an additional 24 lines subject to licensing only. "Agreement on Market Access between the People's Republic of China and the United States of America." One Chinese source published in mid-1999 confirms there were 261 encumbered tariff lines. "WTO Entry," *Nongcun jingji* (Agricultural Economics), June 20, 1999, pp. 4–10, in FBIS-CHI-1999-0811. At that time there were 6,940 tariff lines in China's tariff schedule. Zhang Yan, "Import Tariff Schedule to Be Adjusted," *China Daily*, January 4, 2000, p. 5.

83. National Bureau of Statistics, *China Statistical Yearbook 2000*, p. 126; *China Statistical Abstract 2001* (Beijing: China Statistics Press, 2001), p. 39; and Reuters, "City Unemployment Rate to Be Kept below 5pc," *South China Morning Post*, August 7, 2001 (http://china.scmp.com [August 7, 2001]).

84. Thomas G. Rawski, *Economic Growth in Prewar China* (University of California Press, 1989), pp. 92–105.

85. State Statistical Bureau, *Statistical Yearbook of China 1993* (Beijing: Statistical Publishing House, 1993), p. 410.

86. State Statistical Bureau, *Statistical Yearbook of China 1997*, pp. 412, 430–31. The data on financial losses are for state-owned firms. The employment figures are inclusive of textile workers in state and nonstate firms. In 1991 workers in state-owned firms accounted for two-thirds of the total. The published data on employment in the industry for 1996 are not disaggregated by ownership.

87. Ma Li, "State-Owned Textiles: Reform and Adjustment Are Still Extremely Great," *Zhongguo jingji shibao* (China Economic Times), January 26, 2000 (http://cet8848.net/20000126/YAOWEN/20001264.htm [March 15, 2000]). The word "slight" to characterize profits in 1999 is appropriate since the sum of fixed assets and working capital of state-owned textile firms in 1999 was RMB 247.4 billion. National Bureau of Statistics, *China Statistical Yearbook 2000*, pp. 424–25. Thus profits of RMB 800-900 million represent a rate of return on assets of less than one-half of 1 percent.

88. Xinhua, "State Textiles out of Doldrums," March 6, 2001, in FBIS-CH-2001-0306.

89. Zeng Peiyan, "Report on the Implementation of the 1999 Plan for National Economic and Social Development and the Draft 2000 Plan for Economic

and Social Development," *People's Daily*, March 15, 2000 (www.peopledaily. com.cn [March 15, 2000]).

90. Employment fell from 1,113,000 in 1996 to 890,000 by year-end 1999, a reduction of a little over a fifth. Gong Zhengzheng, "Industry Reshuffle Continues," *China Daily Business Weekly*, July 3, 2000, p. 1.

91. Some analysts were skeptical that the reported improvement in profitability reflected improvements in underlying productivity. They pointed out, for example, that rising prices of petroleum and refined petroleum products boosted the profits of PetroChina and other large, state-owned oil companies. They neglected to note, however, that to the extent these firms sell their output to other state-owned companies rising prices would have no effect on the aggregate profits of state-owned industry. Although there seem to be no systematic data, clearly other state firms are major users of refined petroleum products sold by PetroChina, Sinopec, and other state oil refiners. For example, the state-owned railroad system is a major consumer of diesel fuel.

92. Wu Jinglian and Zhao Renwei, "The Dual Price System in Chinese Industry," *Journal of Comparative Economics*, vol. 11 (September 1987), pp. 309–18; and William Byrd, "Impact of the Two-Tier Plan/Market System in Chinese Industry," *Journal of Comparative Economics*, vol. 11 (September 1987), pp. 295–308.

93. State-guided prices are prices that are allowed to fluctuate with a band around a price fixed by the state. Initially, in the mid-1980s, the band was plus or minus 20 percent.

94. That means the domestic price of these imports was the international price times the exchange rate plus any import duties. As chapter 2 explains, average import duty collections in the 1990s were quite low, so that for many commodities the domestic price converged toward the international price.

95. Editorial Board of the Almanac of China's Foreign Economic Relations and Trade, *Almanac of China's Foreign Economic Relations and Trade 1993/94* (Hong Kong: China Resources Advertising Co., Ltd., 1993), p. 43.

96. Guoqiang Long, "Will China Liberalize Its Grain Trade," Brookings Institution Center for Northeast Asian Policy Studies, Working Paper, Fall 1999 (www.brook.edu/fp/cnaps/papers/1999 [December 21, 1999]); and Economic Research Service, *China: Situation and Outlook Series*, International Agricultural and Trade Reports WRS-97-3 (U.S. Department of Agriculture, June 1997), p. 26.

97. Foreign Agricultural Service, *People's Republic of China: Grain and Feed Annual Report 2000*, GAIN Report CH0009 (U.S. Department of Agriculture, February 2000), pp. 2, 7.

98. Trish Saywell and Kathy Wilhelm, "Seeds of Change," *Far Eastern Economic Review*, June 29, 2000, pp. 44–46; and Stephanie Hoo, "China's Wheat Farmers Already Shifting Crop Mix Pre-WTO," Dow Jones Newswires, June 16, 2000 (www.interactive.wsj.com [June 16, 2000]).

99. World Bank, *China: Foreign Trade Reform* (Washington, 1994), p. 116.

100. Nicholas R. Lardy, *Foreign Trade and Economic Reform in China, 1978–1990* (Cambridge University Press, 1992), p. 91.

101. Dong Jian, "Domestic Oil Prices Go Global," *China Economic News*, vol. 19 (June 22, 1998), p. 2.

102. Kang Wu, "Oil Industry and Market Developments in China: A Short-Term Outlook to 2000," East-West Center Energy Project, Energy Advisory 235 (September 1999), p. 5.

103. "OPEC Crude Hike Won't Weaken Prices, China Imports-Execs," Dow Jones Newswires, June 22, 2000 (http://interactive.wsj.com/archive/retri...00622-000510.djml&template=printing.tmpl [June 22, 2000]).

104. Xu Yihe, "China to Adjust Oil Ptds Prices Every Month-Official," Dow Jones Newswires, June 8, 2000 (http://interactive.wsj.com/archive/retri...00608-002500.djml&template=printing.tmpl [June 8, 2000]). Zeng Huaguo, Fu Gang, and Zhang Yanping, "Perspectives on China's Fifth Upward Adjustment in the Price of Petroleum Products," *Jinrong shibao* (Financial News), July 26, 2000, p. 9.

105. "China to Loosen Up Water Transportation Pricing," ChinaOnline, March 30, 2001 (www.chinaonline.com [April 2, 2001]).

106. Many of these products already had been freely traded in competitive markets. James Kynge, "China Eases Price Control to Help with WTO Entry," *Financial Times*, July 12, 2001, p. 7; Stephanie Hoo, "China Ends More Price Controls Ahead of WTO Entry," Dow Jones Newswires, July 11, 2001 (http://interactive.wsj.com [July 11, 2001]); and Fu Jing, "State Liberalizes Prices on 10 Items," *China Daily*, July 12, 2001, p. 2.

107. For the complete list see World Trade Organization, *Draft Protocol on the Accession of the People's Republic of China*, WT/ACC/SPEC/CHN/1/rev.8 (Geneva, July 31, 2001), annex 4, pp. 166–69.

108. In early 2000 the State Power Corporation, the monopoly owner of the power grid, began buying electricity from producers through an open-bid process known as pooling. The experiment began in Zhejiang and Shandong provinces and in Shanghai. The state expects eventually to buy and sell all electricity through power pooling. Karby Leggett, "China Opens Energy Grid to Limited Competition," *Wall Street Journal*, interactive edition, January 28, 2001 (http://interactive.wsj.com [January 28, 2001]).

109. "Price Change Ahead for Oil, Gas, Water," Reuters, *South China Morning Post*, May 30, 2001 (http://china.scmp [May 29, 2001]).

110. The White House Office of Public Liaison, "Briefing on the Clinton Administration Agenda for the World Trade Organization Material: Summary of U.S.-China Bilateral WTO Agreement," November 17, 1999 (www.uschina.org/public/991115a.html [August 16, 2001]).

111. This point is developed in chapter 3.

## Notes to Chapter 2

1. In 1996 the share of imports subject to limited trading rights (either in the form of a monopoly, sometimes called state trading, or only a few authorized traders, referred to as designated trading), import licensing, import quotas, or price tendering summed to 60 percent. But many product categories were subject

to more than one type of restriction. For example, virtually every product subject to an import quota was also subject to import licensing. Taking into account these redundancies, only 33 percent of all import products were subject to one or more of these nontariff barriers. World Bank, *China Engaged: Integration with the Global Economy* (Washington, 1997), p. 15.

2. The name of this ministry has changed twice since it was established in 1952. In March 1982 it absorbed the Ministry of Foreign Economic Relations (the successor to the Foreign Economic Relations Commission, established June 1964, responsible for China's foreign economic assistance programs), the Foreign Investment Control Commission (established 1979), and the State Import and Export Control Commission (established 1979) to become the Ministry of Foreign Economic Relations and Trade, frequently known by its acronym MOFERT. Since 1993 it has been known as the Ministry of Foreign Trade and Economic Cooperation or MOFTEC. Throughout this book I refer to this organization simply as the Ministry of Foreign Trade.

3. Nicholas R. Lardy, *Foreign Trade and Economic Reform in China, 1978–1990* (Cambridge University Press, 1992), pp. 19–29.

4. Nicholas R. Lardy, *China in the World Economy* (Washington: Institute for International Economics, 1994), p. 2.

5. Nicholas R. Lardy, "Chinese Foreign Trade," *China Quarterly*, no. 131 (September 1992), pp. 695–700.

6. Greg Mastel, *The Rise of the Chinese Economy: The Middle Kingdom Emerges* (M. E. Sharpe, 1997), pp. 103–04.

7. Tariff revenues were a very small share of total government tax revenues and were very small as a percentage of the value of imports. In the First Five-Year Plan (1953–1957) tariff revenues were well under 5 percent of total government revenues and only about 10 percent of the value of imports. In 1975 the numbers were similar, 4 percent and 10 percent, respectively. Ministry of Finance, *Finance Yearbook of China 1998* (Beijing, 1998), pp. 445–46; and State Statistical Bureau, *Statistical Yearbook of China 1986* (Oxford University Press, 1986), p. 481.

8. Lardy, *Foreign Trade and Economic Reform in China, 1978–1990*, p. 47.

9. From March 1986 through the first half of 1991 tariffs were adjusted downward on only eighty-three tariff lines, 1 percent of the total. "Statement by Vice-Minister of MOFERT Tong Zhiguang at the 10th Session of the GATT Working Party on China," in Editorial Board of the Almanac of China's Foreign Economic Relations and Trade, *Almanac of China Foreign Economic Relations and Trade 1992/93* (Hong Kong: China Resources Advertising Co., Ltd., 1992), p. 35.

10. The standard deviation of tariff rates fell from 32.1 percent in 1992 to 13.1 percent by 1998. Elena Ianchovichina, Will Martin, and Emiko Fukase, "Comparative Study of Trade Liberalization Regimes: The Case of China's Accession to the WTO," unpublished manuscript, June 14, 2000, p. 7.

11. For a list of all of the import tax exemptions and reductions in effect in 1994 see Zhang Shuguang, Shang Yansheng, and Wan Zhongxin, *Measuring the Costs of Protection in China* (Washington: Institute for International Economics, 1998), p. 33. A list of import duty exemption programs in effect in 2001 is contained in article 104 of World Trade Organization, *Draft Report of the Working*

*Party on the Accession of China to the World Trade Organization*, rev. 7 (Geneva, July 10, 2001), pp. 27–28 (www.insidetrade.com [July 16, 2001]).

12. Lardy, *Foreign Trade and Economic Reform in China, 1978–1990*, p. 42.

13. Between 1988 and 1991 processed exports produced with inputs purchased from abroad more than tripled, from $6.4 billion to $19.5 billion. Over the same period total exports rose by just 50 percent. World Bank, *China: Foreign Trade Reform* (Washington, 1994), p. 12.

14. The State Council announced in late 1995 that this exemption from tariffs and import-related taxes would be eliminated on April 1, 1996. It provided an exemption for foreign-invested enterprises approved before April 1 to allow them additional time to take advantage of tariff-free imports. For projects involving total investment under $30 million the exemption was until December 31, 1996; for those over $30 million the exemption was until December 31, 1997. See State Council, "Circular on Reforming and Readjusting Import Taxation Policies (Summary)," in Editorial Board of the Almanac of China's Foreign Economic Relations and Trade, *Almanac of China's Foreign Economic Relations and Trade 1996/97* (Hong Kong: China Economical Publishing House and Economic Information and Agency, 1996), pp. 211–13. These deadlines turned out to be quite soft, and eventually the import duty exemption program was formally reinstated. However, in the new regime a small number of commodities, for example, automobiles, microcomputers, televisions, and digital telephone switchboards are no longer eligible for duty-free import. "Catalogue of Imported Commodities Not Entitled for Tariff Exemption for Projects with Foreign Investment," December 29, 1997, in Editorial Board of the Almanac of China's Foreign Relations and Trade, *Almanac of China's Foreign Economic Relations and Trade 1998/99* (Beijing: China Economics Publishing House, 1998), pp. 158–59.

15. General Administration of Customs of the People's Republic of China, "Tentative Provisions on the Exemption of Import Duty and Tax for Special Articles Used by the Disabled," April 10, 1997 (http://ntsvr.emart.com.hk/Chinalaw [July 12, 2000]).

16. "Several Policies for Encouraging the Development of Software Industry and Integrated Circuit Industry," Xinhua, July 11, 2000, in Foreign Broadcast Information Service, *Daily Report: China* (hereafter FBIS-CHI) 2000-0711 (http://wnc.fedworld.gov).

17. In the first half of 2000 only $38.99 billion of $102.1 billion in total imports was subject to any duty. "Customs, Import Tax Revenue Hits U.S.$12.1 Billion in First Half," ChinaOnline, July 12, 2000 (www.chinaonline.com/topstories [July 13, 2000]); "China IH Imports Up 36.2% to $102.1 Billion-Customs," July 12, 2000 (interactive.wsj.com [July 13, 2000]).

18. These illegally diverted imported parts and components are known as "flying materials" *(feiliao)*.

19. Lardy, *Foreign Trade and Economic Reform in China, 1978–1990*, p. 44.

20. Rajesh Chada, Drusilla K. Brown, Alan V. Deardorff, and Robert M. Stern, "Computational Analysis of the Impact on India of the Uruguay Round and the Forthcoming WTO Trade Negotiations," unpublished manuscript, May 2000, p. 1.

21. In 1992 out of a total of 6,940 tariff lines, 1,247 were subject to licenses or quotas or both. Long Yongtu, "Continuous Progress Made in Negotiations of

China's Accession to WTO in 1997," in Editorial Board of the Almanac of China's Foreign Economic Relations and Trade, *Almanac of China's Foreign Economic Relations and Trade 1998/99*, p. 39; and Zhang Yan, "Import Tariff Schedule Adjusted," *China Daily*, January 4, 2000, p. 5.

22. "Memorandum of Understanding between the Government of the United States of America and the Government of the People's Republic of China concerning Market Access," October 10, 1992.

23. Ministry of Foreign Trade and Economic Cooperation, *Zhongguo duiwai jingji maoyi baipishu 1998* (China's White Paper on Foreign Trade and Economic Cooperation 1998) (Beijing: Economic Science Press, 1998), pp. 93, 522–39.

24. "WTO Entry," *Nongcun jingji* (Agricultural Economics), June 20, 1999, in FBIS-CHI-1999-0811. The annex of the "Agreement on Market Access between the People's Republic of China and the United States of America," November 15, 1999, lists the 261 eight-digit tariff lines.

25. World Trade Organization, *Draft Report of the Working Party on the Accession of China to the WTO*, rev. 6 (Geneva, July 18, 2000), p. 32 (www.insidetrade.com [July 28, 2000]).

26. Mark O'Neill, "Tobacco Giant in Training for WTO," *South China Morning Post*, August 28, 2000 (www.scmp.com [September 6, 2000]).

27. Mark O'Neill, "Clinton Wants WTO Triumph for the Record," *South China Morning Post*, September 5, 2000 (www.scmp.com [September 5, 2000]); and National Bureau of Statistics, *China Statistical Yearbook 1999* (Beijing: China Statistics Press, 1999), p. 445.

28. For an analysis of smuggling see chapter 5.

29. Lardy, *Foreign Trade and Economic Reform in China, 1978-1990*, p. 39.

30. Ministry of Foreign Trade and Economic Cooperation, *China's Foreign Trade and Economic Cooperation White Paper 1999*, p. 191. The announcement of the licensing of private firms for foreign trade came in early 1999. James Kynge, "China Eases Access to Foreign Trade," *Financial Times*, January 6, 1999, p. 7; and Gao Wei, "Firms Get Trading Rights," *China Daily*, February 10, 1999, p. 1.

31. Ministry of Foreign Trade and Economic Cooperation, "MOFTEC Notice on System of Registration of Nation's Large Industrial Enterprise Import-Export Trading Rights," *People's Republic of China Ministry of Foreign Trade and Economic Cooperation Bulletin*, January 22, 1999, pp. 5–7, in FBIS-CHI-1999-0828.

32. Initially eligible firms had to have registered capital and net assets with a combined value of RMB 8.5 million and had to have supplied commodities worth a minimum of $1 million to trading companies for export during the previous two years. In 1999 the state reduced the capital requirement to RMB 5 million in coastal areas and RMB 3 million in other areas and eliminated the requirement to demonstrate a minimum level of sales for export. Wai Mao, "Entrepreneurs Enter Foreign Trade Sector," *China Daily Business Weekly*, December 14, 1998, p. 1; Wu Feng, "State Lowers Requirements for Foreign Trade License," *China Daily*, June 23, 1999, p. 5; and Gan Lu, "China to Loosen Control on Foreign Trade Right," *China Economic News*, vol. 22 (May 28, 2001), p. 8.

33. Jason Dean, "China to Ease Limits on Foreign Trade by Private Cos," *Dow Jones Newswires*, December 10, 2000 (http://interactive.wsj.com [December 11, 2000]).

34. Ministry of Foreign Trade and Economic Cooperation, *China's White Paper on Foreign Trade and Economic Cooperation 1999*, p. 192.

35. Zhang Yan, "Access to Trade Rights Expands," *China Daily*, February 23, 2000, p. 5.

36. "1,000 Private Enterprises Get Permission to Export," Xinhua, December 9, 2000, in FBIS-CHI-2000-1209.

37. There are more than 7 million manufacturing firms in China and millions more in construction, transport, and commerce.

38. Only four companies, along with their subsidiaries and branch organizations, are authorized to trade in crude oil and refined petroleum products: China National Chemicals Import and Export Corporation, China International Petroleum Chemicals Allied Corporation, China Petroleum Allied Corporation, and Zhenrong Company. Ministry of Foreign Trade and Economic Cooperation, "Measures for Organizing the Implementation of the Import of Crude Oil and Finished Oil," in Editorial Board of the Almanac of China's Foreign Economic Cooperation and Trade, *Almanac of China's Foreign Economic Relations and Trade 2000* (Beijing: China Foreign Economic Relations and Trade Publishing House, 2000), pp. 116–20.

39. Will Martin, "WTO Accession and China's Agricultural Trade Policies," unpublished manuscript, June 1999.

40. Ministry of Foreign Trade and Economic Cooperation, "Notice on the Checked and Ratified Import Commodities Operating the Five Commodities (Steel Included) and Relevant Issues," in Editorial Board of the Almanac of China's Foreign Economic Relations and Trade, *Almanac of China's Foreign Economic Relations and Trade 2000*, pp. 152–63.

41. General Agreement on Tariffs and Trade, "China's Foreign Trade Regime: Note by the Secretariat" (Geneva, 1988), p. 21. In 1998 imports for which trading rights were monopolized, sometimes referred to as state-traded imports, were 7.1 percent of total imports. Designated imports were 3.8 percent of total imports. The proportion of imports subject to state and designated trading combined in 1996 and 1997 was 14.8 percent and 14.9 percent, respectively. U.S. International Trade Commission, *Assessment of the Economic Effects on the United States of China's Accession to the WTO*, Publication 3229 (Washington, September 1999), pp. 3-15, 3-17.

42. U.S. Trade Representative, *1989 National Trade Estimate Report on Foreign Trade Barriers* (Washington, 1989), p. 44.

43. One reason for the lack of studies is the absence of systematic information about the system. It appears that the regulation establishing the system and the list of commodities it covered was never published. The 1992 announcement of the abolition of the system by the vice minister of foreign trade appears to be the only official public statement that the system even existed. None of the annual almanacs of the Ministry of Foreign Trade published between 1987 and 1992, which are usually reliable guides to major regulations affecting imports, ever included anything about the import substitution system other than the announcement of its elimination (see next note).

44. "Statement by Vice-Minister of MOFERT Tong Zhiguang at the 10th Session of the GATT Working Party on China," in Editorial Board of the Almanac of China's Foreign Economic Relations and Trade, *Almanac of China's Foreign Economic Relations and Trade 1992/93* (Hong Kong: China Resources Advertising Co., Ltd., 1992), pp. 33–37.

45. State Planning Commission, Ministry of Foreign Trade and Economic Cooperation, People's Bank of China, General Administration of Customs, and the State Administration for Foreign Exchange Control, "Provisional Procedures for the Administration of the Automatic Registration for the Import of Special Commodities," in Editorial Board of the Almanac of China's Economic Relations and Trade, *Almanac of China's Foreign Economic Relations and Trade 1995/96* (Hong Kong: China Resources Advertising & Exhibition Co., Ltd., 1995), pp. 115–17.

46. An admonition to comply with the provisions of the system was contained in State Development Planning Commission, Ministry of Foreign Trade and Economic Cooperation, and the General Administration of Customs, "Notice concerning the Adjustment of the Catalogue (Tariff Number) of Some Import Commodities Subject to the Management of Quotas of Import of General Commodities and Specific Registration Commodities," in Editorial Board of the Almanac of China's Economic Relations and Trade, *Almanac of China's Foreign Economic Relations and Trade 1999/2000*, pp. 179–93. Chinese trade negotiators in meetings of the working party on China's accession in Geneva in 2000 also acknowledged the system of automatic registration was still in operation and would be reformed to be consistent with article 2 of the WTO Agreement on Import Licensing Procedures. The chief requirement of article 2, which covers automatic import licensing, is that "approval of the application is granted in all cases." World Trade Organization, *Draft Report of the Working Party on the Accession of China to the WTO*, rev. 6, p. 33 (www.insidetrade.com [July 28, 2000]).

47. "Memorandum of Understanding between the Government of the United States of America and the Government of the People's Republic of China concerning Market Access," October 10, 1992. The products in question are listed on pages 6–9 of the annex to the agreement.

48. Ian Dickson, *China's Steel Imports: An Outline of Recent Trade Barriers*, Working Paper 96/6, Chinese Economy Research Unit, University of Adelaide, July 1996, p. 10.

49. Ibid., p. 22.

50. Imports of steel products measured in millions of metric tons followed this path: 1991–3.67; 1992–7.10; 1993–30.26; 1994–22.83; 1995–13.97. Editorial Board of the Almanac of China's Economic Relations and Trade, *Almanac of China's Foreign Economic Relations and Trade 1992/93*, pp. 548–49; *Almanac of China's Foreign Economic Relations and Trade 1994/95* (Hong Kong: China Resources Advertising Co. Ltd., 1994), pp. 610–11; *Almanac of China's Foreign Economic Relations and Trade 1995/96*, p. 601; and *Almanac of China's Foreign Economic Relations and Trade 1996/97* (Hong Kong: China Economics Publishing House and Economic Information and Agency, 1996), p. 641.

51. National Bureau of Statistics, *China Statistical Yearbook 2000* (Beijing: China Statistics Press), p. 65.

52. The only period since the establishment of the People's Republic of China in which prices surged more was in the aftermath of the Great Leap Forward in the early 1960s.

53. The November 1999 U.S.-China bilateral agreement identifies one hundred separate lines of China's tariff schedule as products for which tendering is required. At that time there were about 7,100 lines in China's tariff schedule. Thus tendering restricted 1.4 percent of all tariff lines.

54. Ministry of Foreign Trade and Economic Cooperation, "Circular on Adjusting Eight Specific Mechanical and Electrical Products for International Tenders," in Editorial Board of the Almanac of China's Foreign Economic Relations and Trade, *Almanac of China's Foreign Economic Relations and Trade 1999/ 2000*, pp. 194–95.

55. Originally this office was under the State Council. Subsequently it was subordinate to the State Economic and Trade Commission and, in 1998, it was moved to the Ministry of Foreign Trade.

56. U.S. Trade Representative, *1999 National Trade Estimate Report on Foreign Trade Barriers* (Washington, 1999), p. 60.

57. In May 2000 China notified the World Trade Organization of statutory inspection requirements on 144 products covering 755 tariff lines, about 10.9 percent of the total. The 21 products subject to safety standards covered 74 tariff lines. World Trade Organization, *Draft Protocol on China's Accession to the WTO Submitted to the Working Party*, annex 7a, "Products Subject to Statutory Inspection" (Geneva, June 6, 2000) (www.insidetrade.com [August 4, 2000]).

58. U.S. Trade Representative, *1999 National Trade Estimate Report on Foreign Trade Barriers*, p. 58.

59. Of the total, state-traded exports were 3.3 percent, designated exports 0.6 percent. The much smaller role of designated trading on the export side compared with imports simply reflects the fact that most of the products on the designated trading list are imports. The portion of exports subject to state and designated trading in 1996 and 1997 was 5.7 percent and 5.4 percent, respectively. U.S. International Trade Commission, *Assessment of the Economic Effects on the United States of China's Accession to the WTO*, pp. 3-16–3-17.

60. All goods subject to export quotas are also licensed. There are a few goods subject to licensing for which the amounts that can be exported are not restricted by quotas. The latter includes a variety of chemicals that are controlled by international conventions. Editorial Board of the Almanac of China's Foreign Economic Relations and Trade, *Almanac of China's Foreign Economic Relations and Trade 1993/94*, p. 50.

61. Liu Xiangdong, ed., *Zhongguo duiwai jingji maoyi zhengce shouce (1994– 1995)* (A Handbook of China's Foreign Economic and Trade Policies (1994–1995) (Beijing: Economic Management Press, 1994), p. 25, pp. 408–96. In 1991 textile and apparel exports accounted for about one-fourth of China's total exports, suggesting that practically all of China's exports were subject to licensing or quota

controls. However, not all textiles and apparel were subject to export quotas and those that were subject to such quotas were not subject to such restrictions in all external markets. State Statistical Bureau, *China Statistical Yearbook 1992* (Beijing: Statistical Publishing House, 1992), p. 630.

62. Editorial Board of the Almanac of China's Foreign Economic Relations and Trade, *Almanac of China's Foreign Economic Relations and Trade 1993/94*, p. 50.

63. Editorial Board of the Almanac of China's Foreign Economic Relations and Trade, *Almanac of China's Foreign Economic Relations and Trade 1999/2000*, p. 61.

64. Guo Maofu, "Thoughts on the Present Situation and Development of China's Foreign Trade," *Guoji shangbao* (International Business Daily), July 25, 2000, p. 2.

65. Lardy, *Foreign Trade and Economic Reform in China, 1978–1990*, pp. 24–29, 66–69.

66. The official exchange rate continued to be used for nontrade transactions on the current account, such as tourism and other services, and for capital account transactions.

67. Hassanali Mehran and others, *Monetary and Exchange System Reforms in China: An Experiment in Gradualism*, Occasional Paper 141 (Washington: International Monetary Fund, 1996), p. 56.

68. The unification of the two rates moved the official exchange rate from about 5.8 to 8.7, a change of about 50 percent. However, since before the unification of the two rates, about 80 percent of all foreign exchange transactions occurred at the swap market rate, the effective devaluation of the currency was only about 10 percent.

69. Measured on the basis of the real effective exchange rate, that is, on a trade-weighted basis and adjusted for the rate of inflation in China relative to its major trading partners. International Monetary Fund, *People's Republic of China—Recent Economic Developments* (Washington, 1996), p. 50a.

70. Since at the time more than 80 percent of all foreign exchange transactions were in the secondary market, it does not appear that thin trading depressed the value of the domestic currency.

71. For most export goods China is a price taker, that is, it has no market power. Thus indirect taxes on exports can not be passed on to buyers, reducing the profits that exporters earn from the sale of their products in international markets.

72. Lardy, *Foreign Trade and Economic Reform in China, 1978–1990*, pp. 48–50.

73. State Council, "Value-Added Tax, Tentative Regulations," December 13, 1993, *China Law and Practice*, January 31, 1994, p. 30.

74. "Rate Increases See Export Tax Rebates Almost Double," Xinhua, in *South China Morning Post*, October 31, 2000 (www.scmp.com [October 31, 2000]).

75. The first type is called *"lailiao jiagong"* usually translated in English language sources published in China as "inward processing or assembly"; the second

is *"jinliao jiagong,"* which is usually translated as "processing with imported materials." Barry Naughton, "China's Emergence and Prospects as a Trading Nation," *Brookings Papers on Economic Activity,* 1996, no. 2, pp. 298–300.

76. Lardy, *Foreign Trade and Economic Reform in China, 1978–1990,* p. 42.

77. The exemption initially covered all raw materials, materials, auxiliaries, spare parts, components, assemblies and packing materials. It subsequently was extended to cover equipment supplied by foreign firms to Chinese firms when the equipment was needed to fulfill processing contracts. To be eligible for this latter exemption from import duties 70 percent of the output produced using the machinery had to be sold in the export market. General Administration of Customs, "Provisions of the Customs Governing the Import of Materials and Parts Needed by Enterprises with Foreign Investment to Perform Product Export Contracts," in Editorial Board of the Almanac of China's Foreign Economic Relations and Trade, *Almanac of China's Foreign Economic Relations and Trade 1987* (Hong Kong: China Resources Advertising Co., Ltd., 1987), pp. 137–39; General Administration of Customs, "Regulations Governing Customs Control on the Importation and Exportation of Goods for Inward Processing," in Editorial Board of the Almanac of China's Foreign Economic Relations and Trade, *Almanac of China's Foreign Economic Relations and Trade 1989,* pp. 135–38; State Council, "Circular on Adjustment of Imported Equipment Taxation Policies," in Editorial Board of the Almanac of China's Foreign Economic Relations and Trade, *Almanac of China's Foreign Economic Relations and Trade 1998/99,* pp. 133–34; and Ministry of Foreign Trade and Economic Cooperation and General Administration of Customs, "Relevant Issues in Imported Equipment for Processing Trade," in Editorial Board of the Almanac of China's Foreign Economic Relations and Trade, *Almanac of China's Foreign Economic Relations and Trade 1999/2000,* pp. 118–20.

78. Francis Ng and Alexander Yeats, "Production Sharing in East Asia: Who Does What for Whom and Why?" World Bank Working Paper 2197, October 1999.

79. Chin Chung, "Division of Labor across the Taiwan Strait: Macro Overview and Analysis of the Electronics Industry," in Barry Naughton, ed., *The China Circle: Economics and Technology in the PRC, Taiwan, and Hong Kong* (Brookings, 1997), pp. 182–87.

80. "42% of Taiwan Desktop PCs Made in—and Sold from—China," *Taiwan Weekly Business Bulletin,* August 16, 2000, p. 6.

81. "King Computer Moves Monitor Plant to China," *Taiwan Weekly Business Bulletin,* August 2, 2000, p. 8.

82. Mark O'Neill, "Mainland Output Boosts Taiwan," *South China Morning Post,* January 29, 2001 (http://china.scmp.com [January 29, 2001]); Edward Chen, "70% of M'land's IT Products Said from Taiwan-Invested Firms," Central News Agency, April 16, 2001 (wnc@fedworld.gov [April 16, 2001]); and "China Displays Buying Power at Taiwan Computer Show," Dow Jones Newswires, June 6, 2001 (http://interactive.wsj.com [June 6, 2001]).

83. "Taiwan Will Produce 60% of World's Notebook PC's in 2000," *Taiwan Weekly Business Bulletin,* August 16, 2000, p. 6.

84. "Compaq to Procure over U.S.$10 Billion from Taiwan Next Year," *Taiwan Weekly Business Bulletin*, October 11, 2000, p. 7.

85. Sonia Tsang, "HK Legend Plans to Sell Computers in Europe 3Q 01," *Dow Jones Newswires*, June 5, 2001 (http://interactive.wsj.com [June 5, 2001]).

86. Bloomberg News, "Quanta Plans Mainland Parts Plant," *South China Morning Post*, September 5, 2000 (www.scmp.com [September 5, 2000]); and "MOEA Okays U.S.$292 Million in China Investments," *Taiwan Weekly Business Bulletin*, August 2, 2000, p. 7.

87. Jia Hepeng, "IT Funds Spill across Straits," *China Daily Business Weekly*, April 24–30, 2001, p. 3.

88. "42% of Taiwan Desktop PCs Made In—and Sold from—China," *Taiwan Weekly Business Bulletin*, August 16, 2000, p. 6.

89. Dermot Doherty, "Taiwan's Chip Designers Edge towards China," Dow Jones Newswires, October 8, 2000 (http://interactive.wsj.com [October 9, 2000]).

90. "Chip-Maker Tests Rule on Cross-Strait Spending," *South China Morning Post*, September 6, 2000 (http://scmp.com [September 6, 2000]).

91. Mure Dickie, "Move to Span Gulf between Taiwan and China," *Financial Times*, September 12, 2000, p. 1.

92. "Taiwan Business Leader Urges Opening to PRC Market," Central News Agency, October 26, 2000, in FBIS-CHI-2000-10-26.

93. Valerie Cerra and Anuradha Dayal-Gulati, "China's Trade Flows: Changing Price Sensitivities and the Reform Process," IMF Working Paper 99-1 (Washington, January 1999), p. 16.

94. Lardy, *China in the World Economy*, p. 2; and World Trade Organization, *International Trade Statistics 2000* (Geneva, 2000), p. 2.

95. "Export Gainers and Losers: The 1990s in Perspective," *Global Data Watch*, August 11, 2000 (New York: Morgan Guaranty Trust Company), p. 15.

96. Nicholas R. Lardy, "Chinese Foreign Trade," *China Quarterly*, no. 131 (September, 1992), pp. 695–700; and Zhang Xiaoguang and Peter G. Warr, "China's Trade Patterns and Comparative Advantage," in *China: Trade and Reform* (Canberra: Australian National University, National Center for Development Studies, 1991), pp. 46–72.

97. State Statistical Bureau, *Chinese Statistical Yearbook 1983* (Hong Kong: Economic Reporter Publishing House, 1983), p. 405; *China Statistical Yearbook 1985* (Beijing: Statistical Publishing House, 1985), p. 484; and National Bureau of Statistics, *China Statistical Abstract 2000* (Beijing: Statistical Publishing House, 2000), p. 140.

98. General Agreement on Tariffs and Trade, *International Trade Statistics 1991–92* (Geneva, 1993), pp. 57, 62; and World Trade Organization, *1999 Annual Report: International Trade Statistics* (Geneva, 1999), pp. 126, 133.

99. The European Union maintained quotas on some types of Chinese footwear, tableware, and kitchenware. As part of the bilateral negotiation between China and the EU the latter agreed to phase out quotas on these products by 2005. WTO Secretariat, "Language for Draft Protocol and Working Party Report Emanating from the EU-China Bilateral Agreement" (Geneva, June 15, 2000), p. 6.

100. State Statistical Bureau, *China Foreign Economic Statistics, 1979–1991* (Beijing: Statistical Information and Consultancy Service Center, 1992), p. 32; and National Bureau of Statistics, *China Statistical Yearbook 1999*, p. 582.

101. These data are for toys only. Chinese exports of toys, games, and sporting goods, division 95 in the harmonized commodity description and coding system, were $7.76 billion or 4.2 percent of total exports in 1998. State Statistical Bureau, *China Foreign Economic Statistics, 1979–1991*, p. 132; National Bureau of Statistics, *China Statistical Yearbook 1999*, p. 588; and General Administration of Customs, *China Customs Statistics Yearbook 1998* (Hong Kong: Goodwill China Business Information Limited, 1999), p. 94.

102. World Trade Organization, *1998 Annual Report: International Trade Statistics* (Geneva, 1998), pp. 124, 131, and *1999 Annual Report: International Trade Statistics*, pp. 125, 132.

103. These world market share data are for toys, games, and sporting goods. China has not released 1980 data for this HS category. It has been estimated as the sum of exports of toys, recreation articles, and sports articles. State Statistical Bureau, *China Foreign Economic Statistics, 1979–1991*, p. 132; General Administration of Customs, *China Customs Statistics Yearbook 1998* (Beijing, 1999), p. 84; and United Nations, *1998 International Trade Statistics Yearbook* (New York, 1999), p. 226.

104. World market share data calculated from data on Chinese exports reported in the previous paragraph and data on world exports contained in the following sources: United Nations, *1987 International Trade Statistics Yearbook* (New York, 1989), pp. 765–66, and *1998 International Trade Statistics Yearbook* (New York, 2000), p. 214.

105. Government Information Services Department, *Hong Kong 1982* (Hong Kong, 1982), pp. 56, 276.

106. Ibid., p. 278. Industry Department, The Government of the Hong Kong Special Administrative Region, *Xianggang gongshangye 2000* (Hong Kong Industry and Commerce 2000) (Hong Kong, June 2000), p. 88.

107. Government Information Services Department, *Hong Kong 1982*, p. 276. Census and Statistics Department, Hong Kong Government Press releases, "Employment and Vacancy Statistics for December 1995–99" (www.info.gov.hk/censtatd [July 24, 2000]).

108. Most of these were not production workers but headquarters staff of firms that had moved their factories to China. Industry Department, the Government of the Hong Kong Special Administrative Region, *Xianggang gongshangye 2000*, p. 8.

109. "Hong Kong Official Meets with Japanese Firms on Entering PRC Market," Xinhua, August 31, 2000, in FBIS-CHI-2000-0831; Thomas P. Rohlen, "Hong Kong and the Pearl River Delta: 'One Country, Two Systems' in the Emerging Metropolitan Context," Stanford University Asia/Pacific Research Center Discussion Paper, July 2000, p. 15.

110. Dow Jones Newswires, "Taiwan Helps China Achieve Social Stability," September 27, 2000 (http://interactive.wsj.com [September 27, 2000]).

111. State Council, "Anti-Dumping and Anti-Subsidy Regulations of the People's Republic of China," in Editorial Board of the Almanac of China's Foreign Economic Relations and Trade, *Almanac of China's Foreign Economic Relations and Trade 1998/99*, pp. 97–100.

112. Constantine Michalopoulos, "The Integration of Transition Economies into the World Trading System," World Bank Policy Research Paper 2182, September 1999.

113. The formal name of the WTO agreement on antidumping is "Agreement on Implementation of Article VI of the General Agreement on Tariffs and Trade." GATT Secretariat, *The Results of the Uruguay Round of Multilateral Negotiations: The Legal Texts* (Geneva, 1994), pp. 168–96.

114. General Administration of Customs, *China Customs Statistics Yearbook 1996*, p. 782; and *China Customs Statistics Yearbook 1997*, p. 889.

115. "China to Take Measures against Imported Newsprint," Xinhua, July 9, 1998, in FBIS-CHI-98-191; and Ma Li and He Jiangtao, "A Briefing on the Preliminary Ruling on the Newsprint Antidumping Case Was Held on the 16th in Beijing," *Guoji shangbao* (International Business Daily), July 17, 1998, in FBIS-CHI-98-217.

116. Ministry of Foreign Trade and Economic Cooperation, "Preliminary Ruling in the Anti-Dumping Investigation of Newsprint Imported from Canada, Korea and the United States," *Guoji shangbao* (International Business Daily), July 10, 1998, p. 2, in FBIS-CHI-98-259.

117. Ministry of Foreign Trade and Economic Cooperation, "Announcement No. 4 1999," June 3, 1999, in *Zhonghua renmin gongheguo duiwai maoyi jingji hezuo bu wengao* (Gazette of the Ministry of Foreign Trade and Economic Cooperation of the People's Republic of China), no. 26 (June 8, 1999), pp. 10–18.

118. Nicholas R. Lardy, "China and the International Financial System," in Elizabeth Economy and Michel Oksenberg, eds., *China Joins the World: Progress and Prospects* (New York: Council on Foreign Relations Press, 1999), pp. 211–12.

119. "PRC Willing to Cooperate on Government Procurement," Xinhua, July 15, 1999, in FBIS-CHI-1999-0715.

120. State Council, "Provisional Procedures on the Administration of Government Purchases," April 17, 1999, *China Economic News*, vol. 20 (June 28, 1999), pp. 8–13, 23–25; and National People's Congress Standing Committee, "The Law of the People's Republic of China on Invitation and Submission of Bids," August 30, 1999, *China Economic News*, vol. 20 (November 29, 1999), pp. 8–14, 22–26.

121. The broad scope is a function of the broad definition of large-scale infrastructure, public utilities, and other projects of public interest or public security (the scope outlined in the Bidding Law) and of the very low minimum thresholds that under the law trigger the requirement that bidding be used in the award of a contract. Infrastructure projects are defined by the implementing regulations to include all energy, transport, post and telecommunications, urban infrastructure, environmental, and other infrastructure. Utility projects include all municipal works, commercial housing, sporting and tourist, health and social welfare, and other utility projects. The minimum standards are a construction contract of more

than RMB 2 million ($241,000); a single piece of equipment or materials procurement contract of more than RMB 1 million ($120,500); a single survey, design, supervision, and management, or other service contract of more than RMB 500,000 ($60,250); or any project for which the price of a single contract is less than these three standards but for which the total investment is more than RMB 30 million ($3.61 million). These low minimums ensure that every significant public project will be subject to the bidding requirement. Freshfields Bruckhaus Deringer, "Analysis: Infrastructure," *China Notes*, October 2000, pp. 2–3.

122. "Latest Regulations to Further Regulate Public Bidding Activities," July 7, 2000 (http://ce.cei.gov.cn [August 30, 2000]).

123. The requirement for approval of purchases of foreign goods contained in the 1999 regulations appears to represent a liberalization of the 1994 Ministry of Finance temporary regulations on government procurement. The 1994 regulations restricted government purchases to domestic goods. Ai Mai, "Opening Institutional Purchases around the Corner," *China Economic News*, vol. 21 (January 31, 2000), p. 2.

124. Ai Mai, "Opening Institutional Purchases around the Corner," *China Economic News*, vol. 21 (January 31, 2000), p. 2.

# Notes to Chapter 3

1. Dianne E. Rennack, *China: U.S. Economic Sanctions* (Washington: Congressional Research Service, October 1, 1997).

2. Six countries regarded as transition economies were founding members of the World Trade Organization—the Czech Republic, Hungary, Poland, Romania, the Slovak Republic, and Slovenia. Of these only the Czechoslovak Republic, which in 1993 divided to become the Czech and Slovak republics, was a founding member of GATT. The others, with the exception of Slovenia, became members of GATT in the 1960s and 1970s. Slovenia became a member in 1994. Between the founding of the World Trade Organization on January 1, 1995, and the end of 2000 eight additional transition economies became WTO members—Albania, Bulgaria, Croatia, Estonia, Georgia, the Kyrgyz Republic, Latvia, and Mongolia.

3. On this incident and the role of domestic interest groups and public opinion in shaping China's WTO negotiating posture see Margaret M. Pearson, "The Case of China's Accession to GATT/WTO," in David M. Lampton, ed., *The Making of Chinese Foreign and Security Policy in the Era of Reform, 1978–2000* (Stanford University Press, 2001), pp. 337–70.

4. "U.S. Resists China Efforts to Begin Expedited Talks on GATT Protocol," *Inside U.S. Trade*, vol. 10 (October 30, 1992), pp. 1–2.

5. World Trade Organization, "WTO Successfully Concludes Negotiations on China's Entry," WTO press release (Geneva, September 17, 2001), p. 2.

6. For a convenient summary of the services commitments China made in its bilateral agreement with the United States in November 1999 see General Accounting Office, *World Trade Organization: Status of China's Trade Commitments to the United States and Other Members* (May 2000), app. I, pp. 25–27.

7. Foreign investors have been able to buy shares in China Telecom (Hong Kong), the Hong Kong listed arm of China Telecom, since its initial offering on the Hong Kong Stock Exchange in the fall of 1997. In the spring of 2000 China Telecom was divided into three separate companies. See note 11. Subsequently, China Telecom (Hong Kong) was renamed China Mobile (Hong Kong). A number of foreign telecommunications companies in the mid-1990s sought to evade China's ban on direct investments in the industry through investment structures that came to be known as Chinese-Chinese-foreign. In 1999 the Ministry of Information Industry ruled that these arrangements violated Chinese regulations and must be abandoned.

8. Valued-added services specified in China's November 1999 bilateral agreement with the United States included electronic mail, voice mail, on-line information and data base retrieval, electronic data interchange, enhanced/value-added facsimile services, code and protocol conversion, and on-line information and data processing. Internet services are subsumed within value-added services. In August 2001 China's Ministry of Information Industry promulgated a new catalog of value-added telecommunications services that is somewhat broader than that outlined in the November 1999 agreement. It is not clear whether the additional value-added services also are subject to the liberalizing steps outlined in China's WTO agreement.

9. Under the bilateral agreement China negotiated with the United States in 1999 the limits on foreign ownership of providers of mobile telecommunications services were 25, 35, and 49 percent at 1, 3, and 5 years after accession, respectively. That schedule was accelerated in bilateral negotiations between China and the European Union. "The Sino-EU Agreement on China's Accession to the WTO: Results of the Bilateral Negotiations" (www.europe.eu.int/comm/bilateral/China/res.pdf [June 13, 2000]).

10. Many observers believe that operationally the separation is not yet complete.

11. In March 1999 the Chinese government divided China Telecom into three independent telecom companies: China Telecom, handling fixed-line telecommunications; China Mobile Communications; and China Satellite Communications. At the national level China Telecom Corporation and China Mobile Communications Corporation began to operate as separate businesses on April 20, 2000. The separation of the companies at the provincial level ensued over the following months. The start-up of China Satellite Communications Corporation awaits further approvals. Wang Chuangdong, "Telecom Sector Reorganized," *China Daily*, April 21, 2000, p. 5.

12. The Ministry of Information Industry issued regulations governing the interconnection of networks between and among telecommunications companies on October 29, 1999. Among other things it established the right of customers to choose their long-distance carrier.

13. The term "foreign banks" refers to foreign branch banks, that is, the branches of Hongkong and Shanghai Bank, Standard Chartered Bank, Bank of East Asia, Citibank, and so on, as well as a smaller number of foreign-funded and joint venture banks, all of which are authorized to provide banking services, such as taking deposits and making loans. See table 4-1 for details on the number of

these institutions in the 1990s. "Foreign banks" excludes the much more numerous representative offices of foreign banks, which cannot offer banking services.

14. Jia Mulan, "Greater Area for RMB Business," *China Economic News*, vol. 20 (August 30, 1999), pp. 3–4; and Zhang Dingmin, "Foreign Banks Enter RMB Business," *China Daily*, March 4, 2000, p. 1.

15. The first domestic-currency syndicated loan with foreign bank participation was a loan of RMB 80 million to Shanghai Tire and Rubber Company made at the end of 1998. The three participating foreign banks, each of which contributed RMB 10 million to the loan, were Standard Chartered Bank, Credit Agricole Indosuez, and the International Bank of Paris and Shanghai. Three Chinese banks also participated in the loan. Dow Jones Newswires, "Foreign Bank Leads China's First Syndicated Yuan Loan," December 22, 1998 (http://interactive.wsj.com [December 28, 1998]).

16. Banks were required to purchase these domestic currency funds with foreign currency from the central bank at the official exchange rate.

17. James Kynge, "China Acts on Interbank Liquidity," *Financial Times*, January 25, 2000, pp. 17, 38. In many countries the interbank market is limited to very short-term transactions, mainly overnight borrowing and lending. In China interbank lending maturities are overnight, 7 days, 20 days, 30 days, 60 days, 90 days, 120 days, and, starting in 2000, one year. The lengthening of the available maturities made the interbank market a somewhat better source for foreign banks to fund their domestic currency lending.

18. Domestic banks, however, lobbied the central bank to limit the ability of foreign banks to borrow on the interbank market by limiting their domestic currency lending to a fixed multiple of from four to six times their operating capital. James Kynge, "Fears over Curb on Renminbi Lending," *Financial Times*, February 1, 2000, p. 4; and Karby Leggett, "Beijing May Place New Limits on Lending by Foreign Banks," March 2, 2000 (http://interactive.wsj.com [March 2, 2000]). Perhaps because of foreign bank protests this proposed restriction was not implemented, but foreign banks still face a limit on the ratio of domestic to foreign currency deposits, discussed in the text.

19. T. K. Chang, "Loosened Restrictions on Foreign Bank Rmb Business," *China Law and Practice*, October 1998, p. 32. The announcement was contained in the People's Bank of China guidelines opening Shenzhen to domestic currency business by selected foreign banks.

20. People's Bank of China, *China Financial Outlook 2000* (Beijing, 2000), p. 39.

21. Nicholas R. Lardy, *China's Unfinished Economic Revolution* (Brookings, 1998), p. 135.

22. Xu Binglan, "Wider Bank Access Mooted," *China Daily Business Weekly*, April 27, 1998, p. 3; and People's Bank of China, *Quarterly Statistical Bulletin*, no. 3 (Beijing, 1999), p. 14.

23. People's Bank of China, *China Financial Outlook 2000*, pp. 39, 90.

24. The sequencing negotiated in 1999, when it was assumed that China's WTO entry would probably be in 2000 or 2001 was as follows: *on entry*: Dalian and Tianjin in addition to Shanghai and Shenzhen; *January 1, 2001*: Guangzhou,

Qingdao, Nanjing, and Wuhan; *2002:* Jinan, Fuzhou, Chengdu, and Chongqing; *2003:* Kunming, Zhuhai, Beijing, and Xiamen; *2004:* Shantou, Ningbo, Shenyang, and Xian; *2005:* no geographic restrictions. These commitments, since they are date specific, did not slide as China's WTO entry was delayed. In its bilateral negotiations with the EU China agreed to bring forward the date of opening in Zhuhai. Thus China had to open eleven additional cities within weeks of entering the WTO in December 2001.

25. The People's Bank also requires that a foreign bank operate a representative office in China for three years before it can apply for a license to operate a branch. It is not clear whether this regulation will remain in place. In any case it would not appear to represent a significant restriction on the expansion of foreign banks. As early as August 1996, besides 126 foreign branch banks, there were 526 representative offices of foreign banks operating in China. Lardy, *China's Unfinished Economic Revolution,* p. 125.

26. At year-end 1999 the government had issued twenty-four licenses to fifteen foreign insurance companies from eight countries. There were four joint venture insurance firms. Szu Liang, "China's Insurance Sector Faces Tough Competition after WTO Accession," Zhongguo tongxun she (China News Agency), May 29, 2000, in Foreign Broadcast Information Service, *Daily Report: China* (hereafter FBIS-CHI) 2000-0529 (http://wnc.fedworld.gov).

27. "PRC to Relax Insurance Industry Investment Restrictions to Greet WTO Entry," *Ta Kung Pao,* October 5, 2000, in FBIS-CHI-2000-1005.

28. In November 1998 the People's Insurance Company of China was reorganized along product lines. The new companies are the China Reinsurance Company, the People's Life Insurance Company of China, the People's Insurance Company of China (focusing on property insurance), and the China Insurance Company (the former Hong Kong PICC Ltd.). Li Sin, "A Reshuffle in the Insurance Sector," *China Economic News,* vol. 20 (May 10, 1999), p. 6.

29. Besides meeting the same prudential criteria that would be applied to licensing additional domestic insurance companies, foreign insurance firms must meet three other criteria. They must have operated in a WTO member country for thirty years, had a representative office in China for two consecutive years before applying for a license, and have global assets of more than $5 billion.

30. Foreign firms will not be allowed to compete with domestic firms for commercial insurance policies below a defined threshold, determined by the annual insurance premium. The threshold will be reduced from $120,000 to $50,000 over a three-year period. "U.S., China Settle Outstanding Problems for WTO Accession," *Inside U.S. Trade,* vol. 19 (June 15, 2001), pp. 1, 21.

31. In the final phase of China's WTO accession negotiations the interpretation of this grandfathering clause was hotly contested. U.S. negotiators argued that the grandfathering provision gave the American Insurance Group the right to open additional branches in new locations that also would be 100 percent foreign owned. The European negotiators, however, argued that the grandfathering clause entitled the AIG to continue to operate its existing branches on a 100 percent foreign owned basis but that the AIG would be able to open additional offices only on the basis of joint ventures in which their ownership is restricted to the

same 50 percent limit that applies to other foreign insurance firms. China's accession package left this issue unresolved, and each side maintained that its terms supported their point of view. U.S. Trade Representative Robert Zoellick stated that the "commitments establish China's obligation to permit insurance companies to set up new branches with the same ownership basis as before its WTO accession." Office of the U.S. Trade Representative, "U.S. Trade Representative Robert B. Zoellick Welcomes Developments on China's WTO Accession," press release, September 17, 2001 (www.ustr.gov [September 19, 2001]). The EU claimed, "The one outstanding issue of interest to the EU, notably the terms under which life insurance companies can operate in China, was successfully resolved in the final text." "EU Welcomes Conclusion of Work to Ensure China's Accession to WTO," press release, September 17, 2001 (http://europea.eu.int/comm./trade/bilateral/china/pr170901.htm [September 19, 2001]).

32. For example, the partner of foreign firms had to be a retailer, imported goods could constitute no more than 30 percent of the value of sales, and each venture had to balance its foreign exchange through exports. Steven Shi and Anne Stevenson-Yang, "Retail Roundabout," *China Business Review*, vol. 25 (January–February 1998), p. 43.

33. Local governments had approved a much larger number, approximately 300. These governments technically had no authority to approve large-scale foreign-invested retail projects. Carrefour's strategy to ramp up its retailing extremely rapidly after its entry in 1995 was to rely on local approvals. Shi and Stevenson-Yang, "Retail Roundabout," p. 44.

34. The scope of China's distribution commitments is broad, extending far beyond simply wholesaling and retailing. For details see U.S. Trade Representative, "Distribution," fact sheet distributed in 1999, especially annex 1, in which the complete scope of distribution services is laid out.

35. In the November 1999 bilateral agreement with the United States, China restricted foreign ownership to less than a majority share for stores with more than 20,000 square meters or chain stores with more than thirty separate locations. In negotiations with the EU the Chinese agreed to majority foreign ownership of both these types of retail establishment. "The Sino-EU Agreement on China's Accession to the WTO: Results of the Bilateral Negotiations," p. 3. China subsequently argued that chain stores included all retail operations with two or more stores. If that definition had stood, China would have been able to preclude foreign firms from operating networks of wholly foreign-owned automobile dealerships, gasoline stations, and similar operations that are not normally considered chain stores. In negotiations in June 2001 the Chinese agreed that chain stores were stores that sell different types of goods and brands from different suppliers, that is, stores like Wal-Mart, Carrefour, and so forth. Thus automobile dealers and distributors of refined petroleum products will not be subject to the chain store limitation and will be able to have more than thirty wholly owned stores. Office of the U.S. Trade Representative, "USTR Releases Details on U.S.-China Consensus on China's WTO Accession," June 14, 2001 (www.ustr.gov/releases/2001/06/01 [June 19, 2001]).

36. "The Sino-EU Agreement on China's Accession to the WTO: Results of the Bilateral Negotiations," p. 4.

37. In the draft U.S.-China bilateral agreement rejected by the Clinton administration in April 1999 China agreed to allow the importation of at least forty motion pictures on accession and to increase this number by five each year over the next two years. The April agreement allowed these imports to be on either a revenue sharing or flat fee basis. The U.S. film industry strongly prefers the revenue sharing arrangement and agreed to a large reduction in the number of films imported for distribution in exchange for the assurance that all of this smaller number would be shown on a revenue-sharing basis.

38. "The Sino-EU Agreement on China's Accession to the WTO: Results of the Bilateral Negotiations," p. 4.

39. The White House China Trade Relations Working Group, "Agriculture–General," February 15, 2000 (www.chinapntr.gov/agricultue%fact%20sheets/agriculture%20general.htm [March 14, 2000].

40. Clothing is an important processed export, but the imports for this processing are in the form of fabric, not raw cotton.

41. Tariff-rate quotas were also established for wool, sugar, palm oil, rapeseed oil, and chemical fertilizers.

42. The Agreement on Agriculture specifies that the base period for these calculations is 1986 through 1988.

43. For grains the 1 percent tariff rate applies to unprocessed products. For partially processed products the rates are higher, for example, 6 and 9 percent for wheat and rice flour, respectively.

44. The percentage figures in the text were calculated by dividing the quota levels into consumption in the base period. Consumption is assumed to equal production plus net imports. If data on inventories of agricultural products were available, one could improve the estimate by assuming consumption equals production plus net imports plus changes in inventories. In negotiations with the United States in 1999, which established most of China's tariff-rate quota commitments, the base period was taken to be 1995–97.

45. General Agreement on Tariffs and Trade, *The Results of the Uruguay Round of Multilateral Trade Negotiations: Market Access for Goods and Services: Overview of the Results* (Geneva, 1994), p. 25.

46. The reason that the provision for private trading will not permanently limit the ability of the Chinese government to raise the price of agricultural commodities significantly above the world level is that the right of private traders to import products subject to tariff-rate quotas applies only to the quota amount. Over time, as domestic demand rises beyond the sum of the quota plus the amount of domestic production forthcoming at the world price, the government at the margin will regain control of the grain trade and could choose to limit imports above the quota amount and raise domestic grain prices above the world level.

47. General Accounting Office, *World Trade Organization: Status of China's Trade Commitments*, p. 23.

48. "Agreement on Market Access between the People's Republic of China and the United States of America," section 1-B, "Tariff Quotas."

49. World Trade Organization, *Report of the Working Party on the Accession of Latvia, Pt. I-Schedule of Concessions and Commitments on Goods, Schedule CXLIII.*

50. D. Gale Johnson, "The WTO and Agriculture in China," *China Economic Review*, vol. 11, no. 4 (2000), p. 403.

51. General Agreement on Tariffs and Trade, *Uruguay Round of Trade Multilateral Trade Negotiations: Legal Instruments Embodying the Results of the Uruguay Round of Multilateral Round of Trade Negotiations Done at Marrakesh on 15 April 1994*, vol. 11, (Geneva, 1994), p. 9,730.

52. Calculated using the exchange rate of 94 yen per U.S.$, the average rate prevailing in 1995. Unit prices for rice traded in international markets calculated from data in United Nations Food and Agriculture Organization, *FAOSTAT.*

53. William Drozdiak, "Poor Nations May Not Buy Trade Talks," *Washington Post*, May 15, 2001, p. E1.

54. General Agreement on Tariffs and Trade, *The Results of the Uruguay Round of Multilateral Trade Negotiations: Market Access for Goods and Services: Overview of the Results*, app. table 6.

55. U.S. Trade Representative, "Market Access and Protocol Commitments," undated manuscript distributed by USTR after Premier Zhu Rongji's April 1999 visit to the United States, p. 6.

56. Gary Clyde Hufbauer and Daniel H. Rosen, "American Access to China's Market: The Congressional Vote on PNTR," International Economics Policy Briefs, 00-3 (Washington: Institute for International Economics, April 2000), p. 21 (www.iie.com [May 1, 2000]).

57. Only 11 members of 122 have made commitments in as many as eleven or twelve of the total of twelve different types of services. World Trade Organization, "Summary of Specific Commitments" (www.wto.org/wto/services/websum.htm [June 12, 2000]).

58. Charlene Barshefsky, "U.S. Trade Policy in China," Hearings before the Senate Finance Committee on the Status of China's Application to Join the World Trade Organzation, April 13, 1999 (www.fnsg.com).

59. China seems to be the only country that has included in its schedule of commitments both the WTO Telecommunications "Reference Paper" and the two chairman's notes of the WTO Group on Basic Telecommunications. These documents specify assumptions applicable to the scheduling of commitments in telecommunications and details on the regulatory framework for telecommunications services, such as competitive safeguards, interconnection rights, universal service, public availability of licensing criteria, and regulatory independence. The inclusion of these documents will provide foreign telecommunications firms with a substantial advantage in their ventures in China.

60. The countries are Ecuador, Mongolia, Bulgaria, Panama, Kyrgyz Republic, Latvia, and Estonia. World Trade Organization, *Technical Note on the Accession Process,* WT/ACC/7/rev.1 (Geneva, November 19, 1999), p. 22.

61. The average for the seven is 12.4 percent versus 8.9 percent for China. However, Estonia at 6.6 percent and Kyrgyz Republic at 6.7 percent had lower tariff bindings than China. Ibid., table 3.

62. Greg Mastel, *Section 201: Reviving the Forgotten Trade Law* (Washington: Center for National Policy, November 1999), p. 6.

63. In the multilateral negotiations in Geneva members of the working party in late 1994 demanded that China accept, without time limit, what is referred to as a general safeguard. Its terms are even more onerous than those outlined below for the transitional product-specific safeguard. The general safeguard would have allowed all members to suspend the WTO benefits that they extend to China if it failed to implement any of its WTO commitments. Although it never was agreed to, this provision remained in drafts of China's protocol of accession dated as late as May 28, 1997.

64. Hufbauer and Rosen, "American Access to China's Market: The Congressional Vote on PNTR, " pp. 13–14.

65. Charlene Barshefsky, "China's WTO Accession: American Interests, Values, and Strategy," Hearings before the Senate Committee on Finance, February 23, 2000, p. 9 (www.finance.senate.gov/W2-23-0 [September 13, 2000]).

66. "Statement by General Counsel Davidson to U.S.-China Security Review Commission," U.S.-China Security Review Commission Hearings on Bilateral Trade Policies and Issues between the United States and China, August 2, 2001 (www.uscc.gov/testav.htm [August 9, 2001].

67. World Trade Organization, *Draft Protocol on the Accession of the People's Republic of China*, WT/ACC/SPEC/CNN/1.8 rev. (Geneva, July 31, 2001), p. 120.

68. "Working Party Sets Rules to Protect Markets from Chinese Exports," *Inside U.S. Trade*, vol. 19 (July 6, 2001), p. 21.

69. According to U.S. Trade Representative Barshefsky the product-specific safeguard that China has agreed to "exists for no other country in the world." Charlene Barshefsky, "Briefing to the National Conference of Editorial Writers at the U.S. Department of State," March 10, 2000. However, when Hungary, Poland, and Rumania joined the General Agreement on Tariffs and Trade, they were required to make safeguard commitments that went beyond those that applied to other members at the time. General Accounting Office, *World Trade Organization: Status of China's Trade Commitments*, p. 39.

70. Initially it was proposed that the textile safeguard would be available only for those countries that maintained restrictions on the import of Chinese textiles and apparel by means of quotas under the Agreement on Textiles and Clothing on the day before the entry into force of China's WTO accession agreement. Many developing country members of the working party objected to this limitation, and the provisions of the textile safeguard were made available to all WTO members.

71. "Agreement between the United States of America and the People's Republic of China concerning Trade in Textile and Apparel Products," February 1, 1997 (www.insidetrade.com/sec [June 26, 2000]). This agreement was never publicly released by the U.S. government, and thus the fact that it provides the general terms of the textile safeguard incorporated into China's working party report is not well known.

72. Immediately upon a request for consultations by the United States or another member the Chinese government has agreed that it will limit shipments of products in the notified categories. The limit is an amount no greater than 7.5 percent above the amount that entered the United States in the first twelve months

of the most recent fourteen months preceding the month in which the request for consultations was made. For wool products the limit is 6 percent. "Language for Draft Protocol and Working Party Report Emanating from the U.S.-China Bilateral Agreement," Informal WTO Secretariat Document, June 15, 2000 (www.insidetrade.com [July 28, 2000]). This language subsequently was incorporated into China's accession package.

73. China proposed, at a working party meeting in early July 2001, to exempt textile products from coverage under the transitional product-specific safeguard. This proposal was not accepted by the working party.

74. The most commonly selected surrogates in U.S. antidumping cases against Chinese firms have been Brazil, India, Indonesia, Pakistan, and Thailand. Per capita gross national product in Thailand and Brazil is about three and five times, respectively, the level in China.

75. Scott Anderson, "Significant Change or Status Quo? The Potential Impact on Chinese Producers and Exporters to the United States from the Draft Chinese Accession Protocol Provisions Regarding Special Anti-Dumping and Product and Textile Safeguards," paper prepared for a World Bank seminar in Beijing, October 25, 2000, p. 18.

76. Ibid., p. 6.

77. Ibid., p. 11.

78. Ibid., p. 10.

79. Dow Jones Newswires, "China's Huarong to List Revamped State Cos in '01," December 18, 2000 (http://interactivewsj.com [December 19, 2000]); and Wang Huidong, "Debt-to-Equity Swaps Trade SOEs out of Plight," *China Daily Business Weekly*, July 10–16, 2001, p. 6.

80. *Uruguay Round Trade Agreements, Texts of Agreements, Implementing Bill, Statement of Administrative Action, and Required Supporting Action*, vol. 1, H. Doc. 103-316, 103 Cong. 2 sess. (Government Printing Office, 1994), p. 913.

81. World Trade Organization, *Draft Protocol on the Accession of China* (Geneva, July 10, 2001) (www.insidetrade.com [July 16, 2001]), p. 6. If China had joined in the 1990s subsidies for research by universities, or higher education or research units; for assistance to disadvantaged geographic regions; and to assist in meeting new environmental requirements would have been nonactionable since subsidies for these purposes are identified in World Trade Organization "Agreement on Subsidies and Countervailing Measures" as nonactionable. But article 31 of the agreement specifies that the exemptions of these subsidies expire five years after the WTO agreement entered into force. Thus since December 31, 1999, these subsidies also have been actionable. I am indebted to C. Christopher Parlin for calling this to my attention. See GATT Secretariat, *The Results of the Uruguay Round of Multilateral Negotiations: The Legal Texts*, pp. 264–314.

82. "Agreement on Subsidies and Countervailing Measures," article 29.

83. Richard Eglin, director, WTO Secretariat, *Challenges and Implications of China Joining the WTO: What WTO Accession Means*, p. 29 (www.worldbank.org/wbiep/trade/papers_2000/China-Challenges.pdf [January 29, 2001].

84. World Trade Organization, *Report of the Working Party on the Accession of Bulgaria, September 20, 1996*, WT/ACC/BGR/5.

85. Privatization subsidies for developing countries are covered in article 27.13, and the other provisions China gave up are covered in articles 27.8 and 27.9 of the "Agreement on Subsidies and Countervailing Measures." See "Working Party Sets Rules to Protect Markets from Chinese Exports," *Inside U.S. Trade*, vol. 19 (July 6, 2001), pp. 1, 21.

86. World Trade Organization, *Draft Protocol on the Accession of China* (Geneva, July 10, 2001), pp. 10–11.

87. "Job Creation and Preservation," fact sheet distributed by U.S. Trade Representative.

88. Anderson, "Significant Changes or Status Quo?" p. 10.

89. *Uruguay Round Trade Agreements, Texts of Agreements, Implementing Bill, Statement of Administrative Action, and Required Supporting Action*, vol. 1, pp. 60–64.

90. Ministry of Foreign Trade and Economic Cooperation, *Zhongguo duiwai jingji maoyi baipishu 2000* (China's Foreign Economic and Trade White Paper 2000) (Beijing: Social Science Publishing House, 2000), p. 208. In 1999 the value of agricultural output (as measured by its contribution to gross domestic product) was RMB 1,445.72 billion. National Bureau of Statistics, *China Statistical Yearbook 2000* (Beijing: China Statistics Press, 2000) p. 53. News coverage of the Geneva debate placed Chinese agricultural subsidies at less than 2 percent of the value of agricultural output. The lower figure is because the average annual domestic agricultural support in the base period 1996–98 was used in the multilateral negotiations. Apparently domestic agricultural support was lower in those years than in 1999.

91. Eglin, *Challenges and Implications of China Joining the WTO*, p. 18

92. U.S. Trade Representative, "USTR Releases Details on U.S.-China Consensus on China's WTO Accession," June 14, 2001 (www.ustr.gov/releases/2001/0601-38htm [June 19, 2001]).

93. Countries with larger agricultural export subsidies were the EU, Austria, United States, Poland, Mexico, Finland, Sweden, and Canada. General Agreement on Tariffs and Trade, *The Results of the Uruguay Round of Multilateral Trade Negotiations: Market Access for Goods and Services: Overview of the Results*, app. table 12.

94. General Agreement on Tariffs and Trade, *Uruguay Round of Trade Multilateral Trade Negotiations: Legal Instruments Embodying the Results of the Uruguay Round of Multilateral Round of Trade Negotiations Done at Marrakesh on 15 April 1994*, vol. 4, (Geneva, 1994), pp. 3,587–596.

95. For example, in WTO Secretariat, "Language for Draft Protocol and Working Party Report Emanating from the U.S.-China Bilateral Agreement" (Geneva, June 15, 2000) (www.insidetrade.com [July 28, 2000]), there is no mention of agricultural export subsidies.

96. General Agreement on Tariffs and Trade, *The Results of the Uruguay Round of Multilateral Trade Negotiations: Market Access for Goods and Services: Overview of the Results*, p. 22.

97. "Agreement on U.S.-China Agricultural Cooperation." The English language version of this agreement was signed in Washington on April 10, 1999, at

the time of Premier Zhu Rongji's visit to the United States. Although Ambassador Charlene Barshefsky and other administration officials stated that it would be implemented immediately, the text of the agreement was not released. Following the U.S. bombing of the Chinese embassy in Belgrade in May 1999 the Chinese government took no steps to implement the agreement. In the fall of 1999, at the abortive WTO ministerial meeting in Seattle, the two sides signed the Chinese language version of the agreement, and the full text subsequently was made public. Before the working party concluded its negotiations with China in September 2001 China had also concluded a bilateral agreement on sanitary and phytosanitary standards with the EU.

98. The agreement provides that the Animal and Plant Health Inspection Service will suspend export of all citrus within a specified distance from any point at which there has been an outbreak of pests. The distance is initially set at seventeen miles but will be reduced two years after a pest outbreak to 4.5 miles unless scientists from both countries agree on a different size quarantine zone. The agreement has many other detailed provisions, including the periods of the year and the density with which monitoring for Medfly presence must be conducted in different growing areas; shipping of certified fruit under closed conveyance, and so forth.

99. U.S. Trade Representative, *1998 National Trade Estimate Report on Foreign Trade Barriers*, p. 50.

100. Anita Narayan, "China Ends Ban on U.S. Leaf Tobacco Imports," ChinaOnline, February 8, 2001 (www.chinaonline.com [February 10, 2001]).

101. "China Opens Its Market to Imports of U.S. Citrus, Meat, and Wheat," U.S. Trade Representative, press release, March 22, 2000 (www.ustr.gov/releases/2000/03/00-20.pdf [March 24, 2000]).

102. Dow Jones Newswires, "Florida Fetes Start of Citrus Shipments to China," March 28, 2000 (http://interactive.wsj.com [March 28, 2000]); and Jeff Bater, "Citrus, Wheat Recently Shipped to China," Dow Jones Newswires, April 3, 2000 (http://interactive.wsj.com [April 4, 2000]).

103. *Uruguay Round Trade Agreements, Texts of Agreements, Implementing Bill, Statement of Administration Action, and Required Supporting Statements*, pp. 1342–43.

104. International Trade Commission, *Assessment of the Economic Effects on the United States of China's Accession to the WTO* (Washington, September 1999), pp. 3–14.

105. These commodities are identified in further detail in annexes 2a1 and 2a2, respectively, of World Trade Organization, *Draft Protocol on the Accession of the People's Republic of China*. WT/ACC/SPEC/CHN/1/rev. 8 (Geneva, July 31, 2001), pp. 131–14.

106. Ibid., annex 2a1, p. 135.

107. A single national-level foreign trade corporation usually monopolizes trade in products subject to state trading. Products subject to designated trading are traded by a larger number of foreign trade companies, typically including a number of provincial and local trade companies.

108. World Trade Organization, *Draft Report of the Working Party on the Accession of China to the WTO*, rev. 7 (Geneva, July 10, 2001), p. 23 (www. insidetrade.com [July 16, 2001]).

109. Recall from chapter 2 that foreign-invested enterprises have always had the right to import raw materials, parts, and components needed for their own production and the right to export the goods that they produce. The trading right referred to here is the right to import and export without any restriction on the goods involved.

110. U.S. Trade Representative, "USTR Releases Details on U.S.-China Consensus on China's WTO Accession," June 14, 2001 (www.ustr.gov/releases/2001/06/01-38.htm [June 19, 2001]).

111. This represents a continuation of a process that has been under way for some time. As discussed in chapter 2 in the text and in chapter 2, note 32, the minimum capital requirement for trading rights was first cut in 1999. World Trade Organization, *Draft Report of the Working Party on the Accession of China to the WTO* (Geneva, 2000), p. 22.

112. In that memorandum the Chinese government also agreed that it would only enforce those laws, regulations, or other measures that have been published. China reiterated that commitment in its WTO agreement.

113. GATT Secretariat, *The Results of the Uruguay Round of Multilateral Negotiations: The Legal Texts* (Geneva, 1994), p. 499.

114. World Trade Organization, *Draft Report of the Working Party on the Accession of China*, WT/ACC/SPEC/CHN/1/rev. 8 (Geneva, July 31, 2001), pp. 11–12.

115. GATT Secretariat, *The Results of the Uruguay Round of Multilateral Negotiations: The Legal Texts*, pp. 398–99.

116. Developed countries and least-developed countries had two and seven years, respectively, to phase out trade-related investment measures.

117. General Accounting Office, *World Trade Organization: Status of China's Trade Commitments to the United States and Other Members* (May 2000), p. 45.

118. General Agreement on Tariffs and Trade, *The Results of the Uruguay Round of Multilateral Trade Negotiations: Market Access for Goods and Services: Overview of the Results*, p. 56.

119. "WTO Protocol on Government Procurement: Member Observers" (www.wto.org/english/tratop_e/gproc_e/memobs_e.htm [September 13, 2001]).

120. World Trade Organization, *Draft Report of the Working Party on the Accession of China*, WT/ACC/SPEC/CHN/1/rev. 8 (Geneva, July 31, 2001), p. 104.

121. General Accounting Office, *World Trade Organization: Status of China's Trade Commitments to the United States and Other Members*, p. 45.

122. World Trade Organization, *Draft Report of the Working Party on the Accession of China*, rev. 8, p. 66.

123. The list of products and services subject to state price control is contained in annex 4 to the draft protocol on the Accession of the People's Republic of China. World Trade Organization, *Draft Report of the Working Party on the Accession of China*, WT/ACC/SPEC/CHN/1/rev.8 (Geneva, July 31, 2001), p. 24.

124. "Quality, Inspection, and Quarantine Bureau Formed," ChinaOnline, April 24, 2001(www.chinaonline.com/topstories/010424/1/c01041808.asp [April 26, 2001].

125. World Trade Organization, *Draft Protocol of the Accession of China* (Geneva, July 10, 2001), p. 7 (www.insidetrade.com [July 16, 2001]).

126. U.S. Trade Representative, *1999 National Trade Estimate Report on Foreign Trade Barriers*, p. 60.

127. "Scientific Equipment," February 15, 2000, and "Construction Equipment," February 15, 2000, fact sheets distributed by the U.S. Trade Representative. The White House China Trade Relations Working Group, "Agricultural Equipment," February 15, 2000 (http://chinapntr.gov/industry%20fact%20sheet/agricultural%20equipment.htm [March 14, 2000]).

128. The four largest trading entities (counting the EU as one) are reviewed every two years, the next sixteen largest trading countries are reviewed every four years, and the rest are reviewed every six years. One exception is that an even less frequent interval may be specified for countries classified as "least developed." GATT Secretariat, *The Results of the Uruguay Round of Multilateral Negotiations: The Legal Texts*, p. 435.

129. These are the Council for Trade in Goods, Council for Trade Related Aspects of Intellectual Property Rights, Council for Trade in Services and Committees on Balance of Payments Restrictions, Market Access, Agriculture, Sanitary and Phytosanitary Measures, Technical Barriers to Trade, Subsidies and Countervailing Measures, Antidumping Measures, Customs Valuation, Rules of Origin, Import Licensing, Trade Related Investment Measures, Safeguards, and Trade in Financial Services.

130. World Trade Organization, "The Trade Policies Review Division (TPRD)," (www.wto.org/english/tratop_e/tpr_e/tprdiv_e.htm [July 23, 2001]).

# Notes to Chapter 4

1. At year-end 1998 the Industrial and Commercial Bank of China employed a staff of 567,230; the Agricultural Bank of China had 524,484 staff, Construction Bank of China had 378,523 staff, and the Bank of China 197,547 staff. See Chinese Banking and Finance Society, *Almanac of China's Finance and Banking 1999* (Beijing, 1999), p. 532.

2. Historically tariff rates were much higher. In 1986, when tariffs were first established on passenger cars, the uniform rate was 220 percent. Rates were reduced starting in 1992. By 1994 imported cars with engines less than three liters were subject to import tariffs of 180 percent; cars with larger engines were still subject to an import tariff of 220 percent. On January 1, 1994, the rates were reduced to 110 and 150 percent. On April 1, 1996, the rates went to 100 and 120 percent. Yu Yongding and Zheng Bingwen, eds., *The Research Report on China's Entry into WTO: The Analysis of China's Industries* (Beijing: Social Sciences Documentation Publishing House, 2000), pp. 384–85.

3. State Planning Commission, "Auto Industry Policy," *People's Daily*, July 4, 1994, in Foreign Broadcast Information Service, *Daily Report: China* (hereafter FBIS-CHI) 94-136 (http://wnc.fedworld.gov).

4. State Statistical Bureau, *China Statistical Yearbook 1995* (Beijing: China Statistical Publishing House, 1995), p. 550; and *China Statistical Yearbook 1999*, p. 590.

5. State Statistical Bureau, *China Statistical Yearbook 1995*, p. 542; and National Bureau of Statistics, *China Statistical Yearbook 1999* (Beijing: China Statistics Press, 1999), p. 582.

6. Buicks produced at General Motors' joint venture factory in Pudong in 1999 sold for $41,000 to $45,800, depending on the trim level. Credit Lyonnais Securities Asia, *WTO: A New Deal for China, Industry and Market Analysis* (Hong Kong: Credit Lyonnais Securities Asia Global Emerging Markets, 1999), p. 15. Except for minor details such as an air conditioning outlet in the rear seat, the car is the same as the Regal model sold in the United States.

7. For example, the tariff on large engine cars drops from an initial level of 100 percent to 77.5 percent in the year 2000, a cut of 22.5 percent. In the final year the cut is from 28 to 25 percent, a reduction of 10.7 percent.

8. "Agreement on Market Access between the People's Republic of China and the United States of America," Office of the U.S. Trade Representative, unpublished manuscript, November 15, 1999.

9. Xinhua, "PRC Plans to Restructure Auto Industry," May 14, 1999, in FBIS-CHI-1999-0514.

10. "China's '98 Auto Production Flat on Yr, below Target," Dow Jones Newswires, January 6, 1999 (http://interactive.wsj.com [January 7, 2000]).

11. Mark O'Neill, "Debt Soars at Beijing Auto," *South China Morning Post*, February 11, 1999 (www.scmp.com [February 13, 1999]).

12. In several listings of motorcycle manufacturers and models for 1996 it is possible to identify more than 110 manufacturers. Machinery Ministry, Automotive Industry Corporation, China Automotive Technical Research Center, *China Automotive Industry Yearbook 1997* (Beijing, 1997), pp. 312–16. In 1999 there were 130 factories manufacturing complete motorcycles. U.S. Foreign Commercial Service and U.S. Department of State, "China: Motorcycle Industry," March 4, 1999 (www.tradeport.org/ts/countries/china/mrr/mark0323.html [January 11, 2001]).

13. China National Automotive Industry Consulting and Developing Corporation, "Development of Motorcycle Industry in China in 1999," 1999 (www.cacauto.com [January 5, 2001]).

14. In Taiwan, a world-class motorcycle producer, ten manufacturers produce almost the entire output of the industry of 1.5 million units annually. About one-third of output is exported. That suggests that firms in China with production levels below 100,000 units are not likely to realize economies of scale in motorcycle production. Taiwan Transportation Vehicle Manufacturers' Association, "Industry Updates" (http://ttvma.asiansources.com [January 9, 2001]); and China External Trade Development Council, "Motorcycles and Parts" (www.cetra.org.tw/tp/auto/motor [January 9, 2001]).

15. H. Richard Kahler, Caterpillar Corporation, personal communication, January 22, 2001.

16. Rahul Jacob and Tim Burt, "China's Walls Will Crumble but Only One Brick at a Time," *Financial Times*, May 30, 2000, p. 8; and Development Research Center, State Council of the People's Republic of China, *The Global and Domestic Impact of China Joining the World Trade Organization* (Washington: Center for China Studies, 1998), p. 35. Their number, 498,000, is for road vehicles.

17. Elena Ianchovichina and Will Martin, "Trade Liberalization in China's Accession to the WTO," World Bank Policy Research Working Paper 2228 (Washington, June 2001) (forthcoming in *Journal of Economic Integration*).

18. Development Research Center, State Council of the People's Republic of China, *The Global and Domestic Impact of China Joining the World Trade Organization*, p. 52.

19. Ibid., p. 35; and "Task Group Assesses WTO Accession," *Takungpao*, November 26, 1999, in FBIS-CHI-1999-1204.

20. Nicholas R. Lardy, *China's Unfinished Economic Revolution* (Brookings, 1998).

21. Although the Bank of Tokyo in 1979 was the first foreign bank to receive permission to open a representative office, the first foreign bank to receive approval to conduct banking business in China was the Nanyang Commercial Bank, which opened a branch in Shenzhen on July 17, 1981.

22. Chinese Banking and Finance Society, *Almanac of China's Finance and Banking 1985* (Beijing, 1985), pp. XI-22–XI-23.

23. There were four foreign banks (the Hongkong and Shanghai Bank, Standard Chartered Bank, Overseas Chinese Bank, and the Bank of East Asia) that had branches in Shanghai (Overseas Chinese Bank had a second branch in Xiamen) that were licensed before 1949. These branches were essentially dormant after 1949 but were permitted to resume banking business in the early 1980s, before new entrants were allowed to establish branches in Shanghai.

24. With a 100 percent tariff, the landed price of an imported car in China at the time of the signing of the bilateral agreement with the United States was two times the world price. Beginning July 1, 2006, when the tariff rate will have fallen to 25 percent, the landed price will be 1.25 times the world price. A drop from 2 times to 1.25 times the world price is a reduction of 37.5 percent (1.25/2 = .625).

25. Ministry of Foreign Trade and Economic Cooperation, Foreign Investment Administrative Bureau and State Statistical Bureau, Department of Trade and External Economic Relations, "1997/1998 Top 500 FFEs in China," *China Economic News*, vol. 20, supplement 1 (Hong Kong February 1, 1999).

26. In 1987 only the tires, radio, and antennae of the Santana were produced in China. The value of these parts constituted only 2.7 percent of the value of the car. By 1997 92.9 percent of all components of the Santana were produced in China. Eric Thun, "Going Local: Foreign Investment, Local Development, and the Chinese Auto Sector," unpublished manuscript, May 2001.

27. Credit Lyonnais Securities Asia, *WTO: A New Deal for China, Industry and Market Analysis*, pp. 15–16.

28. Ministry of Foreign Trade and Economic Cooperation, Foreign Investment Administrative Bureau and State Statistical Bureau, Department of Trade and External Economic Relations, "1997/1998 Top 500 FFEs in China."

29. Huang Gang, "Volkswagen to Invest DM3 Billion in China in Coming Five Years," *China Economic News*, vol. 21 (December 4, 2000), p. 5.

30. Clay Chandler, "China Approves Toyota Joint Venture to Build Small Cars," *Washington Post*, May 30, 2000, p. E1.

31. Owen Brown, "China's Tianjin Xiali Fires Latest Salvo in Car War," Dow Jones Newswires, December 13, 2000 (http://interactive.wsj.com [December 13, 2000]).

32. Liu Ping, "Toyota Sets Up Its First Auto Plant in Tianjin," *China Economic News*, vol. 21 (August 14, 2000), pp. 4–5.

33. In 1994 domestic car production was 249,114 units, and imports were 47,681 units. *China Machinery Industries Yearbook 1997* (Beijing: China Machine Press and New York: Springer Verlag, 1997), p. 141; and State Statistical Bureau, *China Statistical Yearbook 1995*, p. 550. "It is now believed by many that the annual volume of cars sold in China could reach 1.25 million in 2000," in Graeme P. Maxton, *The Automotive Sector of the Pacific Rim and China: Moving into the Fast Lane* (London: Economist Intelligence Unit, 1994), p. 14.

34. David Murphy, "China Car Makers Focus on Individual Buyers," Dow Jones Newswires, February 14, 2001 (http://interactive.wsj.com [February 15, 2001].

35. Toyota plans to build a facility with a capacity of 30,000 in Tianjin. Ford Motor Company expects to begin producing a vehicle on the Fiesta platform in its joint venture, which was approved in 2000. The planned initial production capacity is 25,000, growing to 100,000 in phases. Suresh Seshadri, "Ford Sees China Car Launch by Early 2003," Reuters, September 17, 2000 (www.chinaonline.com [September 18, 2000]). Hyundai Motor, South Korea's largest vehicle maker, has permission from Beijing to build a factory with an annual capacity of 300,000 units. Reuters, "Mainland Plant to Play Key Role in Hyundai's Global Expansion," *South China Morning Post*, October 5, 2000 (www.scmp.com [October 5, 2000]); and Karby Leggett, "GM Plans Compact Car for China to Draw Middle Class as Sales Slow," *Wall Street Journal*, October 24, 2000.

36. Thomas G. Rawski and Robert Meade, "On the Trail of China's Phantom Farmers," *World Development*, vol. 26 (May 1998), pp. 767–81.

37. National Bureau of Statistics, *China Statistical Yearbook 2000* (Beijing: China Statistics Press, 2000), p. 116.

38. Jikun Huang, Scott Rozelle, and Linxiu Zhang, "WTO and Agriculture: Radical Reforms or the Continuation of Gradual Transition," *China Economic Review*, vol. 11, no. 4 (2000), p. 400.

39. Xie Ping, "Reforming Banking System and Perfecting Capital Market," unpublished manuscript, 2001.

40. The importance of foreign banks is sometimes measured as a share of loans outstanding from the financial system. Since loans compose a larger share of the assets in foreign banks than in domestic banks, the loan share of foreign banks is slightly higher than their asset share.

41. At year-end 1999 the domestic currency deposits of foreign banks were RMB 5.442 billion, an amount equal to 2.1 percent of their total liabilities. It is unlikely that these banks have other significant RMB-denominated liabilities. People's Bank of China, *China Financial Outlook 2000* (Beijing, 2000), p. 39.

42. People's Bank of China, *Quarterly Statistical Bulletin*, no. 2 (Beijing, 2000), p. 12.

43. People's Bank of China, *China Financial Outlook 2000*, p. 39.

44. Foreign banks' foreign currency loans outstanding at year-end 1999 were 21.831 billion, 12.8 percent of total foreign currency loans outstanding from all domestic financial institutions, including foreign banks in China. People's Bank of China, *China Financial Outlook 2000*, p. 39. At year-end 2000 their foreign currency loans were $18.8 billion, 22.7 percent of foreign currency loans. Yang Shuang and Wang Baoqing, "Raise the Level of Central Bank Regulation and Supervision; Stress Paying Special Attention to the Work of Financial Supervision," *Jinrong shibao* (Financial News), January 16, 2001, pp. 1–2.

45. People's Bank of China, *Quarterly Statistical Bulletin*, no. 1 (Beijing, 2000), p. 55.

46. This calculation ignores risk weighting. To the extent that the average risk weighting of the assets of foreign banks in China is less than one, their total assets could exceed $33.5 billion.

47. Stijn Claessens, A. Demirgüç-Kunt, and Harry Huizinga, "The Role of Foreign Banks in Domestic Banking Systems," pp. 117–37, in Stijn Claessens and Marion Jansen, eds., *The Internationalization of Financial Services: Issues and Lessons for Developing Countries* (London/The Hague/Boston: Kluwer Law International, 2000), p. 132.

48. In 1991–96 the savings rate was 34.9 percent and 35.0 percent, net capital inflow was 7.7 percent and 6.5 percent, and gross domestic capital formation was 42.6 percent and 41.5 percent for Thailand and Malaysia, respectively. Asian Development Bank, *Asian Development Outlook 1997 and 1998* (Hong Kong: Oxford University Press (China) Ltd., 1997) pp. 229–30; and *Asian Development Outlook 1998* (Hong Kong: Oxford University Press (China) Ltd., 1998), pp. 240–41.

49. International long-distance phone charges in 2000 were eight times the level in the United States. Wang Jiahe, "Lowering Monopoly Prices to Stimulate Effective Demand," China *Economic News*, vol. 21 (December 4, 2000), p. 7. Rate reductions that took effect in March and June 2001 reduced international long-distance fixed-line phone charges to a flat rate of RMB 8 a minute regardless of the country called. That rate is about one dollar a minute, still several times rates for most international calls in the United States. At the same time rates on domestic long-distance calls from fixed-line phones were cut. "China Sharply Cuts Phone Rates to Prepare for Competition," Bloomberg News, December 25, 2000, *New York Times*, December 26, 2000, p. C3; and James Kynge, "Beijing Adds to Confusion over Mobile Fees," *Financial Times*, December 27, 2000, p. 2.

50. Development Research Center, State Council of the People's Republic of China, *The Global and Domestic Impact of China Joining the World Trade Organization*, pp. 39, 42.

51. The ITC report was done after the Chinese offer of April 1999 was made but before the final bilateral agreement between the United States and China was reached in November 1999. Although there are serious differences between the offer and the agreement on rules-based issues and services, the tariff schedule in the two is identical. The tariff schedule attached to China's WTO protocol was almost the same as that negotiated with the United States. The EU negotiated for reduced tariffs on scotch that matched those the United States had negotiated on bourbon; the Swiss negotiated a lower tariff on imported watches, and so on. But cumulatively these changes were minor and not likely to affect the ITC estimates.

52. International Trade Commission, *Assessment of the Economic Effects on the United States of China's Accession to the WTO,* p. 6-3.

53. To maintain the pretense that the Multifiber Arrangement and the successor arrangement, the ATC, do not involve import quotas, the administration of the restrictions is the responsibility of the exporting country.

54. *Uruguay Round Trade Agreements, Texts of Agreements, Implementing Bill, Statement of Administration Action, and Required Supporting Statements,* vol. 1, pp. 1398–399.

55. The initial U.S. intention to apply the phase-out provisions of the Agreement on Textiles and Clothing to China was expressed in article 21 of the 1997 bilateral textile agreement. This commitment, which was conditional on China's WTO membership and the application of the World Trade Organization with respect to China by the United States, went unnoticed at the time because the text of the bilateral agreement was not released. It was finally leaked in 2000. "Agreement between the United States of America and the People's Republic of China concerning Trade in Textile and Apparel Products," February 1, 1997, p. 10 (www.insidetrade.com [June 26, 2000]). The U.S. commitment to phase out quotas on imports of textiles and apparel from China subsequently was included in the November 15, 1999, "Agreement on Market Access between the People's Republic of China and the United States of America" and became part of the *Draft Report of the Working Party on the Accession of China to the WTO,* rev.7 (Geneva, July 10, 2001).

56. International Trade Commission, *Assessment of the Economic Effects on the United States of China's Accession to the WTO* (Washington, 1999), p. 8-4.

57. Only the United States, the EU, Canada, and Norway impose quotas on textile and apparel imports. In 1998 these markets absorbed 22 percent of China's textile and apparel exports. Gu Qiang, "Will Springtime Come to the Textile Industry after Entering the WTO?" *Zhongguo jingji shibao* (China Economic Times), February 2, 2000 (http://cet.8848.net [March 15, 2000]).

58. A growth rate of 2 percent was applied to apparel of silk blend fibers and noncotton vegetable fibers. These items accounted for less than 1 percent of the total volume of China's allowable quotas. International Trade Commission, *Assessment of the Economic Effects on the United States of China's Accession to the WTO,* pp. 8-13, 8-18–8-19.

59. According to an analysis prepared for the American Textile Manufacturers Institute, China fills a larger share of its individual textile and apparel quotas than any other country. "Statement of the American Textile Manufacturers Institute,"

Hearings before the House Committee on Ways and Means on the U.S.-China Bilateral Trade Agreement and the Accession of China to the World Trade Organization, February 16, 2000, exhibit A, p. 3.

60. Development Research Center, State Council of the People's Republic of China, *The Global and Domestic Impact of China Joining the World Trade Organization,* p. 48.

61. International Trade Commission, *Assessment of the Economic Effects on the United States of China's Accession to the WTO,* pp. 8-24, 8-26.

62. Will Martin, Betina Dimaranan, Thomas W. Hertel, and Elena Ianchovichina, "Trade Policy, Structural Change and China's Trade Growth," unpublished manuscript, August 2000. In an earlier version of this paper the authors estimated that China would increase its share of the world apparel market to about 60 percent. The revised number takes into account the duty exemptions available to firms engaged in processing for the export market before China's accession to the World Trade Organization. For a complete analysis of the importance of taking previously existing duty exemptions into account in estimating China's gains from joining the World Trade Organization see Elena Ianchovichina, Will Martin, and Emiko Fukase, "Comparative Study of Trade Liberalization Regimes: The Case of China's Accession to the WTO," unpublished manuscript, June 14, 2000.

63. Gu Qiang, "Will Springtime Come to the Textile Industry after Entering the WTO?"

64. This number is for exports of apparel produced in Hong Kong. It excludes Chinese apparel re-exported from Hong Kong. World Trade Organization, *1999 Annual Report: International Trade Statistics* (Geneva, 1999), pp. 122, 132.

65. The deficit in wool averaged about $500 million and in chemical fiber $3,200 million. National Bureau of Statistics, *China Statistical Yearbook 1999,* p. 582.

66. Will Martin, Betina Dimaranan, Thomas W. Hertel, and Elena Ianchovichina, "Trade Policy, Structural Change and China's Trade Growth," unpublished manuscript, August 2000.

67. Yu Yongding and Zheng Bingwen, eds., *The Research Report on China's Entry into WTO: The Analysis of China's Industries,* p. 166.

68. The share of synthetic fiber used in China's textile industry rose from 15.2 percent in 1975 to 28.1 percent in 1985, and 54 percent by 1997. Yu Yongding and Zheng Bingwen, eds., *The Research Report on China's Entry into WTO: The Analysis of China's Industries,* pp. 200–02.

69. Development Research Center, State Council of the People's Republic of China, *The Global and Domestic Impact of China Joining the World Trade Organization,* p. 54.

70. Ibid., p. 35.

71. As of April 2000 the negative list for imports from China maintained by the Board of Foreign Trade in Taiwan included 4,563 products, 45 percent of the total of 10,421 items listed under Taiwan's ten-digit harmonized system tariff codes. Board of Foreign Trade, "Trade Policies and Measures" (www.trade.gov.tw [November 29, 2000]).

72. State Statistical Bureau, *China Statistical Yearbook 1992* (Beijing: Statistical Publishing House, 1992), p. 632; and National Bureau of Statistics, *China Statistical Yearbook 2000*, p. 593.

73. Elliot Spagat, "Mexico Sees Slow Progress toward China's WTO Entry," Dow Jones Newswires, December 20, 2000 (http://interactive.wsj.com [December 21, 2000]); and Andrea Mandel-Campbell, "China Puts Mexican Trade in Line of Fire," *Financial Times,* January 10, 2001, p. 7.

74. Thom Beal, "A Mexican Standoff with China," *Asian Wall Street Journal,* June 1–3, 2001, p. 17.

75. "Mexico Inks Accord with China, Gets Shield for AD Measures," *Inside U.S. Trade* (www.insidetrade.com/secure/specials/sp091401_1.asp [September 17, 2001]).

76. "Language for Draft Protocol and Working Party Report Emanating from the EU-China Bilateral Agreement," Informal WTO Secretariat Document, June 15, 2000 (www.insidetrade.com [July 28, 2000]).

77. Details are spelled out in World Trade Organization, *Draft Protocol on the Accession of the People's Republic of China*, annex 7, WT/ACC/SPEC/CHN/1/rev.8 (Geneva, July 31, 2001), pp. 204–09.

78. Khozem Merchant, "Indian Manufacturers Tremble as Import Barriers Are Set to Be Lifted," *Financial Times*, December 20, 2000, p. 21.

79. National Bureau of Statistics, *China Statistical Yearbook 2000*, p. 593.

80. The criteria and methodology must be notified to the WTO Committee on Anti-Dumping Practices before they are applied. WTO Secretariat, *Draft Report of the Working Party on the Accession of China to the WTO*, rev. 7 (Geneva, July 10, 2001) (www.insidetrade.com [July 16, 2001]), pp. 44–47.

81. On the fiscal challenge of bank restructuring see Nicholas R. Lardy, "When Will China's Fiscal System Meet China's Needs?" in Nicholas Hope, ed., *How Far across the River: Chinese Policy Reform at the Millennium?* (University of Chicago Press, forthcoming); and "China's Worsening Debts," *Financial Times*, June 22, 2001, p. 13.

82. For a comprehensive analysis of the growth of the Chinese computer market and changing patterns of market dominance see Qiwen Lu, *China's Leap into the Information Age: Innovation and Organization in the Computer Industry* (Oxford University Press, 2000).

83. "Dell Places Its Bet," *Business China*, vol. 24 (May 25, 1998), p. 2; and "Shooting Star," *Business China*, vol. 24 (August 17, 1998), pp. 7–8.

84. "The Dynamic Duo," *Business China*, vol. 25 (February 15, 2000), pp. 7–9; and "Only the Best," *Business China*, vol. 25 (November 22, 1999), pp. 3–4.

85. Hou Mingjuan, "Legend Expects a 30 to 40 Percent Growth in Coming Years," *China Daily Business Weekly*, December 25, 2000, p. 5.

86. "Who Needs Competition?" *Business China*, vol. 24 (October 12, 1998), p. 4.

87. "Unlikely Hero," *Business China*, vol. 25 (July 5, 1999), pp.1–3; and "Huawei" (www.huawei.com/english/about%20us/product.htm [March 6, 2001]).

88. Henny Sender, "Beijing Envisions Huawei Becoming the Cisco of China," Dow Jones Newswires, October 5, 2000 (http://interactive.wsj.com [October 6, 2000]).

89. "Huawei to Set Up Production Center in Mexico," ChinaOnline, February 26, 2001 (www.chinaonline.com/topstories [February 27, 2001]).

90. "About Haier" (www.haier.com/englishabout/index/html [December 21, 2000]); and Bing Lan, "Forum: Economy to Benefit from WTO," *China Daily Business Weekly*, April 24, 2000, p. 4; "Taking on the World," *Business China*, vol. 26 (November 20, 2000), p. 3; and Chuan Jiang and Chuan Jiao, "Haier Rises to Global Brand in 16 Years," *China Daily*, December 27, 2000, p. 5.

91. "Taking on the World," p. 3.

92. Wu Lian, "OEM Heat in China's Home Appliances Market," *China Economic News*, vol. 22 (July 30, 2001), pp. 8–9; and Dai Yan, "Galanz Aims to Fuel Flaming AC Price War," *China Daily Business Weekly*, July 10–16, 2001, p.7.

93. Editorial Board of the Almanac of China's Foreign Economic Relations and Trade, *Almanac of China's Foreign Economic Relations and Trade 2000* (Beijing: China Foreign Economic Relations and Trade Publishing House), p. 564; and *Almanac of China's Foreign Economic Relations and Trade 1991/1992* (Hong Kong: China Resources Advertising Co., Ltd., 1991), p. 413.

94. Elena Ianchovichina, Will Martin, and Emiko Fukase, "Comparative Study of Trade Liberalization Regimes: The Case of China's Accession to the WTO," unpublished manuscript, June 14, 2000, p. 7.

95. Exporting countries have used WTO dispute settlement to challenge successfully injury determinations by Mexico, the EU, and Thailand and dumping margin determinations of the United States, the EU, Guatemala, and Thailand. Lawrence Walders and Daniel Price, "Antidumping, China, and the WTO: WTO Rules, Antidumping and the Stakes for Chinese Business," unpublished manuscript, March 8, 2001.

96. Scott Anderson, "Significant Change or Status Quo? The Potential Impact on Chinese Producers and Exporters to the United States from the Draft Chinese Accession Protocol Provisions Regarding Special Anti-Dumping and Product and Textile Safeguards," paper prepared for a World Bank seminar in Beijing, October 25, 2000, p. 4.

## Notes to Chapter 5

1. Author's calculations based on data in Development Research Center, State Council of the People's Republic of China, *The Global and Domestic Impact of China Joining the World Trade Organization* (Washington: Washington Center for China Studies, 1998), pp. 26, 39, and 42; and information supplied by Dr. Wang Zhi, cohead of the research team that produced the Development Research Center report.

2. Ibid., p. 42, table 7.1.

3. Amy Louise Kazmin, Hugh Williamson, and Sheila McNulty, "Foreign Investors Desert South-East Asia for China," *Financial Times*, October 13, 2000, p. 8.

4. Lester J. Gesteland, "Remote Control: Toshiba Shifts TV Production to China," ChinaOnline News, March 19, 2001 (http://chinaonline.com/topstories/010319/1/c01031955.asp [March 20, 2001]).

5. "Beware Chinese Promises," *Washington Post*, October 16, 2000, p. A26.

6. Greg Mastel, "Are Our China Troubles Over?" May 25, 2000 (http://speakout.com/issues/activism/opinions/5255-1.html [September 6, 2001]).

7. "Memorandum of Understanding between the Government of the United States of America and the Government of the People's Republic of China concerning Market Access," October 10, 1992.

8. The precise timetable was set forth in an annex to the memorandum. It identified more than 665 individual tariff lines and the year in which quotas, licenses, and in some cases both quotas and licenses would be eliminated for each product. The schedule for lifting restrictions was as follows: 1992—6 lines or 0.9 percent of the total to be eliminated, 1993—259 lines (38.9 percent), 1994—269 lines (40.5 percent), 1995—110 lines (16.5 percent), 1996—9 lines (1.4 percent), and 1997—12 lines (1.8 percent).

9. U.S. Trade Representative, *1998 National Trade Estimate Report on Foreign Trade Barriers* (Washington, 1998), p. 45.

10. The first batch of twelve internal regulations, dating from 1985 through 1991, was published in Editorial Board of the Almanac of China's Foreign Economic Relations and Trade, *Almanac of China's Foreign Economic Relations and Trade 1992/93* (Hong Kong: China Resources Advertising Co., Ltd., 1992), pp. 91–132. A second batch of internal regulations appeared in *Almanac of China's Foreign Economic Relations and Trade 1993/94*, pp. 87–101.

11. Zhonghua renmin gongheguo duiwai maoyi jingji hezuobu (Ministry of Foreign Trade and Economic Cooperation of the People's Republic of China), *Wenbao (Gazette)*. By the end of 1999 more than 230 issues had been published.

12. U. S. Trade Representative, *1998 National Trade Estimate Report on Foreign Trade Barriers*, p. 48.

13. Ex post facto one could infer the limits from the detailed trade data published by the Chinese General Administration of Customs. And some of the limits were included in the bilateral agreement between the United States and China signed in November 1999.

14. U.S. Trade Representative, *1998 National Trade Estimate Report on Foreign Trade Barriers*, p. 48.

15. "Agreement on Trade Relations between the United States of America and the People's Republic of China," July 7, 1979 (www.insidetrade.com [June 26, 2000]).

16. Michel Oksenberg, Pitman B. Potter, and William B. Abnett, "Advancing Intellectual Property Rights: Information Technologies and the Course of Economic Development in China," National Bureau of Asian Research Analysis, vol. 7 (November 1996), p. 7.

17. "Memorandum of Understanding between the Government of the People's Republic of China and the Government of the United States of America on the Protection of Intellectual Property," January 17, 1992.

18. Margaret M. Pearson, "China's Integration into the International Trade and Investment Regime," in Elizabeth Economy and Michel Oksenberg, eds., *China*

*Joins the World: Progress and Prospects* (New York: Council on Foreign Relations Press, 1999), pp. 172–73.

19. U.S. Trade Representative, *The 1996 Trade Policy Agenda and 1995 Annual Report of the President of the United States on the Trade Agreements Program* (Washington, 1996) (www.ustr.gov).

20. U.S. Trade Representative, "United States and China Reach Accord on Protection of Intellectual Property Rights, Market Access" (Washington, February 26, 1995) (www.ustr.gov/releases/1995/02/95-12 [March 16, 2000]). This release contains a summary of the bilateral agreement.

21. SID codes are "signatures" that identify which particular CD press produced an individual CD, allowing inspectors to quickly determine whether the CD has been produced under a licensing agreement or is pirated product. U.S. Trade Representative, "Chinese Implementation of the 1995 IPR Enforcement Agreement," fact sheet, June 17, 1996 (www.ustr.gov/releases/1996/06/96-53/96-53.fact.html [March 16, 2000]).

22. U.S. Trade Representative, "Statement by Ambassador Barshefsky," June 17, 1996 (www.ustr.gov/releases/1996/06/96-53.html [March 16, 2000]).

23. Charlene Barshefsky, U.S. Trade Representative, "Foreign Affairs Briefing to the National Conference of Editorial Writers," U.S. Department of State, March 10, 2000.

24. U.S. Trade Representative, *The President's 2000 Annual Report on the Trade Agreements Program* (Washington, 2001), p. 152.

25. U.S. Trade Representative, *1999 National Trade Estimate Report on Foreign Trade Barriers* (Washington, 1999), p. 61; and *2000 National Trade Estimate Report on Foreign Trade Barriers*, p. 50.

26. Among the most important of these imperfections is that the threshold for the application of criminal penalties in copyright cases is too high. Prosecutors must demonstrate that the pirates have earned more than RMB 50,000 in sales before they can recommend that the courts impose criminal penalties. Copyright violators rarely keep records that could be used to document sales volume, and the law does not provide for criminal penalties based on either the inventory or production capacity for pirated product.

27. In 1998 the value of these copyright products was RMB 140 billion or 1.8 percent of gross domestic product. In the United States in 1997 the figure was 6.5 percent, according to data published by the World Intellectual Property Organization. "Copyright Material Nears 5% of GDP," ChinaOnline News, March 30, 2001 (www.chinaonline.com/topstories/010330 [April 2, 2001]).

28. "Beware Chinese Promises," p. A26.

29. Yang Guohua and Cheng Jin, "Bibliography of Chinese Books on GATT/WTO," unpublished manuscript. I am indebted to Professor John H. Jackson for this information.

30. On January 1, 2001, tariffs were cut on 152 tariff lines, including 79 for complete vehicles and 73 for parts and accessories. For example, the Ministry of Foreign Trade cut the import tariff on sedans with engines three liters or larger from 100 percent to 80 percent, while on vehicles with smaller engines the rate went from 80 percent to 70 percent. Xinhua, "China Slashes Tariff for Car Im-

port," February 5, 2001 (www://www.securities.com/cgi-bin/split.../Data/CN/News/ISIH/isih010205.html [February 5, 2001]).

31. If its negotiations for WTO entry had failed, China could have reversed the tariff cuts just described since the new lower rates were not bound. This was reflected in Chinese documents that described the new rates as "interim" (*zheding*). In its WTO accession documents China agreed to bind its new lower tariff levels, meaning it does not have the freedom to raise rates, except under special, negotiated conditions. Binding is discussed in chapter 3. One reason that China cut its tariffs on January 1, 2000, and January 1, 2001, before it entered the World Trade Organization, was the nature of its tariff commitments. These commitments, made originally in 1999, are date specific. That means that if China had not made cuts in 2000 and 2001, it would have had to make catch-up cuts when it entered in December 2001. For example, in 1999 when the tariff on large sedans was 100 percent China agreed to reduce the rate to 77.5 percent in 2000, 61.7 percent in 2001, 50.7 percent in 2002, and so forth through July 2006. Thus when its entry was delayed it was not obligated to make these tariff cuts. But in 2002, shortly after it came into the World Trade Organization, the tariff on large sedans had to be 50.7 percent. Cutting tariffs on sedans voluntarily in 2000 and 2001 thus spread out the cost of adjustment.

32. The other partners are Shanghai Telecom, the Shanghai arm of China Telecom, with a 60 percent stake, and Shanghai Information Investment, an investment firm controlled by the Shanghai municipal government, with a 15 percent share. Richard McGregor, "AT&T in China Breakthrough," *Financial Times*, December 5, 2000.

33. Because there still was a legal ban on foreign ownership of telecommunications companies, the foreign investment in Netcom was through a Hong Kong-registered subsidiary of Netcom. Eric Ng, "China Netcom Offers Private Equity Stakes," *South China Morning Post, Business Post*, December 6, 2000, p. 4; Kenneth Wong, "China Netcom to Raise U.S.$500M via Shr Placement by Yr-End," Dow Jones Newswires, December 5, 2000 (http://interactive.wsj.com [December 5, 2000]); Jason Dean, "China Netcom Closes $325 M Private Equity Placement," Dow Jones Newswires, February 19, 2001 (http://interactive.wsj.com [February 20, 2001]); and Jason Dean, "China Netcom Looks to Form Global Alliances," Dow Jones Newswires, March 1, 2001 (http://interactive.wsj.com [March 1, 2001]).

34. Craig S. Smith, "AOL Joins Chinese Venture, Gaining a Crucial Foothold," *New York Times*, June 12, 2001, p. W1; and Richard McGregor and Rahul Jacob, "China's Internet Portals Need Allies to Survive," *Financial Times*, June 11, 2001, p. 19.

35. James Kynge and Dan Roberts, "China Telecom to Seek Global Profile," *Financial Times*, September 8, 2000, p. 1; Peter Wonacott, "China Telecom Prepares IPO Plans to Get Head Start on Competition," *Asian Wall Street Journal*, December 6, 2000; "China Telecom Plans to Sell Shares Overseas," *International Herald Tribune*, December 6, 2000, p. 17.

36. See chapter 1, note 76, for the precise phase-out schedule.

37. "Several Policies for Encouraging the Development of Software Industry and Integrated Circuit Industry," Xinhua, July 11, 2000, in Foreign Broadcast

Information Service, *Daily Report: China* (hereafter FBIS-CHI)-2000-0711 (http:/ /wnc.fedworld.gov).

38. Zhu Linyong, "Film Industry to Be Reformed," *China Daily*, July 11, 2000, p. 5. Ministry of Culture and State Administration of Radio, Film, and Television, "Instructions on Deepening the Reform of China's Film Industry," cited in "Film Distribution and Exhibition Sectors to Be Opened Wider," July 11, 2000 (http:// ce.cei.gov.cn [August 30, 2000]).

39. "Beijing Further Opens the Construction Market," *Zhongguo jiancai bao (China Building Materials Daily)*, June 29, 2000 (www.chinabmb.com/asp/ cbmdaily/viewtext.asp [July 25, 2000]).

40. "Provisions on Pilot Foreign-Invested Commercial Ventures," cited in Ya Shih, "Foreign Retailers Eye Chinese Market," *China Economic News*, vol. 21 (July 17, 2000), p. 4; and "Retail Giants, Including Wal-Mart, Increasing Investment in China," Xinhua, June 29, 2000, in FBIS-CHI-2000-0629.

41. State Tourism Administration and Ministry of Foreign Trade and Economic Cooperation, "Provisional Measures of Experiments of Sino-Foreign Joint-Venture Travel Agencies," October 29, 1998, in Editorial Board of the Almanac of China's Foreign Economic Relations and Trade, *Almanac of China's Foreign Economic Relations and Trade 1999/2000* (Beijing: China Foreign Economic Relations and Trade Publishing House, 1999), pp. 196–98.

42. "PRC to Open Retail Sector for Joint Ventures," Xinhua, April 22, 1999, in FBIS-CHI-1999-0422.

43. Xu Yihe, "China Energy Watch: Foreign Oil Cos Must Play a Long Game," Dow Jones Newswires, March 22, 2001 (http://interactive.wsj.com [March 22, 2001]).

44. Wang An, "Vast China Petroleum Market Faces a Brutal Fight for Shares," *China Economic News*, vol. 21 (July 31, 2000), p. 5; and Lin Zhi, "Monopoly Is Being Broken," *China Economic News*, Vol. 21 (November 20, 2000), p. 11.

45. Xu Yihe, "Shell, Sinopec Sign China Strategic Alliance Pact-Shell," Dow Jones Newswires, September 11, 2000 (http://interactive.wsj.com [September 12, 2000]).

46. Xie Ye, "Race Is on for Petrol Stations," *China Daily Business Weekly*, February 19, 2001, p. 10.

47. Xie Ye, "Oil Product Markets Open to Overseas Companies," *China Daily*, December 15, 2000, p. 1.

48. "Agreement on Market Access between the People's Republic of China and the United States of America," November 15, 1999.

49. Coudert Brothers, *China Newsletter*, no. 15 (August 2000), p. 1.

50. Details on China's commitments on trading rights are set forth in chapter 3. The rights granted in July 2001 are for exporting only, not importing, and exclude products subject to state trading and export licensing. Meng Yan, "Foreigners' Trade Rights Improved," *China Daily*, July 24, 2001, p. 5; and "MOFTEC Circular on Related Issues of Expanding Import and Export Power of Foreign-Funded Enterprises," *China Economic News*, vol. 22 (August 20, 2001), pp.12–13.

51. "GE Starts New Company in China," Xinhua, September 8, 2000, in FBIS-CHI-2000-0908.

52. "China to Relax Controls on Foreign Investment," Dow Jones Newswires, October 25, 2000 (http://interactive.wsj.com [October 25, 2000]).

53. Zhong Huayan, "A Shares Market to Open Door to FIIs," *China Economic News*, vol. 21 (July 31, 2000), pp. 3–4.

54. "To Win the Project of Sending the Gas from West to East," *China Economic News*, vol. 21 (July 31, 2000), pp. 1–2; and "Protests in the Pipeline," *Business China*, July 31, 2000, p. 4.

55. Wang Yan, "Three Petroleum Giants Purchase SinoPec Shares," *China Economic News*, vol. 21 (November 13, 2000), pp. 5–6; Lin Zhi, "Monopoly Is Being Broken," *China Economic News*, vol. 21 (November 20, 2000), p. 11; Sonia Tsang, "China's CNOOC to Issue 1.64B Shrs in IPO Source," Dow Jones Newswires, December 14, 2000 (http:interactive.wsj.com [December 14, 2000]); and Xie Ye, "CNOOC Launches IPO in HK," *China Daily*, February 16, 2001, p. 5.

56. Peter Wonacott, "Shell Plans $300 Million Investment in China National Offshore Oil IPO," *Wall Street Journal*, interactive edition, November 15, 2000 (http://interactive.wsj.com [November 15, 2000]); and Luo Lan, "Shell Signs a Strategic Alliance Agreement with China Offshore Petroleum Corp," *China Economic News*, vol. 21 (December 11, 2000), pp. 12–13.

57. The list has not been made public, but the official Chinese government news agency referenced its existence. "China Submits Working Documents to WTO," Xinhua, March 21, 2000, in FBIS-CHI-2000-0322.

58. Ni Siyi and Wu Liming, "Li Peng Speaks at Closing Session of NPC Standing Committee Meeting," Xinhua, October 31, 2000, in FBIS-CHI-2000-1031; and Liu Ping, "China Amends Foreign-Funded Enterprise Laws," *China Economic News*, vol. 21 (November 20, 2000), pp. 2–3.

59. Owen Brown, "China Forex Admin Discusses Draft Law Changes," Dow Jones Newswires, November 2, 2000 (http://interactive.wsj.com [November 2, 2000]).

60. James Kynge, "China Gives Citizens Right to Sue Patent Office," *Financial Times*, September 2–3, 2000, p. 2. For a detailed analysis see Jiwen Chen, "The Amended PRC Patent Law, *China Business Review*, vol. 28 (July–August 2001), pp. 38–41.

61. Meng Yan, "Amendments to Better Protect Copyright," *China Daily*, December 27, 2000, p. 2. The amendments of the Customs Law adopted the principle of transaction value as the primary basis for the valuation of imports, which in turn is the base for levying import duties. The amended law also established the right of an importer to demand an explanation of how a customs value has been determined. It also improved the process of appealing such decisions by giving importers the right to appeal rulings directly to the General Administration of Customs in Beijing and, if necessary, to the local courts. Rico Chan, "Customs Law Gets A Facelift," *China Business Review*, vol. 28 (March–April 2001), pp. 30–34.

62. "Telecommunications Regulations of the People's Republic of China," Xinhua, September 30, 2000, in FBIS-CHI-2000-0930.

63. For a detailed analysis of the Telecommunications Regulations see Jamie P. Horsley, "China's New Telecommunications Regulations and the WTO," *China Business Review*, vol. 28 (July–August, 2001), pp. 34–37, 41.

64. "PRC Supreme Court Vice President Says WTO Rules to Prevail over PRC Laws," Xinhua, October 29, 2000, in FBIS-CHI-2000-1029; and Hu Qihua and Shao Zongwei, "Laws Pave Way for WTO Entry," *China Daily*, October 31, 2000, p. 1.

65. Zeng Guohua and Li Fengshuang, "There Can Hardly Be a Winner in Local Protection," Xinhua, July 27, 2000, in FBIS-CHI-2000-0727.

66. Barry Naughton, "How Much Can Regional Integration Do to Unify China's Markets?" Working Paper 58 (Stanford University Center for Research on Economic Development and Policy Reform, August 2000).

67. Chinese interprovincial trade in goods as a share of gross domestic product is about four times higher than the level of either intra-EU trade or intra-ASEAN trade. Services compose an increasing share of gross domestic product as income rises and tend to be traded less than goods. Thus the four times comparison partially reflects the much larger services share of gross domestic product in the EU and in ASEAN than in China. The China-EU comparison cited in the text takes that factor into account.

68. Naughton, "How Much Can Regional Integration Do?" p. 24, figure 6.

69. Ramoncito dela Cruz, "China Maps Out Reforms for New Econ Cycle Report," Dow Jones Newswires, August 25, 2000 (http://interactive.wsj.com [August 25, 2000]).

70. State Council, "Regulations Regarding Prohibition of Regional Blockades in Market Economy Activities," Xinhua, April 29, 2001, in FBIS-CHI-2001-0429.

71. State Council, "Outline of State Industrial Policies for the 1990s," part 1, March 25, 1994; *China Economic News*, vol. 15 (July 25, 1994), pp. 5–8, and part 2, vol. 15 (August 1, 1994), pp. 6–10.

72. State Planning Commission, "Auto Industry Policy," February 19, 1994, *People's Daily*, July 4, 1994, in FBIS-CHI-94-136; and Li Anding, "Vice Minister Discusses Industrial Policies Documents," Xinhua, June 16, 1994, in FBIS-CHI-94-118.

73. WTO Secretariat, "Language for Draft Protocol and Working Party Report Emanating from the EU-China Bilateral Agreement," June 15, 2000, p. 10 (http://www.insidetrade.com [July 28, 2000]).

74. "Shanghai Volkswagen to Produce New Model Cars after PRC's WTO Entry," Xinhua, July 26, 2000, in FBIS-CHI-2000-0726.

75. Zheng Yan, "Shanghai GM to Make Smaller Fuel-Saving Buick," *South China Morning Post*, July 12, 2000 (www.scmp.com [July 13, 2000]).

76. Xin Zhiming, "Cheap Compact Breaks Price Monopoly," *China Daily*, December 21, 2000, p. 4; and Craig S. Smith, "The Race Begins to Build a Small Car for China," *New York Times*, October 24, 2000, p. W1.

77. The other two are the Guangzhou Honda Accord with a 2.3 liter engine and the Audi A6 model, one version of which is equipped with a 2.4 liter engine.

78. Volkswagen appears to believe that this paves the way for it to buy out its joint venture partner, Shanghai Automotive Industrial Corporation, and become the sole owner of Shanghai Volkswagen. Uta Harnischfeger, "VW Plans China Plant Buyout," *Financial Times*, September 4, 2000, p. 17.

79. Notable mergers were Baoshan Iron and Steel Corporation with Shanghai Metallurgical Holdings; Wuhan Iron and Steel Group Corporation with Huangshi Daye Steel Works and Echeng Steel Mill; and North China Pharmaceutical Group Corporation's takeover of the Tianyuan Pharmaceutical Plant.

80. State Planning Commission Macroeconomic Research Institute, "Several Questions Meriting Attention in the Current Development of Enterprise Groups," *People's Daily*, January 5, 1998, pp. 1, 2, in FBIS-CHI-98-057; "Merger Mania under Scrutiny as Model Goes Awry," *South China Morning Post*, January 6, 1998 (www.scmp.com [January 6, 1998]); "Misunderstandings Affect Enterprise Reform," *China Daily*, January 8, 1998, p. 8; Zhao Renfeng, "Experts Sound Merger Warning," *China Daily Business Weekly*, February 23, 1998, p. 8; and Wu Jinglian and Wei Jianing, "The East Asian Financial Crisis: Impact, Lessons, and Countermeasures," *Gaige* (Reform), no. 3 March 20, 1998, pp. 9–18, in FBIS-CHI-98-127.

81. "Several Policies for Encouraging the Development of Software Industry and Integrated Circuit Industry," Xinhua, July 11, 2000, in FBIS-CHI-2000-0711.

82. China's commitment to the WTO Information Technology Agreement, which requires zero tariff on these items, is discussed in chapter 1. China's import tariffs on imported software were 9 percent on the eve of its entry into the WTO. The rate is scheduled to fall to 6 percent the first year after entry, 3 percent the second year, and 0 the third year.

83. Sang Ke, "China Restricts Foreign Investment in Cellular Phone Manufacture," *China Economic News*, vol. 21 (December 11, 2000), pp. 3–4.

84. At least through 2001 the Ministry of Information Industry seems to have made little attempt to enforce these regulations.

85. "China Submits Working Documents to WTO," Xinhua, March 21, 2000, in FBIS-CHI-2000-0322.

86. For a thoughtful analysis of the development of China's courts and other legal institutions and the prospect that China will be able to comply with article 10 of the General Agreement on Tariffs and Trade, which requires members to publish their laws on trade and administer them in a uniform, impartial, and reasonable manner. See Stanley B. Lubman, *Bird in a Cage: Legal Reform in China after Mao* (Stanford University Press, 1999).

87. International Commentary, "Free Trade China," *Wall Street Journal*, interactive edition, November 16, 1999 (http://interactive.wsj.com [November 16, 1999]).

88. Samuel S. Kim, "China and the United Nations," in Economy and Oksenberg, *China Joins the World*, p. 46. Emphasis in original.

89. In the fall of 1981 the United States cast sixteen vetoes against China's favorite candidate for secretary general of the United Nations, and China cast sixteen vetoes against the favorite candidate of the United States, paving the way for the election of a compromise candidate.

90. Kim, "China and the United Nations," p. 61.

91. "Chief Negotiator Long on Benefits of WTO Membership," China Radio International, April 20, 1999, in FBIS-CHI-1999-0420.

92. Eduardo Lachica, "Minister's Speech Hints at More Vocal China Role," *Wall Street Journal*, interactive edition, December 6, 1999 (http:// interactive.wsj.com [December 6, 1999]); and "Delegation Head Urges WTO to Adapt to Change," Xinhua, December 12, 1996, in FBIS-CHI-96-240.

93. "Chief Negotiator Comments on WTO Investment Agreement," Xinhua, December 12, 1996, in FBIS-CHHI-96-240; "No Place for Labor on WTO Agenda, China Says," ChinaOnline, December 6, 1999 (http://www.chinaonline.com [December 9, 1999]).

94. Annex II, "Marrakech Declaration," adopted at the Ninth Ministerial Meeting of the Group of 77 and China, Marrakech, Morocco, September 1999, pp. 73–81, in *Report of the United Nations Conference on Trade and Development on its Tenth Session*, Bangkok, February 2000 (September 21, 2000) (www.unctad-10.org [June 19, 2001]), p. 77.

95. Robert E. Scott, "China Can Wait: WTO Accession Deal Must Include Enforceable Labor Rights, Real Commercial Benefits," Economic Policy Institute Briefing Paper, May 1999, p. 8.

96. The WTO provisions on antidumping are set forth in the "Agreement on Implementation of Article VI of the General Agreement on Tariffs and Trade, 1994." See chapter 2, note 113. Through July 2001 445 antidumping cases involving more than $10 billion had been brought against Chinese firms. Wang Yan, "Exporters Expected to Win Price Suit," *China Daily*, August 16, 2001, p. 5.

97. Nancy Dunne, "U.S. Subsidy Bill for Farms Nearly as High as Net Income," *Financial Times*, March 15, 2001, p. 6.

99. "Long Yongtu Addresses APEC Ministers' Meeting," Xinhua, June 30, 1999, in FBIS-CHI-1999-0630.

99. Gary Schmitt, "U.S.-China Policy," Project for the New American Century, memorandum of June 21, 1999.

100. Amy Borrus and Pete Engardio with Dexter Roberts, "The New Trade Superpower," *Business Week*, October 16, 1995, p. 56.

101. Bureau of the Census and Bureau of Economic Analysis, *U.S. International Trade in Goods and Services-December 2000*, exhibit 12, February 21, 2001 (www.census.gov/foreign-trade/Press-Release/2000pr/12/exh12.pdf [June 19, 2001]).

102. Although China's statistical authorities publish aggregate data on exports produced by foreign-invested firms, they do not disaggregate these data by individual foreign market (see table 1-1).

103. In the analysis immediately below the numbers on U.S. exports take into account the re-export of U.S. goods from Hong Kong to China. The U.S. Department of Commerce records these goods as exports to Hong Kong. The re-export of U.S. goods from Hong Kong to China, net of the margin added by Hong Kong firms, rose from $1.14 billion in 1989 to $5.68 billion in 2000. These numbers represent 20 percent and 35 percent, respectively, of U.S. exports to China in 1989 and 2000 as reflected in U.S. data, shown in figure 5-1.

104. Nicholas R. Lardy, "Issues in China's WTO Accession," Hearing before the U.S.-China Security Review Commission, May 9, 2001 (www.brook.edu/views/ testimony/lardy/20010509.htm).

105. U.S. International Trade Commission, *Assessment of the Economic Effects on the United States of China's Accession to the WTO*, Publication 3229 (Washington, September 1999), pp. xi–xii, table ES-4.

106. U.S. International Trade Commission, *Assessment of the Economic Effects on the United States of China's Accession to the WTO*, pp. xii, table ES-5, 7-7.

107. Ibid., p. 7-12, table 7-11.

108. Damian Milverton, "As WTO Debate Swirls, China Opens Up to U.S. Ag Exports," Dow Jones Newswires, March 23, 2000 (http://interactive.wsj.com [March 24, 2000]).

109. In 1998, for example, U.S. producers exported 222,180 metric tons of oranges valued at $170 million to Hong Kong, about seven-eighths of Hong Kong's total orange imports. Almost a third of Hong Kong's imports of oranges were re-exported to China. In 1998, for example, Hong Kong re-exported 62,740 tons of oranges, valued at $44.8 million, to China. But China's General Administration of Customs reported that China's orange imports from all countries in the same year were only 3,700 metric tons, valued at $1.3 million. Of these direct imports only 350 tons valued at $120,000, about a tenth of China's recorded orange imports, were of U.S. origin. Thus at a minimum the value of oranges smuggled from Hong Kong to China in 1998 was $43.5 million, more than thirty times the value of imports reported by China. Assuming the share of smuggled oranges from Hong Kong to China that originated in the United States was the same as the U.S. share of Hong Kong's orange imports, the value of U.S. fruit smuggled into China would have been $38 million. Taking into account re-exports of oranges from Hong Kong to China that were not reported to the Hong Kong customs authorities or reported as re-exported to other markets but then smuggled into China, the value of oranges smuggled into China in 1998 may have been several times $43.5 million. Hong Kong Trade and Development Council, *Business Stat Online* (stat.tdc.org.hk [February 1, 2001]). Customs General Administration of the People's Republic of China, *China Customs Statistics Yearbook 1998*, p. 932.

110. The same sources as cited in the previous note report that Hong Kong's re-exports of cigarettes to China in 1998 were valued at $242 million, three and a half times the imports reported by the China General Administration of Customs. For 35mm color film the amount of re-exports from Hong Kong in 1998 was $159 million, five and a half times the imports reported by the China General Administration of Customs. U.S. firms supplied about one-quarter of all cigarettes imported into Hong Kong and a little under a tenth of all 35 mm color film.

111. Jeff Bater, "Citrus, Wheat Recently Shipped to China," Dow Jones Newswires, April 3, 2000 (http://interactive.wsj.com [April 4, 2000]).

112. Agence France-Presse, "China Outlines Need for Free-Trade Zone," *New York Times*, November 26, 2000, p. 4.

113. "PRC Finance Minister Envisions Asian Economic Union, Reluctance on Differences," Xinhua, January 10, 2001, in FBIS-CHI-2001-0110.

114. Kenneth Lieberthal, "U.S. Policy toward China," Brookings Policy Brief 72 (March 2001), pp. 3–4.

115. For a more specific prediction see Henry S. Rowen, "The Growth of Freedoms in China," Stanford University, Institute for International Studies, Asia/Pacific Research Center Working Paper Series, April 2001.

116. J. R. Wu, "China Lures Taiwan Techs but Worries Remain," Dow Jones Newswires, August 24, 2000 (http://interactive.wsj.com [August 25, 2000]).

117. Fred Hu, "One China Is Coming," *Asian Wall Street Journal*, August 25, 2000 (http://interactive.wsj.com [August 25, 2000]).

118. In September 2000 the Taiwan government announced it would allow direct shipping from the mainland to Matsu and Kinmen, tiny islands very near China's coast. Although these direct shipments began in January 2001, since the reshipment of Chinese goods from the small islands to Taiwan is not allowed, they are of extremely limited economic significance. In the summer of 2001 shipping companies were allowed to import Chinese goods directly to Taiwan if they were then shipped onward to a third market.

119. Mark Landler, "China Feud Has New Risks for Taiwan," *New York Times*, July 28, 2001, pp. B1, B3.

120. The estimate comes from the Taiwan Electrical and Electronic Manufacturers Association. "Taiwan Trade Association Urges PRC-Taiwan Shipping Links," Central News Agency, January 6, 2001, in FBIS-CHI-2001-0106.

121. Y. H. Sun, "China Watch: Taiwan to End Discrimination on China Goods," *Wall Street Journal*, interactive edition, June 4, 2000 (http://interactive.wsj.com [June 5, 2000]). Editorial Board of the Almanac of China's Foreign Economic Relations and Trade, *Almanac of China's Foreign Economic Relations and Trade 2000* (Beijing: China Foreign Economic Relations and Trade Publishing House, 2000), p. 542. Taiwan's Board of Foreign Trade reported similar numbers. It placed Taiwan's surplus at $16.7 billion in 1999 and $19.9 billion in 2000. Francy Fang, "Taiwan-PRC Cross-Strait Trade Breaks $30 Billion Barrier," Central News Agency, February 27, 2001, in FBIS-CHI-2001-0227.

122. Jason Dean and Erik Guyot, "Taiwan Panel Backs Firming Economic Links with China," *Wall Street Journal*, interactive edition, August 27, 2001 (http://interactive.wsj.com [August 27, 2001]).

123. In the waning days of the Clinton administration the resumption of the activities of the Trade Development Agency in China was announced. Anita Narayan, "U.S. Trade Agency Reopens Export Assistance Program in China," ChinaOnline, February 1, 2001 (www.chinaonline.com [February 3, 2001]). The program officially reopened in China in July 2001. Associated Press, "China, U.S. Reopen Grant Program Shut Down in 1989," Dow Jones Newswires, July 31, 2001 (http://interactive.wsj.com [July 31, 2001]).

124. "China Announces Largest Judicial Cooperation Program with EU," Xinhua, April 11, 2001, in FBIS-CHI-2001-0411.

125. Author's calculations based on National Bureau of Statistics, *China Statistical Yearbook 1999* (Beijing: China Statistics Press, 1999), pp. 422, 432, 581-82.

126. Yu Yongding and Zheng Bingwen with Song Hong, *The Research Report on China's Entry into WTO: The Analysis of China's Industries* (Beijing: Social Sciences Documentation Publishing House, 2000), pp. 168-69.

127. Development Research Center, State Council of the People's Republic of China, *The Global and Domestic Impact of China Joining the World Trade Organization* (Washington: Washington Center for China Studies, 1998), p. 59; and

"Task Group Assesses WTO Accession." *Ta Kung Pao*, November 26, 1999, in FBIS-CHI-1999-1204.

128. Mark O'Neill, "Japan's Border-Crossing Farmers Straddle Trade War Divide," *South China Morning Post*, March 12, 2001 (http://scmp.com [March 13, 2001]).

129. U.S. International Trade Commission, *Assessment of the Economic Effects on the United States of China's Accession to the WTO*, p. 8-26.

130. Most of the empirical results of the ITC estimates are presented in graphic form. Unfortunately it is impossible to read precisely the change over time in the Chinese shares of the U.S. market for various products. For textiles, the share appears to rise from about 10 percent in 2004 to about 12 percent in 2006 and then declines slightly between 2006 and 2010. The Chinese share of the U.S. textile market in 2010 is stated in the text as 11 percent. U.S. International Trade Commission, *Assessment of the Economic Effects on the United States of China's Accession to the WTO*, pp. 8-26–8-28.

131. Between 1993, the last year before the implementation of NAFTA, and 1999 Mexico's share of the U.S. apparel market rose from 4 percent to 15 percent; China's share fell from 17 percent to 11 percent. U.S. International Trade Commission, Interactive Tariff and Trade Data Web (http://dataweb.usitc.gov [February 6, 2001]). Mexico's preferred access under the terms of the North American Free Trade Agreement has two dimensions. First, unlike China, it is not subject to any quotas on its textile and apparel exports to the United States. Second, it enjoys preferential tariffs on these products in the United States. For example, the normal U.S. import duty rate on cotton T-shirts in 2001 was 17.8 percent. For T-shirts imported from Mexico the rate was zero. U.S. International Trade Commission, *2001 Tariff Database* (http://dataweb.usitc.gov/scripts/tariff2001.asp [February 15, 2001]).

132. U.S. International Trade Commission, Interactive Tariff and Trade Data Web (http://dataweb.usitc.gov [June 18, 2001]).

133. Even after China entered the World Trade Organization Mexico still has the advantage of lower tariffs. The United States is reducing tariffs to meet its WTO obligations. But, for example, the import duty rate on T-shirts by 2004 will fall only about 1 percentage point, to 16.5 percent. Under NAFTA, Mexican producers will continue to enjoy a duty rate of zero. U.S. International Trade Commission, *Tariff Database 2001*.

134. Development Research Center, State Council of the People's Republic of China, *The Global and Domestic Impact of China Joining the World Trade Organization*, p. 60.

135. "Nonfarm Payroll Statistics from the Current Employment Statistics (National) Home Page," U.S. Department of Labor, Bureau of Labor Statistics.

136. GATT Secretariat, *The Results of the Uruguay Round of Multilateral Trade Negotiations: The Legal Texts* (Geneva, 1994), pp. 168–96. The basis in U.S. law for the nonmarket economy provisions is the Tariff Act of 1930.

137. GATT Secretariat, *The Results of the Uruguay Round of Multilateral Negotiations: The Legal Texts*, pp. 545–46.

138. "Commission Decision No 1000/1999/ECSC of 11 May 1999 Amending

Decision No 2277/96/ECSC on Protection against Dumped Imports from Countries Not Members of the European Coal and Steel Community," *Official Journal of the European Communities*, May 12, 1999, pp. L122/35-L122/37.

139. For example, in an EU antidumping investigation of Chinese exporters of integrated electronic compact fluorescent lamps ten producers applied for market economy treatment. Of these the Lisheng Electronic & Lighting (Xiamen) Co., Ltd., was determined to meet the criteria to be granted market economy treatment. Its provisional antidumping duty was set at 0. The antidumping margins of the other firms were set at levels from 6 to 60 percent. The average antidumping margin for firms that did not apply for market economy status was 74.4 percent. "Commission Regulation (EC) No 255/2001 of 7 February 2001 Imposing a Provisional Anti-Dumping Duty on Imports of Integrated Electronic Compact Fluorescent Lamps (CFL-I) Originating in the People's Republic of China," *Official Journal of the European Communities*, February 8, 2001, pp. L38/8-L38/21 (www.europe.eu.int/eur-lex/en/oj/index/html [March 1, 2001])

140. Xiao Hou, "Unicom Subscribers Hit 20.26 Million," *China Daily*, February 14, 2001 (www.chinadaily.com.cn [March 1, 2001]).

141. Wang Chuandong, "China Mobile (HK) Plans U.S.$31 Billion Writedown," *China Daily*, October 16, 2000, p. 5.

142. "China Mobile, Vodafone Strengthen Mobile Connection with R&D Deal," ChinaOnline, March 1, 2001 (www.chinaonline.com [March 6, 2001]).

143. Long Yongtu, "Grasp the Opportunity and Greet the Challenge Brought by China's Entry to World Trade Organization (WTO)," in Editorial Board of the Almanac of China's Foreign Economic Relations and Trade, *Almanac of China's Foreign Economic Relations and Trade 2000*, pp. 27-30.

144. This issue came to a head in the meeting of the working party on China's accession in Geneva in January 2001. China claimed the right to increase agricultural subsidies to as high as 10 percent of the value of agricultural output, the WTO ceiling for developing countries, while the United States, Australia, and some other countries urged that China be limited to the 5 percent ceiling applying to developed countries. China's negotiators presented data showing that domestic agricultural subsidies were under 2 percent of agricultural output.

# Index

Acer Computer, 52, 53

Agreement on Market Access between the People's Republic of China and the United States of America (*1999*). *See* U.S.-China bilateral agreements

Agreements. *See* WTO agreements

Agriculture: citrus, 163, 208*n*98, 227*n*108; commitments for entry into WTO, 65, 75–79; contaminations, 94–95; as dominant supplier, 114; effects of WTO membership, 22, 92, 109–110, 114, 121, 170, 174–76; employment issues, 106, 114; exports and imports, 47, 55, 78, 79, 93–95, 109, 163, 169–70, 176; labor-intensive crops, 169–70; prices, 14–15, 24–25, 30, 77–78; quotas, 76, 79, 109, 203*n*46; sanitary and phytosanitary standards, 94–95; shortage of arable land, 109; subsidies, 91, 92–94, 105, 156, 207*n*90, 230*n*143; tariffs, 22, 75, 76, 78; trading rights, 77–78; transfer of labor out of, 13; value of output, 207*n*90

Airbus, 101

Aircraft industry, 101–02

Alcatel, 131

American International Assurance Co., Ltd., 70

American International Group, 70, 71–72, 147

Antidumping. *See* Dumping

AOL Time Warner, 143

Apparel. *See* Textiles and apparel industry

Argentina, 79, 127

Arima Computer, 53

ASEAN. *See* Association of Southeast Asian Nations

ASEAN plus three, 164

Asia, 51, 134–35, 162

Asian Development Bank, 167

Asian financial crisis (*1997–98*), 2, 16–17, 115, 136, 152. *See also* Economic issues—China

Asian Infrastructure Fund, 147

Association of Southeast Asian Nations (ASEAN), 135, 162, 164

AT&T, 142, 175

ATC. *See* WTO Agreement on Textiles and Clothing

Audi. *See* First Auto Works

Audiovisual services, 74, 143–44, 203*n*37